MW00974606

Lysergic

3rd Edition

By Krystle Cole

Also by Krystle Cole

After the Trip
The NeuroSoup Trip Guide
MDMA for PTSD

Table of Contents

DISCLAIMER

This book focuses on describing events that occurred during the years of 2000 thru 2003. It is mostly factual; however, some parts of the story are fictionalized to protect the individuals involved. It is a sad time when spiritual people must hide out of fear of imprisonment.

Why is this country waging war on itself?

I pray for spirituality to be given the freedom to manifest itself without such a horrifying struggle. We are losing our brothers and sisters everyday. We are getting beaten down by the system. We must stop this trend.

We all are one, most of us have just forgotten.

These are merely my views. I am in no way claiming that I know anything other than what I believe to be true for myself. I realize each person must find his or her own answers. In a sense, I am only recounting how my slice of the infinite cosmic pie tastes.

PART 1: LYSERGIC

Chapter 1 FIRST ROLL

I was raised in a small Kansas town, which is comparable to being sucked into a spiritual black hole. I was surrounded by flat, bleak cornfields farmed by similarly flat, bleak people. They were stuck in a philosophical time warp that held their minds back in the dark ages. At a young age my classmates labeled me as a nerd, causing me to never quite fit in. The first thing that comes to my mind upon reflection is, "Thank God for being an outcast!!!" However, as a small child, it was extremely difficult to deal with. I wanted friends to play with at recess instead of kids who behaved hatefully toward me.

By the time I started high school, my life hadn't gotten much better. My peers were the perfect example of white trash at its worst. The majority of them had already given birth to a couple of children and dropped out of high school because of it. No aspirations existed in their minds beyond the next round of incestuous sex, six-pack of beer, and line of meth. I had nothing in common with those people. In fact, this is why going to college became extremely important to me. I needed to get out of there before I somehow ended up becoming one of them. So I didn't waste any time! I dropped out of high school at fifteen and started going to a nearby community college. Of which, I graduated before my classmates graduated from high school!

I quickly discovered that life as a college student wasn't cheap. From the ages of sixteen to eighteen, I worked at Sonic Drive In as a carhop during the day. At night, I worked at a group home for the mentally handicapped. Going to college full-time and holding two part-time jobs completely wore me out. By the time I turned eighteen, I was willing to do anything that could possibly change my life for the better. So I started working as an exotic dancer. I was tired of being poor and knew that dancing would solve that problem within a few days!

I had long blonde hair, stood five foot eight, and weighed about one hundred and twenty pounds. The guys at the club *loved* me. On some nights, I'd wear my hair in pigtails and look like the innocent country girl next door. On others, I'd dress in black leather and lead myself around the stage with a dog collar and leash.

Of course, the perverts and child molesters were immediately attracted to me. I remember one client commenting on how perky my breasts were and that they probably weren't even developed yet. He drooled over me, knowing he was getting something fresh. YUCK!

Still, in no time, I was able to afford to pay

14

back my student loans, rent my own place, and buy my first car. This was a necessity because my Dad had basically raised me as a single parent since I was twelve. He worked in a bakery for $9 an hour, so we didn't have much money for anything. We were always poor when I was growing up. This wasn't his fault because he tried his best. Yet, it is part of the reason stripping was a welcomed solution.

My life was incredibly predictable. I went to school, work, and then back to my house. I was always alone. Alone and miserable. At night I would sit in my empty house and think. What was the most important thing in the world? What would make me the happiest? These were easy questions for me to answer; I needed to be loved. However, love was not so easy to find with the people I had to choose from.

I yearned for an intelligent conversation to replace the blank looks I'd often receive from everyone around me. I knew someone out there had to be able to actually understand what I was saying and respond with something intelligent. So I waited, and I tried my best to be patient.

After dancing for about six months, the pain of loneliness eventually reached a new depth. Something was missing; I knew my life was supposed to be different somehow. I had tried everything except for prayer. I had never prayed before because I didn't like the scare tactics of Christianity. It also seemed to me that such a definitive answer could never be true. I believed that I would never totally understand, and I was comfortable with not understanding. Yet, no other solution presented itself. And a person has to try everything, right?

I sobbed as I begged for *whatever was out there* to help me find a family. I bargained with it by promising that I would do anything if I could be loved, really loved just once. I didn't want to be alone anymore. I had been isolated my whole life, stuck in a world with non-thinkers and non-feelers. I needed to find people that were like me. I needed it deeply with my whole soul.

The next day Todd walked into the club. He looked like a very well dressed Amish man, which got my attention immediately. My first thought was, "What a sick-o!" Did Amish men actually go into strip clubs? Weird!

Curiosity overcame me. Upon introducing myself, I quickly learned that the only thing he had in common with the Amish was the lack of a mustache. He started our conversation with a unique question. "If you could have anything in the world, what would it be?"

I paused briefly. Should I give him a real answer or just tell him something that he would want to hear and move on? I knew I should say something sexual that would turn him on, if I wanted to make money. But at that moment I didn't care if I made a dime from him. After my crying session the night before, I was simply not in the mood to play the usual games. So out came the truth. "I don't want to be alone anymore. I want to be loved, really loved."

"Don't worry. You will never be alone again." He stared at me for a moment and then smiled lovingly. I knew that he was different than everyone else. The universe had answered my prayers.

We talked for hours about philosophy and religion. The conversation consisted mostly of him asking me what I thought about everything, and then me stumbling through an answer the best I could. As the evening progressed, I started to feel very comfortable with him. He really seemed like he cared about me.

16

Most of the men that came into the club were only there for a cheap thrill. If the money wasn't so good I never would have been there; the whole dynamic of the club disgusted me. I was repulsed by the smelly old men who paid me ten dollars to grind on their laps for five minutes.

Todd was completely different from them. He wouldn't watch me when I was on stage, and he never bought a dance from me. The club made him uncomfortable too. Neither of us were ready for the night to end, so we eventually decided to go back to his place. This isn't like it sounds; we both made it clear that I wasn't going there to have sex with him. We were just friends.

Todd lived in an old decommissioned missile base, which he claimed was supposed to have housed his robotic spring factory and a music-recording studio for big stars like Sting. Though, I never saw any evidence of either.

All in all, this made me even more curious about him. Why would a person want to live in a missile base? Questions started to spin in my mind. How did a person get a missile base? From the government? Who was this strange man?

His missile base was huge. It was like a fortress, surrounded by chain-linked fence and barbed wire. We went to the main room first. He explained that this was where the missile used to be stored when it was at *rest*. So, accordingly, they named it the coffin. The room was about twenty-five feet tall, two semi-trucks long, and one semi-truck wide. There were Persian rugs covering the cement floors, and the walls were painted white. It had a sterile smell, very clean.

Two white leather couches were positioned in the center of the room in front of a complicated looking stereo system. The stereo components were placed side by side on the floor with wires everywhere. Huge speakers were positioned on each side, and hundreds of CD's were stacked randomly in between. Oddly enough, there was also a black baby grand piano located directly behind the stereo and CD's.

"It's a Mark Levinson and Reference system; the most expensive stereo money can buy. Its price totaling around $200,000," Todd boasted, obviously proud of his baby.

"I never heard of a stereo that expensive. It must be really nice!" It impressed me but at the same time I thought it was a little foolish. Couldn't he have done something better with all that money? My Dad didn't make that much money in ten years.

We headed down a long metal tunnel that was also painted white. It connected the main missile bay with the rest of the complex. There were fluorescent lights spread evenly every five feet along the top of it, and the floor was a combination of cement and grating. So each time we would walk down the tunnel our footsteps would echo. Clang, Clang. Clang, Clang. It was wild!

The other side of the complex had the same sterile smell and white walls as the rest of the facility. There were several normal size bedrooms, a kitchen, and a very extravagant bathroom. The bathroom was tiled with granite and marble, and it had a vaulted ceiling. The largest bathtub I had ever seen took up the main part of the space. Ten people could have fit in it! There was a steam bath and a large multi-headed shower too. It looked like he'd modeled it after a bathroom in a spa; it was amazing!

"I hate the smell of cigarettes from the club on my clothes," he grumbled, sniffing at his shirt. "Disgusting! You don't mind waiting on me while I take a bath, do you?" He led me to an empty room, before I could even answer.

"Sure, I'll wait." What choice did I have? I looked around and saw scraps of paper with what looked like phone numbers or notes scattered all over the carpeted floor. There was a lone office chair positioned in the middle of the room, and on it was a silver metal briefcase. He walked directly over to it, put a combination into the lock, and popped it open. It was stacked full of one hundred dollar bills! And that is how he left me. Me and all of that money, alone in a room! I was incredibly nervous. What was I getting myself into?

I was alone in a room with more money than I had ever seen. It was so tempting to just go take a few hundreds, but I didn't. I didn't even go near it. I just sat on the floor and waited - wondering how much was there. Could it have been two million? Possibly three million? Time moved slowly. I stared at the white walls and waited. And waited. And waited some more. Would he ever return? Finally, after what seemed like a lifetime, he came back looking relaxed. He had dressed himself in a polo shirt and khaki pants; he looked much more comfortable. And it was evident that his bath was warm because his cheeks were still red!

* * *

He had a digital lab scale all set up and waiting on us as we entered the kitchen. "Would you like to try some MDMA?"

"What's that?" I asked. The only drugs I'd ever heard of were weed, cocaine, and meth. I thought I had tried everything!

"It's ecstasy." I stared at him blankly. He could tell that I didn't have a clue what he was talking about. "You've never heard of ecstasy? You will like it. It makes your body feel really good, and it makes you happy. Really happy."

"I don't know. I hardly know you. Maybe I should try it some other time." I was nervous. Who was this guy?

"Really you should try it. You will love it. They used to prescribe it in the 80's for marriage counseling. It allows people to bond without nervousness or anxiety. It helps people to open up easily." He looked at me hopefully. I could tell he wasn't giving up anytime soon.

"Well, are you sure I won't have a bad time? I've taken drugs before that I didn't like and felt miserable. Are you sure I'll like it?"

"Yes, I'm sure." He smiled, knowing he had won.

"Okay, but I want a small dose. Very small." I decided to jump in headfirst because he might've been my gift from the universe. And I'd made a deal; I'd promised *whatever is out there* that I would do *anything* for love... I didn't know what was ahead of me, but I had to go for it.

So we stood together in front of his scale. He weighed the white powder - 100 mg exactly. Then he handed it to me lying on a piece of paper. I looked at it with one last second of hesitation, and then poured it into my mouth. It tasted horrible! I will never forget it as long as I live. It had a sharp chemical, slightly alkaloid-like taste with a bite at the end. Absolutely disgusting!

"That was gross!" I squealed, grimacing. My stomach was becoming very queasy, and I thought I might throw up.

"This stuff does taste nasty, but you will love it. I promise," he replied reassuringly as he gulped down his own pile of powder. "Let's go to the bay and listen to some music."

One hour later:

"I can't believe I didn't want to try this!" I was the most happy I had ever felt. The world was uplifting and radiating warmth.

"I told you that you would enjoy it." Todd smiled. He reached out his hand and touched mine. All the while, he never took his gaze away from mine. He had big brown eyes, deeper than any I'd seen before.

"I feel so good!" It was a little difficult for me to talk; my mouth was dry. My skin tingled as it crawled around my body. A comforting fuzzy, cuddly feeling came over me. Yet, my mind was clear.

"I'm so glad to finally find a real friend. You are a dream come true!" I felt like we were better friends already than I usually ever was with any of the people in Kansas. Maybe it was the MDMA that made me feel like this, who knows. But I LOVED it!

We were sitting on one of the couches in the missile bay. Todd's stereo played music in the background that was magnificent; it was better than perfect. It had depth and layers. So much energy rushed through me that sitting was impossible; I had to get up and dance. I felt like a child and twirled around in circles, arms stretched out, embracing the world. I moved with the sound, my soul floating along with the beat. The music took on new shape, twisting, evolving. The highs and lows were more noticeable than before. The voices were singing in another language, yet I understood them perfectly. I was at home. I felt safe.

The room pulsated slightly. There was a large tapestry hanging over a doorway to an area I had not yet seen. The designs on it started to move, crawling around in a wavelike motion. My skin bonded with it all, warm and energized. I felt the love that is always in the universe for the first time. I was happy. I was awakening.

INTEGRATION

MDMA changed me. Not only did it make me feel warm and fuzzy for about three days afterward, but it also altered my consciousness permanently. The realization that love is everywhere was refreshing. My soul was cleansed and reborn into a reality with more possibilities than I had ever imagined. The goodness in life had magically revealed itself, giving me a new sense of hope for the future.

I surveyed my new world with innocence, much like that of a child seeing and hearing for the first time. Sound, no longer clothed with preconceived notions of what it *really* was, stood before me partially undressed. Subtleties in pitch allowed themselves to be heard. My eyes could see new shadows and differences in hue. The beauty in each never-ending moment appeared so quickly.

How had I missed all of this?

I believe this *new vision* occurred from realizing the possibility and instinctively moving toward it. Life only needed to be perceived or conceptualized this way once. By listening and paying attention, I naturally allowed it the space to manifest its radiance again. The mental blocks or constraints that held me in my usual pattern of selective perception were no longer there. Everything was possible!

Chapter 2 MEET L

Todd and I flew into Oakland. This was the second time I ever rode on an airplane. The flight made me a little nervous, but it was uneventful aside from a few bumps. As we got off and headed toward the luggage carousel, a really big grin spread across my face. Giggles exploded out of me every so often; I just couldn't keep all that happiness contained within myself. I was excited to be out of boring, small-town Kansas and in the big city with lots of things to do!

We watched all the other travelers pick up their bags, but ours never came. "Don't worry they'll get them to us," Todd said, grabbing my hand to lead us out of the airport. "We have to go. We're late."

"I don't care. I'm just happy to be here!" I was elated, even if I had to wear dirty clothes for a few days. It was worth it!

Todd and I hurriedly caught a cab and headed to the Warf. We were going to have dinner at one of the famous seafood restaurants there.

The restaurant was extravagant. As we waited for the host, I looked around in awe. I had never been out to eat at a place like this; it was like the restaurants that people went to on TV! There were so many different types of silverware and dishes on the table. Which ones did I use for which dish? My palms started to sweat as I pondered it all.

A feeling of uneasiness crept into me upon noticing that most of the people filling the room were wearing either suits or dresses. People just didn't dress like this in Kansas; they mostly wore jeans and t-shirts! To describe my appearance as underdressed is putting it nicely. I had on black knee high boots, a black leather mini-skirt, and fishnet stockings. A dog collar was proudly wrapped around my neck and thick black eyeliner was under my eyes. I usually dressed "Goth" at home for the sole purpose of giving the bible thumpers a heart attack! But here, now, with these people I felt completely different. I tried to calm my nerves by taking a few deep, relaxing breaths.

The host led us to our table. Todd allowed me to sit down first, pushing my chair in behind me. "A brother of mine will be joining us for dinner."

"Your brother lives in California?" This surprised me; he had never mentioned having a brother.

"He's not really my brother. We've just been business partners for so long it feels like we're brothers. Anyway, please don't speak to him much. He likes his space and privacy." He started shuffling through the metal briefcase of his and pulled out some Plexiglas plaques. "You should look at these before I give them to him. They're worth a lot of money, much more than they say. They have been out of circulation for many years." Smashed in between the Plexiglas for protection were two bills - a ten thousand dollar bill and a five thousand dollar bill.

"I didn't know there was such a thing!" I was impressed, which definitely was his goal. Todd was like that, all about the flash and shock value of things. He loved to feel important, powerful. And he was.

Todd quickly put them back in his briefcase, as he stood up to greet the couple being led to our table by the host. Two people never looked more elegant. They wore black suits, which perfectly complimented their tall, thin statures. The man must have been twice the age of the woman. His wavy, shoulder-length, silver hair helped his face to radiate a grandfather's loving warmth. He gazed at me for a moment and tried to place me. Todd didn't seem to notice that he was politely awaiting an introduction. Instead, he took matters into his own hands. "Hello. This is my fiancée Natasha, and I am Leonard." His voice was as soft and kind as his face.

"I'm Krystle." Their energy drew me to them instantly. Who were they? I wanted to know more, but Todd didn't allow it.

Todd immediately took over the conversation for the rest of the dinner. He rambled on about political happenings and world events. After which, he moved onto talking about springs and the stock market. Sometimes he would say things that were so over my head I had no idea what they were. His monologue was putting me to sleep. I think it was boring everyone else too. They were just better at acting interested!

My presence seemed to cause Leonard and Natasha to be quite reserved. They both sat straight and tall in their chairs with legs crossed in front of them. They tilted their bodies slightly, resting to one side a bit more than the other. Somehow they made themselves look at ease and comfortable. How? It was difficult for me to sit up straight all the time like that. It would hurt my back after a while!

When Natasha ordered, she revealed a beautiful Russian accent. She mentioned to the waiter that neither of them ate meat and asked about a vegetarian meal. I was so excited by this; I rarely met other people that were vegetarians at home! She ordered an appetizer of deep fried tofu for Leonard. I later found out that he ate this at almost every meal; it was a staple in his diet.

I gazed at them across that table. Natasha's long blonde hair and light skinned complexion contrasted attractively with her all black attire. They were so alike. That's how couples that are really in love get. They seem to grow over time to become like each other. Each one picks up the other's habits, word structure, and the like. He smiled slightly, noticing that I was admiring the two of them. My palms started to sweat again. How could I talk to them with Todd droning on?

I had to know more about them. So I eagerly waited the chance to interrupt his discourse and change the subject to something more interesting. What would I say if I got the chance? My heart sped up. I didn't want to say something stupid. What if my midwestern accent made me sound like a hick? These people were obviously more educated than me, what could I say to them? My face flushed.

I ended up chickening out. I felt like a teenage girl trying to talk to the cute guy in school. Why? The courage just never came to me, despite how much I wanted it to. They really intrigued me; I simply had to know more! Maybe next time I would get a chance to talk with them more freely, without Todd's control and my shyness.

Chapter 3 WALNUT CREEK

Two days had passed since we first arrived in San Francisco, and the airline still hadn't found our luggage. "Let's go buy some new clothes!" Todd announced, pacing around our hotel room with so much energy I thought he might burst. "I can't stand wearing these any longer."

"Don't you think we should just wait until they find them? New clothes are expensive." I only got knew clothes twice a year when I was growing up - in the fall for school and the spring for summer. My parents said that it was a waste of money to buy them any other time.

"The money means nothing to me. Feeling clean is much more important than a few hundred dollars." He was already walking out of the door. "Come on sweetie, hurry up."

"Okay," I slipped on my platform boots and headed out after him. "Where are we going to?"

"Nordstrom in Walnut Creek. And if we don't find what we want there, we'll head to Saks Fifth Avenue." He glanced over at me, trying to gauge my reaction.

"Okay." I had never heard of either of the stores before.

"I need to get dress coats and pants. Shoes and socks. Shirts, cufflinks, and ties. Oh and boxer

shorts, I like Nordstrom's boxer shorts." He opened the doors to his Porsche Boxster with his keys by remote. "You've never seen my west coast car. You'll like it. It's a little smaller than the C-4 I have in Kansas, but otherwise it looks the same."

We both hopped in. He cranked the music immediately - Sarah McLaughlin. Then he put the top down. We both loved driving with the top down. The sun shined brightly on us for the half an hour it took to get to the stores. Todd drove a little too fast, but it was fun. After driving like this for a while and not getting in a wreck, I started to feel safe. He obviously knew how to drive at fast speeds.

Nordstrom had many nice things, but everything was so expensive. "Do you want to go look in the women's section while I get what I need? The only thing I ask of you is to pick out something that looks classy. No more trashy Goth clothes. Okay?"

"But I like the clothes I have on." Where did he think he got off telling me what I should dress like? I wasn't going to stand for it.

"You can't dress like that of you want to be around me while I'm doing business," he said curtly. "What will everyone think of me if you're dressed like that?"

"I don't care what people think, screw 'em if they don't like it." My heartbeat pounded in my ears.

"Sometimes in life you have to care what people think of you. I'm not going to ruin a million dollar banking deal because of the way you *like* to dress. You'll either wear appropriate clothing or leave." He turned and walked off in a huff.

I walked around for a long time, but I didn't find anything that seemed to fit my age group. The clothes looked like what grandmas would wear. Every once in a while I went by to check on Todd. It seemed like he would never finish. He must have picked out three new suits, a half a dozen shirts and ties, a dozen socks and boxers, and two pairs of shoes by the time he was finished.

"I didn't find anything I wanted. Can I wait to shop at Saks?" I eventually asked, interrupting his shopping spree.

"Sure, let's go pay for this stuff." Todd motioned for the clerk to take his pile to the cashier.

"Sir, the total is $4,896.24." The cashier waited patiently. The total was obviously nothing unusual. However, I was in shock. His clothes cost as much as my car!

Todd propped his metal briefcase up on the counter and opened it. It looked like a tornado had hit the thing! After digging around in the mess for about five minutes he finally found a stack of cash. Then he nonchalantly counted out forty-nine one hundred dollar bills. He acted like it was nothing, like he did it everyday. And he did...

* * *

We were headed toward Saks with the top down and music blasting again when Todd realized the time. "Sweetie, we don't have time to go to Saks. We have to get to the airport to meet Leonard. We chartered a plane and can't be late. It's business."

"I don't mind. Where are we headed?" This was the first mention of a business trip. What happened to planning things out?

"We have to get to Las Vegas. There are some people coming in from Europe for a big banking deal." He got a serous tone to his already deep voice. "And we're late already. I didn't think shopping would take us so long." The traffic on the freeway was slowing down because we were in rush hour. So Todd sped up and started to drive on the shoulder. He cranked the music up louder to drown out the noise created by the extra wind. I wasn't nervous at all; I really thought Todd was a good driver. I laughed as we went faster and faster. At one point, I looked over at the speedometer and it read 136 mph. I laughed more; it was great. Adrenaline rushed through me. I had never driven that fast.

We drove for several minutes, and then started to exit without slowing down a bit. I thought nothing of it until the back wheels started to slide around. I glanced over at Todd as we began to fishtail. Neither of us had our seat belts on. Luckily we were ahead of all the cars, so we didn't crash into anyone else. The only thing that was in our way was a cement light pole, and we hit it head on. The last thing I heard Todd say before we crashed was, "here we go!" I was screaming as we impacted.

Neither of us blacked out. In fact, we both jumped out of the car almost instantly. Todd started digging his clothes and what looked like wads of hundred dollar bills out of the smashed trunk while I lay down on the ground. My neck was in excruciating pain; I thought it must have been broken. I couldn't see out of my right eye or feel the right side of my face, which ended up being caused by a severe airbag burn.

A commuter passing by called an ambulance for us. Todd kept telling everyone that he didn't need one. He was walking around just fine, like nothing had happened. All the while, people would stop and ask where the fatalities were; it surprised them when they found out that we were the people in the wreck!

When the ambulance arrived, the EMT's stabilized me by strapping me tightly down to a headboard. Who knew lying flat on a hard surface would be that painful? It felt like it was hurting my head a whole lot more than it was helping my neck.

I don't remember much of the ride other than

the EMT's telling me I was okay and to be calm. At the hospital, I was put through x-ray after x-ray, and they found nothing wrong with my neck other than a severe whiplash. Of course, I also had a concussion. But I was lucky! My guardian angel was definitely beside me that time!

* * *

We went back to the hotel for the night, and then flew out to Las Vegas on a chartered jet the next morning. The doctor had prescribed oxycodone for my pain, so I was pretty out of it. I kept nodding off.

During one of these periods, I had a visit from aliens. We were in the air at around 35,000 feet when it all took place. There were seven of them with extra long arms and legs. Their bodies were very thin with heads shaped like pears and gray pasty looking skin. We were all naked, cuddling, and stroking each other. They were different than me, though; they had no sexual organs. We caressed each other more as I figured it out. They were telepathically having sex with me. They don't do it like we do; they do it with their minds! It was too weird! I woke up and quickly looked around me. Thank god nobody noticed!

Chapter 4   A BIG PURPLE FRIEND

Our plane landed on a private runway in Las Vegas. There was a long black limousine waiting to pick the four of us up. Leonard and Natasha were absorbed in a 3-d molecular modeling program on their laptop for the entire flight. Todd and I had both been dozing off periodically. Now that we were on the ground, I felt a little better. I wonder if the altitude contributed to my strange hallucinations. I did have a concussion after all. Who knows...?

The limo drove us to the *secret* entrance of the Mirage casino's villas. They were around the side where no usual gambler could find them. We stayed in number eight - right next to Kevin Costner. There were four bedrooms, three bathrooms, a kitchen, a dining room, a bar, and a pool in the backyard.

The pool was surrounded by little misters that sprayed small amounts of water everywhere to cool the air. The whole idea of outdoor air conditioning astonished me. When I was a kid, we didn't even have air conditioning indoors, let alone outdoors!

"Hey sweetie, look at this. There are Monet's on the walls!" Todd pointed to a painting of a flower scene.

"Cool," I replied. Though, I really could have

cared less. And who was Monet? I thought the painting sucked; flowers were boring.

"So do you like the place?" he asked, plopping down on our bed. We were alone now, since Leonard and Natasha had retired to their portion of the suite.

"It's really amazing. I want to go swimming! I can't believe we have our own pool!" We were in a palace. Something right out of a movie. Suddenly, there was a knock on the door, and the bellman let himself in.

"Good evening Mr. Skinner, Mrs. Skinner." This caught me off guard; no one had ever called me a misses before. It sounded kind of good. "I have your luggage. Would you like me to bring it into the closet?"

"Sure, go ahead." Todd didn't move from his relaxed position, except to hand the bellman a twenty-dollar bill when he was finished.

* * *

The next morning we awoke and ordered room service. A bowl of cereal cost eight dollars! It was a rip off. But "money meant nothing" to Todd, so we lived it up. We ordered enough for the four of us, knowing Leonard and Natasha would be hungry too. By the time the food arrived, we were all waiting in the dining room. Our butler set it up for us. I'm not kidding! Each villa had its very own butler who was at our beck and call.

"L and I have to go to some meetings today," Todd announced. "You guys should explore the city while we're gone." He shoved a huge bite of eggs into his mouth and then another. Todd was inhaling his food faster than I'd ever seen anyone eat. He must have been hungry!

"I need to go shopping for some clothes since they still haven't found my luggage." My clothes were incredibly dirty. "Can I have a few hundred dollars? I don't have any money."

"Sure sweetie. As soon as we're finished with breakfast." He continued to shovel away.

"I think I'll pass on the shopping trip and stay here to rest," Natasha replied. "The combination of the flight and morning sickness really wore me out. I would like to get a few more hours of sleep." Natasha took slow dainty bites out of her bagel, chewing them completely and swallowing slowly.

"I couldn't tell that you were pregnant. How far along are you?" I asked, completely surprised.

"I'm almost three months." A glowing smile covered her face. You could tell she was happy to be a mother.

"Excuse me," Todd interrupted as he got up and walked into our bedroom. His plate was finished even though the rest of ours weren't. He returned as quickly and handed me three one hundred dollar bills. "Now I have to go take a bath."

"Thank you." Clean clothes were on the way!

We finished our food with small talk about the sites I should go see, since I had never been there before. I wasn't old enough to gamble in the casinos but I could check out the shows like Cirque De Soleil. When all of us were through, Leonard politely excused himself to go to the restroom. Afterward he called the butler to come back in and clean up our mess. Then he walked over to me and pulled an envelope out of his pocket. He must have gone into their bedroom to get it when he excused himself to go to the restroom.

"Here you go, baby. Don't tell T that I gave it to you. Just keep it between you and me, okay?" He raised his eyebrows and looked me straight in the eyes.

"Okay. Thank you." How much was there? It was really thick. I peeked inside, and it was all hundreds. There must have been two thousand dollars!

"Go put it up before he gets out of the bathtub," he instructed, motioning toward the bedroom.

* * *

"VIP services," the female operator had an aristocratic tone to her voice.

"Yes, this is Mrs. Skinner in Villa 8." I glanced over at Natasha, who had just woken up from her nap.

"Good evening, Mrs. Skinner. What can I do for you?"

"Could you send a limo around to pick us up?" I almost giggled, but I somehow suppressed it.

"Yes, Ma'am, I'll send him right now. Is there anything else?"

"Oh, yes," I paused, about to burst. "I need to know where the raunchiest sex store in Las Vegas is." I couldn't contain it any more. Laughter spilled out of my lungs. Natasha rolled into the corner of the couch attempting to muffle her cackles; she was laughing hard too. This was her idea, but she expected me to pull it off! How? It was hilarious!

"Let me check into that for you," the operator replied abruptly. Then she hung up.

Minutes later, the limo arrived. The driver held the door open while we situated ourselves. "Where to Ma'am?" He was so polite and uptight it was disgusting. Boy was he in for a treat!

He drove us to several different sex stores; all the while, he kept a straight face. Was he used to this kind of thing? We got all kinds of outfits, including a bunch of bondage gear. I guess Leonard liked that kind of thing. I dressed Goth but wasn't really into bondage. It was fun to act like it, though,

36

to shock people! We also each got a three-foot tall stuffed penis pillow. Natasha's was pink, and mine was purple. We did this mostly to see what the driver's reaction would be, but we got absolutely no response from him.

"Drop us off at the front of the casino," I directed. "We'll walk through it to the villas." If he wouldn't react, someone else would!

We paraded through the floor of the casino. Everyone stared at us as we giggled uncontrollably. We made so much noise that Leonard noticed us and hurried over.

"Well, hello," he looked at us with a smile that radiated warmth from his face. "I see you girls have been busy shopping!" He started to laugh too. "Don't let T see you out here like this; he is such a square."

"We're on our way to the room right now," I reassured. His comment made me nervous. I didn't want Todd to be upset with us.

*   *   *

I woke up in the morning and realized that Todd had never come back to the suite. I had stayed up until three, but I must've fallen asleep some time thereafter. I was a worried wreck as I knocked on Leonard and Natasha's door. "Todd didn't come back last night. Something must be wrong!" A tear rolled down my cheek.

"Oh, come here Beh-beh," Natasha said baby, but her Russian accent always made it sound that way. She wrapped me up in her arms. "Where is T?" she asked, directing her attention to Leonard.

"Let me try and find out." He picked up the phone, seeming annoyed more than worried. He talked to someone for a few minutes and then hung up. "T is staying with Roxanna over at the Bellagio. I am sorry about this baby, but he'll be back in a few days. Don't worry about her. She's just a fling and won't be around for long. You're here to stay. We like you."

I was in shock and quickly left their room to cry in my own. Todd had never mentioned anything about us dating, but I had sort of assumed it. We were traveling together after all. I had fallen in love with him. Didn't he love me? I thought people that loved each other only dated each other. Maybe he didn't love me. I miserably waited in the room and sulked for two days until he finally returned.

Todd could easily see that I was upset, but he offered no explanation. He simply said, "I love you sweetie. You have nothing to worry about with her, believe me." What an asshole. He could have apologized at least!

Leonard's prediction turned out to be correct, though. Roxanna was a one-time thing. She never came back into our lives.

Chapter 5 BEGINNINGS OF AN EDUCATION

Todd left me behind at the missile base, while he went to Tulsa to visit his mother and two children. Before leaving, he explained that he wasn't ready to introduce me to his family and that he was only going to be gone for three or four days. I was a little disappointed about being apart from him, yet I understood completely. Whenever I thought about meeting them it made me nervous too! What would they think of our eighteen-year age difference?

I wasn't alone at the base; the caretaker was also there. Gunnar was forty-five years old, about six feet tall, and slightly overweight. He had the very appropriate nickname of "Mopy-Dopy." It came from the story of the seven dwarves, you know Mopy and Dopy. Gunnar was always one or the other. "Mopy" would start the day really down and depressed. At which point, "Dopy" either took some sort of drug or drank alcohol to escape his feelings. I often wondered why he wasted his life hiding from his problems instead of actually doing something about them.

Needless to say, we stayed out of each other's way for the most part. I tried to use my time productively. So I read a few of the psychedelic chemistry books that Todd had recommended. I started with *Pihkal*, and then I moved on to *Tihkal*. I finished both books in less than two weeks. They were way over my head. I had to refer to both a dictionary and a chemistry textbook in order to even remotely begin to understand them. However, I did gain some knowledge. Most importantly, the books inspired me to learn more. My interest in human biology, neurology, and psychedelic chemistry increased immediately. What were these amazing substances actually doing to us? How were they working in the human body? Were they harmful like the anti-drug campaign claimed? How could they be "bad" when they seemed so helpful psychologically and spiritually?

Two weeks had passed, and there still was no word from Todd. He was supposed to only have been gone for a few days. Was he alright? Did something bad happen to him in Tulsa? I tried to push the worry out of my mind, but it was difficult.

The books were finished so I moved on to the internet. The multitudes of information absorbed me for hours. There was more available than I ever thought possible! I quickly found an incredibly helpful site, www.erowid.org. It had a wide range of information on many different types of drugs. The writers discussed dosage, safety, and legality. They posted people's personal accounts of their trips on different types of psychedelics, which was the most helpful part of the site for me at the time. Unlike the books that I was attempting to understand, they used a language style that was easily readable. Links to sites with more complex technical information were also provided.

One of these *educational* links got me into a little trouble with Gunnar. I accidentally stumbled onto a site that showed pictures of an MDMA lab, and it had synthesis instructions. When I saw this, my heart started to beat a little faster. How could they print that much information? It was amazing! I had never seen anything like this before, so it took me a few minutes to comprehend what it even was. I was pondering all of this when, unfortunately, Gunnar walked up behind me. There was a picture of a flask filled with a red residue on the screen. He immediately knew what I was looking at and was not too happy. "If T knew you were getting on sites like that from the base he would be really upset with you."

"What do you mean? I'm just looking at stuff on the internet, what's wrong with that?" Gunnar had never been upset like this toward me. I really hadn't meant to do anything that would cause a problem.

"Well," he sighed and shook his head in disbelief, "the government tracks stuff like that. They trace your location through the phone lines." His face started to flush and his tenseness obviously increased as he thought about it.

"Who cares? It's just some pictures. What ever happened to the Freedom of Information Act? Anyway, there isn't anything here at the base that's illegal, so why does it matter anyway?" Wasn't he blowing it all out of proportion?

"This is a missile base, and people like to spread rumors about places like this. We don't want to be raided. The cops could come here with search warrants and rip the place apart. We both know that they wouldn't find anything. But the damage could cost T a lot of money." He wasn't going to let me squirm out of it, so I gave in.

"Well okay. I sort of understand. So you won't tell Todd?" I didn't want Todd to be disappointed in me; I honestly didn't understand what my actions could potentially cause.

"I won't tell him as long as you're more

careful from now on," he replied, his lips curving into a slight frown.

"Okay, just please don't tell him! I promise I won't look up any of this stuff from here ever again!" My heartbeat raced. What would Todd think of me if he found out?

*   *   *

Life was weighing me down. Todd had never even called once to talk to me over the phone. His absence was eating away at me more each day. It felt like he didn't care at all. And having Gunnar watch my every move to make sure that I wouldn't screw up again just made the situation even worse. It was all too much to deal with; I needed a change of pace.

Two hours away, in Kansas City, there were raves every weekend. I started going and easily found a new group of friends to hang out with. After a few weekends of this, I decided not to go back to the base. The city was so much fun! I took e-pills, or ecstasy, at least three times a week and went to clubs almost every night. I was out of control; I took more ecstasy than I ever should have. Todd had always warned me to never take it more than ten times during my whole life. I was way over that mark by the second week! But Todd was talking about pure MDMA. E-pills usually didn't have much real MDMA in them. They usually consisted mostly of DXM and meth. So I felt safe taking more of them than he had suggested. All the other party kids ate more pills than I did, and they seemed okay.

I should have listened to Todd, though, because it eventually caught up with me. I started getting what Todd referred to as "back-ends" during the week after my ecstasy experiences. A back-end felt similar to a hangover from alcohol, only it was worse. My head pounded with pain. My energy dropped to almost nothing. I slept for days, and each time I woke up feeling as tired as when I went to sleep. The worst part about it was that I felt stupid. It was like my brain was processing everything in slow motion. Once this started happening to me, I noticed that some of the other ravers were experiencing it too. The *responsible* ravers even had a name for this decrease in IQ; they called the other *careless* ravers, e-tards!

*   *   *

Finally, Todd called me after about six weeks with no contact. I was relieved to hear that he was doing well. At the same time, I was extremely disappointed with him. The way he blew me off had really hurt my feelings. Our conversation was abrupt. He obviously wanted to avoid a stressful interchange and made a sad attempt at an apology. Then he quickly moved on to the actual reason behind his call. "I need a driver. You would have to drive a moving truck, but it would only take an afternoon. Can you do it?"

Did he actually think I would help him after what he did? "No. Maybe some other time. I'm too busy." To get me to stop what I was doing, he would have to try harder than that! I immediately hung up on him to get my point across!

He left several messages on my phone over the next few days. Somehow his persistence started to chip away at my defenses. So when he invited me out to the base to see him, I decided to go. We had both suffered enough. I still wanted to be with him, so there wasn't a reason to keep playing games.

Upon my arrival, I noticed that Gunnar was acting strange. He was walking around outside aimlessly. He was in his own world as I tried to say

43

hello to him. I received no response or indication that he even knew I was there. He just stood there with a blank stare. His eyes were sort of glazed over; they were bulging so far out of his head that they looked like they might pop out. What was wrong with him? He never got that messed up when he was on one of his Mopy-Dopy benders...

Chapter 6 ALD-52

"So you really think you can handle it?" Todd smiled, excited by my boastfulness.

"I've been tripping a lot since you've been gone. I can handle it!" Adrenaline raced through me.

"How long has it been since you have taken LSD?" He said this with an inquisitive look, just like a scientist studying his experiment.

"Well, I had some really bad acid last weekend. It didn't give me any visuals and only made me feel low. I'm not for sure it was even real." I had only taken LSD that one time ever, but he didn't have to know that! Mainly I had just been taking e-pills. You have to fake it until you make it, right?

"Okay," he replied as he furrowed his brow contemplatively. "The weekend was about four days ago, so you probably still have a small tolerance. I guess you can take the ALD-52, an analog of LSD. If you didn't have a tolerance, I wouldn't suggest it because it's still in the extremely potent crystalline form."

"So what does that mean?" He always talked over my head. What was crystalline? Didn't acid only come in liquid or on blotter paper?

"It is extremely potent. It hasn't been broken down to a liquid yet." He seemed to be disinterested with explaining things to me. So he quickly grabbed a large vitamin jar. "We need something to get it out with. Go find a paper clip."

The nearest office in the missile base was only a few steps away. So I hurried to the desk, found a paper clip, and rushed back. "Okay, here it is."

He methodically straightened out the paper clip and then opened the jar. "Come here, you'll want to look at this. Most people never get to see what crystalline ALD looks like. Be careful, just look inside. Don't get too close."

I cautiously peered down inside. The jar was dark opaque brown, so it allowed the crystalline to be seen quite easily. The sides were covered with a gray-white dust. A layer about an inch thick was covering the bottom. How many doses could that have been? A million or so?

After I was finished looking, he dipped in the paperclip. "I'm using the paperclip to control the dose since it has a small surface area. I only want to get the very tip of it covered with the crystalline. The normal dose is 100mcg, so we will *hope* that your dose is only 1000mcg!" He dipped it in, looked at it, and then handed it to me. "Now hold it under your tongue."

The taste was slightly bitter, yet there was hardly enough there to give an adequate description. The paper clip stayed in my mouth for about five minutes. And I could feel it almost instantly!

The world around me started to sparkle. White light, shimmering energy pulsated through everything. The colors around the room became more vibrant than I had ever seen. Each one had an infinite number of shades and hues. I felt incredibly alive. Power surged through my veins. "I want to listen to music!" I exclaimed. And off we went, toward the stereo in the missile bay.

The stereo put out a sound that was ver clear and crisp. Perfect. However, the ALD made the sound take on a new dimension! Todd had put in a Deep Forest CD, which had tribal beats with pygmies harmonizing to them. The pygmies were amazing! I could feel them singing and dancing all around me. Little angelic, sparkly, pygmies! They created mandalas that spiraled through my existence. I became them. I created mandalas. Time began to swirl in a pattern comparable to the mandalas. It started from me, and then expanded out to the world.

My body felt so light, like I was floating on clouds. A fairy, flying around leaving a trail of pixie dust behind! I wondered how much further I could go. How much more beautiful could it get? I contemplated this for a while, lost in wonderment. Eventually I asked Todd if I could have another dose.

He was sitting next to me on the couch and looking very skeptical. "Well, I guess so. Don't you think you are high enough already?"

"No, I want more, MORE! I feel wonderful!"

"Okay, but you might not feel it since you are building a tolerance."

"Oh well. Can we just try anyway?"

"Okay, okay. But you have to drink some juice before you take it. You need to keep your blood sugar up." And with that, we got up and headed to the other side of the complex.

First, however, we had to walk through the tunnel. And it was amazing! Claaaaooueeng, Claaaoooeeeaaang. The world was spiraling out of control. Our footsteps created rainbow light prisms that bounced off the sides and reverberated everywhere. Claaaouueeeng, Claaeeeeaaaouuoongg, Cleeeaaaoouueeaanng.

got to the kitchen, I immediately went
rator to drink some apple juice. It was
than I thought it would be. I picked
and was instantly sucked into it. My
_ _ connected with the cold moist glass. We
were apart of each other. I was the glass and the
apple juice, and they were me. There was no
difference, no separation. Swallowing myself was
quite a challenge!

As I drank, I felt like I might choke. I just
couldn't swallow normally now that I could see it
from both angles. This oneness was strange, very
confusing. Yet, it felt as though I always knew our
world was set up this way - only I had forgotten for
some reason.

When my struggle eventually finished, I
noticed that Todd was laughing at me. My
consciousness was so absorbed in the apple juice
unity thing, that I had forgotten he was even there.
"Are you sure you want another paper clip sweetie?"
He just kept giggling.

"Yes, I do. And stop laughing at me!"

So he prepared another paper clip, the same
as before. Then we headed back down the spinning
rainbow tunnel to listen to music and await the
results. Where did I end? I was expanded, whole.
Time moved slowly, yet seemed to be in the natural
flow of things.

I could see the *real* reality. Amazing texture
and depth. People started to remind me of dogs. A
dog can only see in black and white, so the dog
thinks the world has no color. The dog is obviously
mistaken because, as humans, we always see in
color. Still, how do we explain to a dog that the
world is *really* this way? There is a language and
comprehension barrier between us. The dog's mind
is set on its course, as limited as that may be. My
visions showed me the next step; they revealed what

48

people don't usually get to see. My words could never come close to describing the magnificence of the entheogenic headspace.

* * *

"I don't think I'm getting any higher. Can I have another paperclip?"

"I think you've built up a tolerance, so no amount will affect you. Anyway, it's getting late, or shall I say early! I think you should take something that will bring you down so we can rest." He was lying on the couch looking exhausted. I don't think he had taken anything so far. How did he stay awake this long?

"I don't want to come down. This is so much fun! I'll trip by myself. I know you're tired. You can go to sleep. Don't worry about me. I can amuse myself!" I didn't want it to end. I mean, that's why I'd asked for more. Didn't he understand that?

"I don't want you to have to trip alone. But I have to take something if I am going to stay up with you." He paused, thinking for a moment. "How about we both take some 2C-B? You won't be tolerant to it because it works on dopamine, unlike LSD which works mostly on serotonin."

"What's 2C-B?"

"You haven't heard of 2C-B in the rave scene?" Todd looked a little shocked. "Well, it's sort of like MDMA, only mellower. Music doesn't sound as good on it, but it's peaceful. Very warm."

"I am up for anything!" I loved to try new drugs and get another notch on my belt.

One hour later:

"Please take me with you when you leave Kansas this time." I gazed over at him with pleading

49

eyes. "You don't know how hard it is to be away from you. I love you."

"I won't leave you behind, but if you are going to be around I have to tell you something." He fidgeted nervously. "I have to tell you who I really am."

"Okay." I already knew that his facility wasn't a *spring factory.* He had excessive amounts of money and was far too paranoid to only be an investment banker. Plus, Gunnar had gotten overly upset about my internet research. I suspected that something was up. My questions might finally get answered.

"Follow me." We walked into a storage area next to the missile bay and headed toward a row of large green metal boxes. "Do you know what these are?"

"They look like storage containers to me."

"You're partly right. I got them from the military."

"Why do you have military storage containers?"

"Camouflage!" He chuckled a bit as he popped the lid off one of them. He reached in and pulled out a large flask with dark residue in it. "I am the head of security for the Brotherhood of Eternal Love." He carefully put the flask back into the container as he continued. "The Brotherhood has been around since the 60's. You've probably heard of Owsley and Nickie Sand. We are the ones that supply the world with LSD."

"I knew something was going on." I couldn't believe he was finally telling me all of this!

"I just got finished tearing down this lab and moving it here for storage. You see, the other missile base is where the lab was operational."

"You have another missile base?"

"Well, indirectly. Do you remember Tim? You

50

know the guy's funeral I had to go to last month? Anyway, he was letting us use his facility. That is, until he committed suicide. We had to move everything because his family now owns the place."

"Is that why you called and asked me if I could drive for you last week?" I started to put together the pieces.

"Yes, but it's alright. We managed without you." He started to laugh really hard. "It was a wild ride though, driving those big trucks when I was tripping that hard!"

"So you got dosed when you were taking it apart?"

"Oh, of course. The LSD crystals were everywhere. Leonard made such a mess. Gunnar picked up a flask and somehow got dusted. He has been tripping for almost three days! He shit in my bathtub that asshole! All I can do is just keep giving him valiums to try to bring him down. I had a tolerance going from finishing up some chemistry, so luckily I didn't get nuked out like he did!"

I hadn't even suspected Leonard to be involved until now. I thought he was just another rich "investment banker" friend of Todd's. Whenever I saw him, he was always wearing a black suit with the confident elegance of someone very educated. I think he said something about going to Harvard. He just didn't seem like he was into drugs. I never did any with him anyway.

I struggled to remember anything that would go along with what Todd was saying. Leonard always called the base and said he was an hour and a half away. I thought that meant that he was driving from the KCI airport, having flown in from San Francisco where he lived. He must have actually been at the lab. Amazing. How had I missed that?

Three or four hours later:

We both lay on the bed, cuddled up. Todd went to sleep the moment his head hit the pillow. Now he was lightly snoring; it was methodic. I lay very still with my eyes closed trying to relax. It wasn't working. I had been tripping for about fifteen hours so far. I was getting a little tired, but it just wouldn't end. I kept seeing scenes of things happening when I closed my eyes. I saw a bustling city, the ocean, and horses running in a field. Then I discovered that I could see any scene I wanted to see. I would think of a scenario, and then it would act itself out in front of me. It was pretty cool. I had a personally directed movie inside my head! Finally, after an hour of movie making, I drifted off. Content. Home.

Chapter 7 PUTTING TOGETHER THE PIECES

Out of nowhere, Todd told us to pack down the missile base. Todd almost always had an entourage of people around him to do his laundry, grocery shopping, and run little errands. He was too stuck up to do any of those tasks himself. He'd been spoiled by a wealthy upbringing, which included fulltime maids and cooks, and this apparently carried over into his adult life.

So, anyway, Todd didn't explain why we had to move; he only said that we had to hurry. It seemed so urgent that no one even asked him why. We all just assumed we were about to get busted. We didn't move the containers holding the lab for some reason; we only moved what Todd felt were the most important things like his stereo and his clothes. When he told us we were moving to Mendocino, California, we forgot about the stress of the move immediately. We were all so excited about living on the beach!

I recruited two of my raver friends from Kansas City to help drive some of the moving trucks. I had never driven across the country before and was excited! Todd wasn't going to be making the drive; he was flying out there ahead of us to get everything ready. This didn't bother me that much, because my friends were coming along. Also, Todd seemed to slow things down sometimes. He liked to sleep in late, eat three full meals a day out at restaurants, and talk on the phone for hours at a time. This wouldn't be a good combination with all the miles we needed to travel!

Before Todd left for the airport, he gave me a stack of cash and said, "You're in charge, go for it." This shocked me. Didn't he know that I had absolutely no experience with this type of thing?

* * *

The trip was long and boring. To spice things up, we decided to do what we called "nudity across America". It was funny; we would stop in opportune  spots and take a few snapshots of ourselves showing some skin! We shot photos in the mountains of Colorado, the desert of Nevada, a McDonald's somewhere, next to a huge three story tall cross, in a cemetery, and by a metal sculpture of a tin man. It made my adrenaline rush, as I would look around before taking off my shirt or lifting up my skirt. No one ever saw us; I would have laughed excessively if they had!

We pulled up to our new house on the beach about four days after we left Kansas. Well, the property had three houses actually. There was the main house, a guesthouse, and an apartment over a two-car garage.

I had never seen the Pacific Ocean before, and we could see it from our living room. The view was breathtaking. The air was thick with moisture and the smell of saltwater, yet it was still cool on my skin. I loved it. We were surrounded on both sides with National Parks, which created a quiet and peaceful environment.

Once we got settled in, I started to notice that something was different somehow. Todd spent a lot of time alone. It looked like he was thinking about something, deeply. He kept taking long walks through the nearby trails in the parks. He meditated every day. I had never seen him isolate himself this way. He didn't want anyone to talk to him and disturb him; his only request was to be left alone. What was up with him?

Todd left several times in the first month we lived there for "meetings". They were very secretive, because he wouldn't say where or for how long he was going. The first two were only for a couple of days. So this time, when he had been gone for almost two weeks, I started to get worried. He never explained where he kept going; he just went. What was he doing? I hated being kept in the dark.

I was surfing on the net and surprisingly found the following article about an LSD lab on the

Topeka Capital Journal's website. I knew it pertained to us and read it immediately. It was dated November 11, 2000, which was only a couple of days earlier. Was Todd okay? Did he get busted trying to move the lab? I nervously read more:

> For years, the whispers have suggested something secretive, even illegal, was taking place at an old missile complex outside of town. The people working there told the curious they were making springs for the space shuttle and the F-16. Top secret stuff, they said... ...On Saturday, a knot of DEA and other law enforcement vehicles clustered outside a building on the grounds of the former missile complex. They were dismantling a 'large non-operational clandestine LSD laboratory,' ... ...Agents wore chemical-resistant clothing to protect them against solvents, acids and other chemicals that might be present...
>
> ...The dismantling of the lab follows the arrest of two San Francisco men earlier this month in Pottawatomie county. William Leonard Pickard, 55, and Clyde Apperson, 45, were indicted Nov.8-9 by a Federal grand jury in Kansas City. They are charged with one count of conspiracy to manufacture, distribute and dispense LSD. The charges carry a minimum of 10 years and a maximum of life in prison without parole...
>
> ...When DEA agents stopped Pickard and Apperson on Colombian Road on the west side of Wamego the evening of Nov. 6, the two had just left the former missile site. One of the men was driving a car and the other a

truck, Seager said, and the truck reportedly contained equipment for the LSD lab. 'We don't know if anything was being manufactured there, just that the lab (equipment) had been there,' the police chief said. 'The equipment for the lab was going to be moved. That's why they (DEA Agents) attempted to stop the car and the truck.' The former missile complex was owned by the Wamego Land Trust. DEA agents had been staking out the missile complex site for several days before they tried to apprehend Pickard and Apperson. When they stopped the vehicles, Apperson was taken into custody, but Pickard fled on foot. An 18-hour manhunt ensued. He was arrested the next day near a farmstead four miles west of town after a farmer called authorities when he saw Pickard enter his equipment shed and get into the cab of his truck...

I was in shock! It didn't say anything about Todd; I hoped he wasn't arrested too. Was he there at the site when all of this happened? I also wished Leonard would've gotten away. And who was Clyde? I had never heard of him before. My thoughts were scattered and raced through my mind. How could all of this have happened?

Todd finally called a few days later and assured me that he wasn't going to jail. He ended the phone call more abruptly than I would have liked, but at least I knew he was okay. He was at the missile base with the DEA when it all happened, but he told me that he had immunity and wasn't in any trouble. How did he get immunity? Is that even possible? He couldn't be a narc, could he?

I slowly started to put it all together. Todd had been acting really stressed for the past month. I remembered one evening where he made everyone leave the house except for me. In my mind it was so we could trip together, but it turned out that he had some "work" to do.

Noticing my disappointment, he gave me a dose of MDMA to rectify things. Then he told me to go listen to music in the other room while he sifted through a bunch of paperwork that was spread out over the top of the kitchen table. He told me not to look at any of it. Instead, I was supposed to stay in the other room and have a good time.

After a couple of hours, I started to get lonely and poked my head into the kitchen. "Can I come in there with you?" I asked. "If I don't look at anything?"

"You can if you sit over there." He motioned to the couch at the opposite side of the room.

As I walked by him, I saw pictures, sort of like passport photos but a little larger, scattered around on the table. Most of them I didn't recognize, but I saw Leonard's easily. It was the one on top with the most copies. Now that I look back on it, it is apparent that Todd was preparing to turn Leonard in to the DEA. Why else would he have immunity now and have had all that information laid out like that back then? How long had he been planning this? I tried to remember more about that night, knowing that it could hold the answers.

I sat there for a while. Then Todd eventually got up and handed me a pile of paperwork. "You should read this while you can. It will show you that your good friend Leonard isn't so good."

I looked down at the papers he handed me. They had classified written on them. Operation Infrared??? I thumbed through it, disinterested. I was in no headspace to read. I wanted to have fun! Didn't he remember that he had given me ecstasy? "Can I read it later?"

"No, you must read it now. This will be your only chance. It is important."

I tried to read some of it, but truthfully I only remember the highlights. Basically, Leonard was working for the CIA. He knew some guy named Dostum from Afghanistan and was trying to trade a stinger missile of Dostum's for a heroin dealer serving time in a U.S. Federal Prison. The file ended by reporting that the trade was successful. "So Leonard knew some guy in Afghanistan and worked for the CIA, who cares?"

"They are really pissed at Leonard over that mission. He did the trade alright, but he also imported a large quantity of heroin, using the trade as a cover." Todd looked disgusted. "Heroin is evil; we are better then that. We don't use or deal substances that are addictive. Those drugs hurt people, and we're not supposed to involve ourselves in such things. We are only here to help by being a positive force in the world."

* * *

On November 21, 2000 another article came out in the Topeka Capital Journal. Todd had bragged to me when we were on ALD that his group produced the world supply. At the time I thought he must be exaggerating, but this article confirmed it:

Drug Enforcement Administration officials in Wamego worked Monday to collect evidence from what experts are calling one of the largest LSD drug laboratories in the world...
...investigators have discovered enough chemical ingredients found to produce between 36 million and 60 million doses of LSD. 'They are predicting that this laboratory could have been supplying a third of the LSD

59

in the United States and maybe the world,' Armstead said. 'This particular laboratory is one of the biggest labs that has ever been seized in this country.'

...On Friday, U.S. District Court Judge Richard D. Rogers ruled to allow Apperson to post bond of $200,000 under the agreement that he will forfeit property for failure to appear in court. Co-defendant Pickard was denied bond...

After reading it, I wondered why Leonard was denied bond. Was an LSD charge really that serious? They usually give murderers a bail. Is LSD possession worse than murder? It made no sense to me...

Chapter 8 SHAMANIC COLONIC

Remembering the first time I smoked DMT, or dimethyltryptamine, is as easy as taking a deep breath. Smoking it is the most common method of ingestion but, after my experience, I don't understand why. Todd gave me a small amount of the orange crystalline rock already loaded into a glass pipe. Its stench seeped out, smelling exactly like mothballs. I lit it and inhaled several times. The smell changed to burnt plastic, and it felt like razors cutting my lungs. I tried to hold the smoke in, but I only could cough uncontrollably. It was the worst substance I ever inhaled. My lungs ached!

My consciousness only shifted slightly. It was euphoric, yet it was not what I'd always heard about. No elves dancing around my head. No aliens. Todd explained to me that, if I smoked a few more hits, I would feel the full effect. Still, my lungs could not take any more torture despite what my heart wanted. They hurt for two days afterward; every breath was painful!

* * *

"There is no way I am going to smoke it again!" The memory of my previous discomfort was still fresh in my mind.

"You can do the shamanic colonic!" Todd

smiled really big, knowing that I had no clue what he was talking about. "That means that you take it anally."

"Yuck, I don't think so." The thought of taking a drug that way petrified me.

"It really will be a good experience, I promise. It's the only other way to take DMT without taking an MAOI (monoamine oxidase inhibitor). And your system isn't clean enough to take an MAOI; you've been drinking coffee." He smiled reassuringly.

"Okay," I said hesitantly. "But this is weird." What was I getting myself into?

"First the DMT needs to be dissolved so that it can absorb through the membranes in the anus. DMT is fat soluble, so mixing it with any form of oil or butter will allow it to dissolve." I cringed as Todd pulled a stick of butter out of the refrigerator and put it into the microwave to melt. "The dosage of 200-600mg varies among people because of body weight, MAOI activity, and substance purity. I think you should start out on the low side and titrate up."

So he used three different large spoons to dissolve a total of 600mg of DMT (200mg in each spoon) with the butter by heating it slowly with the flame from the stove. "It should only be heated until it is dissolved, not more." Then he sucked up each mixture with a different syringe. Therefore, this resulted in three syringes with 200mg of DMT in each syringe. This way, I could use one and then keep adding more if the first one wasn't strong enough.

Todd also explained that the DMT solution would soak in more efficiently if I did an enema first. My head was spinning with nervous energy. Weren't the syringes bad enough by themselves? I looked at him in agonizing discomfort as he handed me the enema kit. What was I doing? Is it really going to be worth *all this?*

My soul felt completely uncentered when I finished in the bathroom. I headed toward the living room filled with apprehension. Impending thoughts of the syringes horrified me as I took off my pants and thong. Todd directed me to position myself with my ass in the air, propped up by some pillows, so nothing would ooze out. Yuck! Then he squirted in the first syringe. My anus was on fire!

"Hold it for as long as you can, even if you have to stand on your head!" Todd instructed.

"It burns! Is it supposed to burn this bad?" It was amazing how horrible it felt. Maybe DMT just wasn't my thing.

About five minutes passed and I felt no head change. So in went the second syringe. And it burned worse! I could barely feel the DMT in my system, although it did seem to be coming on stronger.

Todd suggested using the third one. He said, "If it doesn't hit you quickly, then you haven't done enough." So off I went on 600mg of DMT.

Up until this point I was cocky, fearless, and thought I could handle anything. I *really* believed that I was a *master tripper*! This was incredibly foolish of me. I had only been tripping for about a year and never really had a bad trip. I guess it was my time for an awakening, and believe me, it was not an easy one...

Twisting, turning, fragmented-mirror tunnels with no time or space. I rolled through them, tunnels to nothingness, empty white-light space. I rolled like a child sliding down an endless tube slide. I felt like a ball. I could feel my ear tucked in tight next to my foot. Different parts of me touched the cosmic slide at different times, scrambled, rolling uncontrollably. I was afraid. In silence and white light. No color or sound. Sterile, crisp.

How long had I been rolling? Would I ever

63

return? Was anything wrong with me? Was I going to be okay? Who am I? Where am I? What was my last thought? I'm scared. **Help! Can anyone hear me?**

Alone, empty, tunnels. Try to think. Try to get a hold of yourself. Sliding, rolling, tunnels. Who am I? Where am I? Fear, everywhere. Alone. No one here to help me. How long had I been rolling? Time, what is time? Who am I? Remember, try to pull it together. Why? Tense, no control, rolling to nowhere yet everywhere. What does that mean?

Suddenly, I smelled an orange. Todd was kneeled down, peeling it, in front of my face. The smell was vibrant, so vivid. I had never smelled a smell better than this one! Finally I was back!!! **Reality! Thank God!** "How long have I been tripping for? Am I okay?"

"You're alright, sweetie. You've only been tripping for about half an hour. Are you having a good time?" He was amused by my discomfort and sort of chuckled. He obviously thought it was time for an attitude adjustment too.

"I'm scared. When will it stop?" I was shaken to my core and wanted the nightmare to end. It felt as if something else was in control of my mind.

"Well, it usually lasts about an hour and a half, so you're a third of the way through it. Just relax. What happened to my little super-tripper? Don't you remember wanting to take it? DMT is a little different than LSD isn't it?" He started to laugh really hard and then added, "Really, sweetie, you're alright. Just breathe."

"Oh no! Here it goes again!" And with that thought I was sucked out of my body and back into the tunnels. Empty timeless folds of my consciousness. Time stopped...

I don't remember much of the rest of the trip, other than the fear that overtook me. I sort of blacked out or something. My memory was totally blank. It was an uneasy feeling, being blank. I kept wondering what happened and if I'd ever remember it.

I returned to reality about two hours after the nightmare began. Humbled, changed completely. Forever reverent and extremely afraid of DMT! During my previous trips, I had been stuck in *pretty colors world* and *warm-fuzzy world*. DMT changed me. Now I had anxiety - a lot of it! So I started to pray before every trip. I didn't want to go back to that headspace ever.

INTEGRATION

My housemates commented on my apparent shift of personality. I changed from a cocky, know-it-all tripper to a very humble soul. I didn't speak much for about three days. Obviously, this was a consequence of never being that scared in my life. Also, having forgotten the trip made me feel low, unsure of myself. Was I really cut out for this? My trips always used to be fun. Why was this one so different?

I eventually realized that tripping is like learning to ride a bike, except you never totally master it. When you first start out you fall down a lot. And it's awfully frightening when you fall down for the first time. Each fall after that gets a little easier, though. Since you know that it can happen, you're sort of prepared for it. At the same time, you have to remember that you never actually master it. You will probably always have little bumps and bruises along the way.

Also, set and setting are crucial. I went into this trip afraid and shell-shocked from the enema. It was a bad idea to even continue at this point. Set and setting has as much to do with your mental state as it does with your surroundings. If you're not in a positive and safe headspace, you should never trip. I should have made sure that I was centered and comfortable. I should have listened to my soul/body and let it guide me, instead of Todd.

Remember that once you go...you never come back the same. It is called a *trip* for a reason! Continual positive evolution is essential for the soul/body. It is your responsibility to allow that positive change to manifest. Change can go both ways if you're not mindful. However, with a pure heart, you are in control of your life. You are the one interpreting the visions. You are also the one integrating those visions into your reality. Believe anything you intuitively feel that you should, since *it is all true.* Tripping is helpful in this way because life lessons can be learned quickly, saving time.

Fears came to the surface during this trip that I didn't even know were there. Looking back on it, the fears were always there; they were just suppressed, forgotten about. I was afraid of being alone and of losing control. If I couldn't control what was going on in my mind, then how could I control my heartbeat or breathing? I was alone and no one was there to help me. This fear nudged my trip to unfold in the direction it did.

I didn't like my experience, yet I needed to learn that I would be totally safe no matter what. Safety is at the root of *reality* because love is always *here.* Love might shift around a bit, but love never ends. Love only grows, like all of us.

Hopefully, this trip gave me sufficient time and experience to work through my fears. I'm skeptical about this though, especially since my memory has seemed to repress most of the visions. It is important to work through things like this completely, so they will end. The last thing anyone wants is to be haunted by fear driven trips! I think I simply needed to realize that fear doesn't exist. Fear is an illusion created by the mind, just like everything else.

The ego can get in the way of learning, so you must surround yourself with humility. I needed to be humbled; it made me much stronger. It helped prepare me for a more universal education. And no one has all of the answers. If you think you know, then you are wrong. Learn from each other and from yourself, for there is no difference between the two. If you don't know, then how can they? And likewise, if they don't know, then how can you? Thus, humility is essential for true knowledge to be obtained.

Prior to this trip, I thought psychedelics were just like every other drug. They had one purpose; they were a fun way to see a different version of reality. How did I walk down the road and miss the city? Were there paths to choose from that I couldn't see? Sometimes the worst (least fun) trips teach you the most; therefore, they really are the best. These substances, entheogens, should be revered. They are of a higher way of being. They are sacred and must be consumed with the purest intentions. I'd suggest praying before each trip, but each person must make his or her own way...

My soul was shaken too deeply to immediately regain the courage that was needed to trip again anytime soon. Sometimes it takes along time to process a trip. You must allow yourself plenty of time to fully integrate where you have been. You will not benefit as much from the experience if you rush yourself. What is time to an egoless co-creator anyway?

I had to make sure I did trip again, though, at some point. If I didn't, I thought I might always fear tripping. And holding onto fear is not a positive and beneficial thing for a person to do.

It's just like when you were a kid and were learning to ride that bike we talked about earlier. Remember that fearless, brave child. No matter what happened, or how many times the child fell down, he or she always got back up. You knew that if you kept trying you would learn how. In some ways this is a poor comparison because as a child you knew exactly what you had to do, to get the end result you sought. I know tripping isn't that simple. You will never know exactly what you need to do or where you will be going.

You are a blind man being led by love, and love alone. Still, don't stop traveling on the psychedelic journey just because you can't see the end. One day you will understand. Let the love guide you and keep you safe. Entheogens, or psychedelics, are in no way here just for fun. They reveal the whole of reality, the good and the bad. Happiness cannot exist without sadness. Security cannot exist without anxiety. Being whole cannot exist without being alone. Namaste.

Chapter 9 ANOTHER MOVE

About a month later, Todd's DEA contact, Karl, called to warn us about a potentially threatening situation. Somehow a few members of the Brotherhood had found out where we were living. This put us in extreme danger since Todd was solely responsible for Leonard and Clyde getting busted. *No one likes a rat.* Needless to say, for our safety, we had to leave Mendocino immediately. If Todd intended on turning in the lab, then why did he move us to the bay area in the first place? He always said that most of the brotherhood lived around there. Did he really even know what he was talking about? Who knows...?

Everything happened so quickly. We rented two of the largest trucks from the only moving truck rental location in town. When the company rented them to us, they explained that the largest truck of the two, "Big Jim," couldn't leave town. It was an older truck that wasn't in very good condition. We had no choice but to lie to them. We needed trucks right then, not in a few hours. So we promised them that the trucks would be used in town only.

Everyone in the group, seven at the time, worked for twenty-two hours straight in order to pack up our three houses. We threw our belongings in boxes, trash bags, and even packed stuff loosely around other items already in "Big Jim". There was no time to be wasted on making things look pretty. Each minute that passed could have brought us closer to danger.

At some point during this time, Todd got out an Atlas and asked us to all gather around. "Where do you guys want to move?"

We all looked at each other, confused. We didn't know; he was the one who made all the decisions. Why was he asking us? He noticed our ambivalence. "Okay, first let's eliminate where we do not want to live. We can't live in California."

"I don't want to live in the Midwest," I chimed in.

"How about the east coast?" Todd asked.

Our discussion went on like this for about an hour. Eventually, we decided to move to Tucson, Arizona. It seemed perfect. The weather was sunny and warm, which was a nice contrast to the cold, foggy climate of the coast. Todd had lived in Tucson in his early twenties for a few years too. So, since he already knew people there, it would be an easy transition. Most importantly, however, we were far away from the Bay Area.

As we got on the highway, we quickly found out that "Big Jim" was a disaster! It could only go 50 mph at top speed. It took us two days to get to the California-Arizona border. Todd and I followed the trucks in a state of total boredom. We must have looked like a motley crew! The two old, barely running moving trucks billowing black smoke were followed by a $130,000 C-4 Porsche and my regular old Pontiac Grand Am. Driving in the caravan was exhausting, literally! Every minute seemed to last ten times as long as it usually did. And the smoke was disgusting.

As we traveled through the desert, "Big Jim" caught on fire periodically. It was a hilarious sight to see! Lupe, our illegal Mexican worker, rode shotgun as Gunnar drove. Every time the engine would catch fire he would jump out and blast it with a fire extinguisher. This whole process slowed us down to a crawl. Black smoke swirled out of the exhaust; it was wild! We finally arrived in Tucson five days after we started. It should have only taken us two, but that's how life goes sometimes, right?

When we got into town, Todd immediately called Karl. He told him about the truck situation and that it was the DEA's responsibility to fix it. Karl was really pissed off when he heard that we basically stole the trucks, almost burnt one on the way, and then were not going to return them! He complained a bit, but he ended up straightening it all out for us. We were no longer an enemy of the DEA. They needed Todd's criminal record to be as clean as possible for when he would testify for them. This was just the first in a long list of incidents that they covered up for us. We learned that they would do anything to win a big case - even drop a few other smaller cases.

As we started to look for a house, we turned to the DEA for help. Because of "possible danger" they had no choice. Karl arranged for us to get a house under a different name with no credit check. He evidently had a connection with Long Realty and sent us to them. Upon our arrival, Karl verified who we were and gave the okay. And it was as easy as that. By the end of the day, we were moving into our new house. No one could track us, so we were safe. It's pretty cool what the government can do if they want to!

We rented a luxurious house in the foothills of the Catalina Mountains. We overlooked the entire city. There was a huge heated pool and Jacuzzi in our backyard. The house was amazing. There were five bedrooms and two bathrooms. Todd and I got the master bedroom and bathroom - complete with our own hot tub. Lupe got a room next to some friends visiting from California. Gunnar took a room off the garage. And our other friends, visiting from Kansas, took the room at the opposite end of the house. Everyone fit, although, it was a houseful.

Chapter 10 TELEPATHY ON NEW YEARS

The excitement had been building among the entourage. There were five members currently, including myself. And Todd had us running in all directions. He wanted his New Years party to be amazing! We were only expecting five guests, but with the six of us already there we totaled eleven. This was a large group for us. We usually just tripped with the entourage; new people were risky.

We planned to dose on MDMA first, then "Candy flip" with either LSD or ALD-52. The group congregated in the kitchen as everyone arrived. Todd and his lab scale were our focus. He weighed out 120mg of MDMA for each of us on little pieces of paper. Having been through this before, I got some juice out of the refrigerator to chase it with. It didn't help much. As everyone else took their doses, they gagged and complained about the taste. The agonizing looks on their faces were priceless! Todd attempted to divert our attention and ushered us out to the pool.

He put on an Enigma CD as we headed out. The pool was warm and comfortable. The music floated around us, creating quite an ambience. I was still a little nervous. My DMT trip had really shaken me; I didn't want to have a bad trip again. I felt the

MDMA coming on. Its energy combined with mine. Love surged through me. The silky water began to shimmer, reflecting the stars. I smiled as the world came to life, completely forgetting about feeling nervous. Who needed to be nervous on this stuff? I felt SO GOOD!

"It has been about forty-five minutes since we took the first dose. It's time to flip," Todd announced as he started handing out the little golden nuggets. They were each dosed with 250mcg of LSD. Some people took two or three; some people took five. Whatever each person wanted, they received.

"You have to chew them up," Todd said. "Because LSD absorbs best in the mouth."

Cautiously, I only took one. I was feeling great but still remembered what a bad trip was like. I didn't want to freak out in front of so many people. It was okay if it was just Todd and I, but I didn't want everyone else to see me like that.

Thirty minutes later:

The shimmering water started to twinkle, glistening in a new way. My visual field was overtaken by movement. Everything started to twist and vibrate. The world started to dissolve; I could no longer see its form. No separations. No divisions. Everything was made up of the same basic substance. It reminded me of what molecules might look like in constant Brownian motion. Which is air and which is water? I couldn't tell the difference because there was no difference. Should I be in the pool? My heart started to beat a little faster. Everything was one, the same. Am I breathing in air or water? How do I know which is which? *Should I be in the pool?*

And with that, I sufficiently freaked myself out. I got out of the pool and began shivering, very cold and wet. My teeth chattered. Where were my clothes? In the bedroom. Where was my bedroom? What was I just thinking about? Cold. Clothes. Everything was Technicolor. The colors were so beautiful! Dripping wet. Clothes. The lights were too bright; they hurt my eyes. I needed a shirt and pants. Shirt and pants. Fuzzy shirt. Warmer. Pants. Aah, finally. Less shaking.

Where was everyone else? Where was I? In the bedroom, shaking. Warmer. I heard voices. I didn't want to be alone. I heard voices. I followed them. The living room. The couch. Sit, try to look normal. Was everyone else as high as I was? I didn't want to freak out. Be calm.

DMT headspace. Be calm. This trip was somehow linked to the DMT trip. Time folded back on itself. I could see myself then, my whole headspace. I could remember! I had seen myself now, in this trip, then. That's why I blacked out. I had seen into my future. Maybe I just wasn't ready for it then. Was I ready now? Are the future and the past really linked through my trips? What about my dreams? Heartbeat raced. Breathe. Is this time travel? My lungs felt tight. Am I crazy? No one will ever believe me. Hands tingled. Relax, don't freak out.

Todd plopped down right beside me. "How are you doing, sweetie?" He threw his giant arm around me, bringing me close to him.

"Okay." Talking was difficult. I felt love radiating from him. Safety. Security. I would be okay now.

Everyone circled around us; some people sat in chairs and some were on the floor. Most of the others looked a little nervous as well. This made me feel a little better; I was glad I wasn't the only one.

Todd talked to us in a monologue. He told funny stories about his life. I couldn't follow them very well. I kept spacing out, going into my own world. I just laughed when everyone else did, which was a lot. He sort of grounded us with his stories. They gave us a common focus, which kept us together even though our minds were wandering through the cosmos in a million directions at once.

Then Todd started pulling me through a vortex. It was intense. I held onto his arm tightly and went along. We ascended. He and I, One. I don't think anyone else got there, to the cosmic divine. We were home. Loved and safe. The Godhead, enlightenment, knowledge that WORDS COULD NEVER DESCRIBE. It must be experienced to be known. We are our heritage and our end. Time's immortal creation and death. What an illusion we live in! If everyone only knew. If everyone only got to see, remember. No more war. No more hate-crimes. No more violence. No more pain. Only love. We are all the same, there is no you or I. Just ONE. Created by LOVE.

I could hear both of our thoughts in my head. It was like I was talking to myself, and then he would answer. Was this really happening? Wow! Can he really hear me? Or is this just in my head? It's probably just in my head. 'No, its not.' Okay, if he can hear me, he'll show me a sign. Todd turned to me and winked. Oh my GOD! I felt elated. Telepathy, something I had always heard about, amazing. What else was possible?

Todd kept a conversation going with me in my head and still kept verbally telling stories to make everyone laugh. He was on 5000 mcg! How did he do it? I was only on 250 mcg and I could hardly concentrate enough to think two of the same thoughts in a row!

Everyone started to leave around 3am. They looked a little shaken. I thought these people had tripped a lot before? I guess they weren't used to

taking this much or something. Wh
tripped all the time, and I still had anxie

'Why?' I asked Todd telepathicall'
was listening in on my thoughts.

'Anxiety is part of tripping for yo
has difficulties. Right now yours is anxiety. Go into
it, and you will be able to get rid of it.'

'What do you mean go into it?'

'Whenever you are having a problem, or you
are in a corner, make yourself feel it more, deeper.
Deliberately try to increase your anxiety. Once you
have worked through it, you will never be in that
corner again. That doesn't mean that you won't get
stuck again in a different corner, but you won't have
trouble with the same one again.'

'How do you know so much?'

'I have been tripping a long time, sweetie.'

Todd and I seized the opportunity to cuddle
in our soft king size bed. As we started to caress
each other our unified consciousness grew stronger.
We were already one with each other and god, yet
sexuality amplified it all. Our souls not only touched
for a brief moment, but were one for a timeless
eternity. Really one. Our senses were heightened,
and the pleasure we shared was amazing. We knew
how deeply we loved each other. No questions. The
deepest love ever, a sacred love. We worshipped
each other as divine interlocking pieces of god. We
were Creation and would never be apart. We were
each other, completely.

We cuddled up close. I could see my lineage,
back through this time and space. And see its
relation to the non-space, non-time universal
consciousness, which unites us all. I felt like we
were both part of a tree. The tree of life. I could see
leaves and shades of green floating around us. I
followed its branches, the timeless picture of
existence, and I could move myself into time

.erever I wished. I could get a glimpse of a .elative's past or my future. What an illusion time is. Everything is extremely interconnected. A tree has one trunk. All the leaves share it, yet each one thinks that they are alone, an individual. We are all little pieces of the same self-reflecting divinity.

Everything is so big, huge. Complex, yet simple. Very simple. ONE. Then LOVE, then LIGHT, then LANGUAGE.

INTEGRATION

The New Year's candy-flip helped rebuild my confidence. Not only did I not fall off my bike, I discovered that I could make it fly. The amount of abilities a person has that are just lying dormant are amazing. All you have to do is think it, and you can create it. Anything imaginable is possible! *Just think it into being.*

My telepathic connection with Todd changed our relationship totally. All our doubts about the depths of each other's love were eliminated. Immediately we both felt secure. We knew what we both felt and thought. We knew we loved each other, like we loved ourselves. We were no longer separate people; we were one.

During those three or four hours of telepathy, I was the happiest I had ever been. For the first time in my life I really wasn't alone anymore. There weren't communication barriers. We thought the same things immediately. It was so natural and safe. I felt whole; I knew that this is how we are supposed to be. The boundaries that separate us are illusions. Look past them and you will see yourself.

For the next few weeks, I was ecstatic. I felt like I was floating on air. I had always dreamt of telepathy, somehow sensing that it could be attained. I had yearned for the gift, but I never actually thought it would happen. I had always thought that it was something on a science fiction movie, but not something that happened in reality. If telepathy exists, then what else is possible? Aliens? Remote viewing? Levitation?

I was eager to trip with Todd again. I wanted us to get back to that headspace. I felt more love during those unifying moments than I ever thought was possible. It was what I had been missing in my soul. The hole that always haunted me had been filled. I wanted to go back there, to that space, so we could see how much further we could take it.

* * *

As I look back on this journey years later, I know that this type of experience is not always a positive thing. It can easily become damaging, so you should only pursue this type of connection with someone you really trust. The person must have good character and values similar to your own. Telepathy will bond the two of you together forever. It can create a tight bond that will probably never be broken. So you should proceed carefully.

I should have been more cautious about choosing Todd. I became more loyal to him than to myself. This loyalty made me incredibly vulnerable. I was easily controlled and manipulated. He pushed me into involving myself in situations that I wouldn't have otherwise. He knew how to get me to do what he wanted; he had seen everything inside me. He was me - except he loved himself more. He put his needs first. This was the risk I took when I got that close. Yet, I had no idea before it happened that something bad/negative could occur. Since I grew up in Kansas, I was used to people telling the truth. Honesty is part of the wholesome Midwestern way of life. When Kansans say they are one way or another, they usually are. I had no way of knowing that Todd was different, and I wish that I had chosen more carefully.

Chapter 11 MESCALINE

"Everyone gets to pick their own dose. You are your own guide," Todd said, standing at his scale once again. He looked to each of us; no one was prepared for this. What happened to the usual routine?

"I've never done mescaline before. How should I know what the dose is?" I asked. Todd normally just handed it out.

"Why don't you look in *Pihkal?* Sasha describes what it is. But keep in mind that what we have is mescaline hydrochloride, not sulfate. So it's a little stronger." He handed me the thick book.

Right away, I opened it to the second half and found its entry, #96. Sasha reported that the dosage for the mescaline hydrochloride salt was between 178-356mg. "I guess I'll take 250mg."

"Sounds like a good dose. Remember that mescaline should be adjusted by bodyweight and you're small." He seemed cautious, although he tried to appear reassuring. Could he tell that I wasn't ready for a dose that size?

"I know I'm taking a good-sized dose. I want a heavy trip!" My previous journey had empowered me. I was ready for the next bike ride!

"Okay. Here it is." He handed the crystalline prisms to me on a sheet of paper like always. "Get it down."

"I hope it's not as gross as MDMA." My stomach was feeling reluctant already; however, I swallowed it anyway. The taste wasn't that bad. It tasted kind of like an alkaloid. My mouth felt weird, like it had been rinsed with an astringent.

Each person, the same group from New Year's, asked for their dose. Some of them had taken mescaline before, yet they all took doses around 180mg. As usual, Todd took the highest dose, 650mg. How could he handle that much? Isn't there a toxicity problem? I was on the second highest dose and was the smallest person there! Great, I was in for a *good* one! I should have asked for my dose last, in order to compare mine with theirs. Now I would be the highest one at the session; I knew it.

The acidity was increasing in my stomach as we all went for a swim. I thought that the warm silky water might ease my increasing discomfort. I had the feeling that the trip wouldn't be as wonderfully telepathic as last time. My stomach just kept getting queasier and queasier. I didn't want to throw up. **God please keep me from throwing up!**

"I feel sick!" And with that I got out of the pool and ran inside to the bathroom. I held my head in the toilet, but nothing came out except for drool. The salty taste in my mouth increased along with dizziness. Was this feeling anxiety, or was it a side effect? The smell of the chlorinated toilet bowl took on a new dimension. It was disgusting. Why couldn't I just throw up and get it over with? The fumes were intense. People are not supposed to be around chlorine!

Lying in the toilet only made me feel worse, so I moved onto the floor. As I stared up at the ceiling, it slammed me. The world morphed into pixie dust land. Everything was immersed in a twinkling white light dust. It sounds nice, but it wasn't. My consciousness was fragmented. The only way to describe it is to compare it to looking at yourself in a broken mirror that had been hit with a baseball or something. The shattering of my psyche started in one spot or vortex. Then it spread out, divided and fractured. Everything looked slanted, causing my perception of size to be off, way off.

My legs started to tremor slightly. Then my teeth started to chatter. Where were my clothes? I stood up to go look for them. My legs were wobbly. I walked at a slant, along with the world. It reminded me of trying to walk while being really drunk, only with size distortion. I kept falling down. Falling into things. Cold. Naked. Finally I made it to the bed, and grabbed a sheet. A little better, but where were my clothes? I looked at some clothes in the sparkling closet. They were all huge, too huge for me. I went to a dresser, too small. Where were my clothes?

I wandered out into the living room where everyone else had collected. "Can't find clothes." I could barely talk; it felt like I was slurring slightly. Everyone started laughing. Why were they laughing at me? I didn't like being laughed at. I didn't want anyone to think I was a bad tripper and freaking out. Because I wasn't. I wasn't freaking out! My balance was totally out of control. I toppled over and rolled around on the floor in my sheet, shaking. They laughed harder. This sucked. "Can someone help me find my clothes?" Desperation overtook me. One of the guests brought me a change of clothes. I looked up at them, confused. "They are too big." Everyone laughed harder.

I crawled into another bedroom and looked into the closet. Too big. Why weren't there any clothes that fit? I collapsed onto the floor to sulk. Why was everyone laughing at me? Don't they realize that nobody likes to be teased? They were out there, cackling away still. Was my discomfort really that funny?

Todd came into the room after what seemed like a lot of time had passed. "What's wrong, sweetie?"

"I can't find my clothes. And everyone is laughing at me."

"We gave you a change of clothes that fit, but you wouldn't put them on."

"No you didn't. You gave me giant clothes; they wouldn't have stayed on. And you did it to tease me." I started to sob. Why were they all so mean? Why were they making fun of me?

"Here, sweetie, stop crying. Put these on." Todd held out what looked like jumbo-sized sweatpants.

"They won't fit. Stop being mean." I sobbed harder.

"Really, they will fit." He looked at me kindly with reassuring patience.

"No they won't." Why was he putting me through this? They were too big; it was obvious!

"Try them on then, just so you can prove to me that they won't fit. If they don't, I will go find you something else."

I reluctantly put them on, knowing that they would just fall right off. Asshole, teasing me like this. Wait a minute... They fit! It was a miracle! How did they all of a sudden shrink? This totally twisted my already scrambled mind.

"I told you they would fit didn't I? Now here's a shirt, try it." He was smiling, patiently holding out a t-shirt.

I put the shirt on and it fit also. Warm and comfortable. I had stopped crying, but still felt petrified because of everyone teasing me with the wrong clothes. Why had they given me clothes that were too large? Just to laugh at my reaction?

"Okay, now let's go have a good trip. Okay?" He started laughing again.

"Why do you keep laughing at me?"

"Baby, I'm not laughing at you. I'm just laughing, to laugh. That's what mescaline does, it makes you laugh." His big frame plopped down beside me with a sigh.

"Everyone out there was laughing at me too." Why did people always do stuff like this to me?

"No they weren't. They were just laughing, because they were laughing. No reason other than they just couldn't keep from it." He reached over and hugged me. "Everyone here loves you. None of us would laugh at you or tease you. Did other children make fun of you when you were young? Is that what this is all about?"

"Yes, they were mean. They would always single me out and embarrass me. They would get such enjoyment out of my pain. Why are people like that? Why does it lift them up when they tear someone else down?" I squeezed him tighter and was comforted by his loving energy.

"I don't know, sweetie. People are mean sometimes. They just don't know what life is all about. They don't know that loving each other is the only way to attain true happiness. You never have to deal with heartless people again, though. We all love you; we are your family."

He always could calm me down. Maybe they weren't laughing at me. Why would they be? Like Todd had said, they were my family.

INTEGRATION

At a young age, I began using drugs and alcohol like most of my peers. I was only fourteen when I started drinking vodka. My habit grew quickly to a pint every day. I would keep it in my locker at school and use the orange juice from breakfast as a mixer. Marijuana came next and then cigarettes. I think I partly did this to escape my dad's temper and his verbal abuse that would sometimes escalate into physical confrontations. But I mostly did it to forget about my miserable childhood.

To say I didn't fit in with the rest of my classmates would be an understatement. Not only was I the nerdy kid with glasses, but I was also the poorest kid in school. I went to a semi-private elementary school where everyone else's parents were upper middle class. My dad supported my Mom and me on $125 a week. Even in the 1980s, this wasn't much money. So I had to wear garage sale clothes, which helped with my popularity, I'm sure! I was the  unfortunate outcast that the rest of the kids threw balls at during recess. They loved to do this. They always aimed at my head and tried to knock off my glasses. It was a fun game for them. Sometimes they would spit on me; they would laugh so hard. *Why?*

To my detriment, I also thought faster and learned quicker than my classmates. Being an only child with no friends gave me ample time to learn. We didn't have cable television at home, so it wasn't a distraction either. Eventually, the school placed me in gifted classes that were supposed to challenge me. All that did was cause me to be singled out and made fun of even more. I learned that it was much easier to get drunk and be the "bad" kid in school, than get tormented for being the smart one.

At fifteen, the combination of never-ending boredom and harassment caused me to drop out of high school. I knew how crucial it was to continue my education to get out of my current situation, though. So I started by getting my GED. My scores were high enough that I was offered a full scholarship to a nearby community college.

I snapped the opportunity right up, and I was a fulltime college student by my sixteenth birthday. I also stopped drinking, smoking cigarettes, and using drugs. It was useless to numb myself out. I saw what it did to those around me. It held them back and kept them stuck in the misery of poverty.

I thought moving on with life and going to college healed my feelings of rejection. Evidently, the pain of humiliation was still there hiding deep within my psyche. Was I over it now? Did the mescaline allow the pain to fully manifest itself, so that I could completely heal?

Entheogens can be very confusing. The visions are often difficult to interpret. Every person sees a small part of the same infinite divinity, yet there are many different people. So there are many different views. Essentially, we relate what we see to what we've experienced in life in order to understand it. This makes understanding the *nature* of reality complex. Each person sees the same thing, yet we all see different things.

Another important lesson I learned from this trip was that there's no way to totally predict or control what will happen while on a psychedelic. You can try to move yourself in the desired direction once you are there. Still, if something is going to come up, it will stick around until you process it. You cannot turn away from it. You have to deal with it, and then you can move on.

This trip also left me feeling fractured and

sad for about a week afterward. One reason for this might be that I was hoping for telepathy again and was let down. Another reason might've been dopamine and/or serotonin depletion. Both mescaline and MDMA affect serotonin and dopamine levels in the brain - each in slightly different ways. I suffered from severe hangovers, or back-ends, every time I took MDMA. I would not only be extremely depressed for about a week afterward, but I'd also feel like I'd been hit by a truck. Could mescaline have done the same thing to me? Could it have caused my neurotransmitters to be depleted?

Chapter 12   TIGHT WORLD

We had planned to trip with some friends of ours, Joe and Mary, before we left Tucson for the summer. But we kept pushing it off for one reason or another. Time had almost run out. We finished moving out of our house yet stayed anyway, specifically for this trip. So there we were - the four of us in a hotel room at the Weston La Paloma Resort. Todd had been working on making a new legal psychedelic, and he was eager for us to try it.

"I promise it won't give you a back-end like MDMA does." Child-like excitement emanated from him.

"Are you sure I won't have a back-end?" I asked, wanting to make sure before I took it.

"It shouldn't. 2C-I works on the same neurotransmitters as MDMA. But has a different mechanism of action, so I don't think it will give you a hangover. Come on, you've never tried it. You should give it a chance at least." Todd was pushing pretty hard.

"Are you sure it won't make me stupid like MDMA?" Mary questioned. "I have finals in two weeks. I can't afford to mess those up."

Mary was twenty years old. She stood there, tall and thin, letting her long brown hair hang midway down her back. She rarely tripped, so this was quite a step for her. She usually had a full schedule with college classes and work, and she simply never had the time for anything else.

"I promise you won't feel bad afterward," Todd assured. "Let's just get started before it gets too late." He had weighed out the doses earlier in the week, before we left the safety of our house. Without wasting any more time, he handed us each a capsule with a very small amount of white powder inside.

Mary and I hesitated, looking at each other nervously. We both new what the consequences would be if it gave us a hangover like MDMA did. Eventually we took the pills, even though we were nervous about the outcome. A person should seize every possible opportunity. *Right?*

Thirty minutes later:

The four of us sat in a circle on the floor. There was no stereo in the hotel room, so we didn't have music this time. I had never tripped without music before. What was it going to be like? Music always comforted me. It gave me someplace to go and float around. I could swim down deep into it or just float along the surface. I could concentrate on it and center myself.

Todd started telling stories again. I had heard them all before, but they still made me laugh. It was good to laugh, as it eased the initial transition. Sometimes, especially on new molecules, it helps ease the tension if you push your mind into a light-hearted and fun direction. The stories were good for this, just like music would have been if we would've had any. Like a bird, I glided carefree over the top of each word. Then I ran along them like a child playing hopscotch or a frog jumping across its lily pads...

Then my chest started to feel tight. Not again!

I was so tired of having anxiety. I couldn't seem to get rid of it. Okay, breathe. Relax. Mary glanced at me; she looked tense also. At least I wasn't alone! I tried to move my mind somewhere else, but just felt tense. The tension spread from my chest into my jaw. I started to grind my teeth, often a side effect of poor quality MDMA. "My teeth are grinding, Todd. I do not like this."

"Here, take a Valium. It should help with that." Todd handed me a little blue pill, and then turned to Mary who was also looking uncomfortable. "You should take one too. I didn't realize that you guys had damaged yourselves to this extent. You guys were right; you both have used way too much MDMA." He paused to think, and then continued. "Joe and I are not having the same reaction. It's not my chemistry that's causing this. Your reaction must be damage related."

The walls started to move as pastel colored patterns crawled around the surface. Uncomfortably compact paisley prints. Constantly morphing, developing new colors and depth. The prints started to build, become deeper, more complex. They crunched in, tightly, and squished themselves. More stacked on top of each other, layered. Moving, turning, transforming into new tighter, more complex paisley universes.

"I feel so tight. Even my hallucinations are tight. I can't believe it." As Mary spoke she shaped her hands in a small circle. I could sense that she wasn't very happy with Todd's little experiment!

"I'm sorry, guys. Let's try flipping with some LSD. It might ease the tension by increasing your serotonin." Todd pulled out the little golden nuggets and handed each of us one of them.

I looked at it in my hand. Should I take this potent little pill? I would be on quite a ride if I did. Was I ready for it? No. Would I ever be totally ready?

No. I decided to take the acid and roll the dice. It might not be an easy trip, but I would learn something from it at least. Then one last thought came to my mind, "Are you sure it won't make the tension worse?"

"It should help the tension, but if it doesn't you can take another Valium."

"Okay, here goes." I chewed it up, prepared for a ride in whichever direction the universe would guide me.

Joe crunched his up right away too. "I don't see what your guys' problem is. This is great! Todd can I have another one of the nuggets? I want to trip hard."

"That means you'll be on 500mcg. Are you sure?" Todd glanced at Joe with a skeptical look.

"I want to *really* go there. I don't want to just reach the edge." Joe looked like a model with short spiky blonde hair and a really buff body. It was difficult for me not to stare at him as he sat Indian style with perfect posture and his hands resting in his lap.

A few moments later, Todd handed him another nugget. As Joe chewed it, he began to morph. It was beautiful, divine. He wasn't moving from his seated position, but he was changing somehow. It was subtly deep. It was cosmic, yet difficult to describe with words. He was moving through time's folds, remembering his lineage. He reminded me of a great yogi, sitting up straight and tall. He was obviously empowered by the universal oneness that joins us all.

Todd looked over at Mary, who was still holding her nugget. "I think you should take it. It will help. Really."

"Well I guess it can't make my back-end any worse than it's already going to be. I just hope I don't screw up my finals." She smiled uncertainly as she took it.

Some time later:

I sat in the bathroom. Alone. The tension was still there chipping away at my patience. Would it ever leave? I was trying to relax when the words started to flood out of me. **TELLELELELAHH-OOH LETETWAH**. The words brought soothing relief as they floated off my tongue. **TELLELELELAHH-OOH LETETWAH**. Breathing was easier. There was less tension. Again. **TELLELELELAHH-OOH LETETWAH**. Even less! What was this magical language? Where did it come from? I felt safe chanting the phrase, comforted. Somehow I felt in more control; it was empowering. A much-appreciated gift from the cosmos.

I don't know how long I was in the bathroom, but when I came out the trip had completely evolved. It was beautiful, incredibly peaceful, and universal. The four of us molded together. My consciousness started to roll into each of theirs. It was out of my control. I felt what they were feeling as I passed through each of them. My heart was only connected with each of their hearts for a brief instant, and then I would move on to the next person around the circle, over and over again.

Eventually this expanded. We became more interwoven, closer. We all knew what we were feeling. We molded together until there were no boundaries. This feeling evolved into knowing and being. It was just like hearing my own voice in my head, but I heard everyone's voice at once. We were all the same mind, thinking to ourselves. Separation is such an illusion!

MARY'S INTEGRATION

Mary ended up tripping for three days afterward. She simply didn't come down. I guess her body processed the chemicals that way. Who knows. After she came down, she wanted to totally change her life. She wanted to quit school, quit her job, and run off into the sunset! Sometimes a drastic change like this happens.

After about a week or two her life returned to normal, though. She decided to continue going to school and work. A good thing because some of her other friends were starting to get upset with us for causing this sudden shift in her personality!

The lesson I learned from this is that you should never change your life on a whim recently after a trip. Wait a few weeks and then make the decision to change things up. Always follow your heart, and you will be going in the right direction.

Chapter 13   A NEW LANGUAGE

What was the language that I had spoken during my trip? Where did it come from? My intuitions led me to follow my heart and believe what it told me. However, this was difficult to actually do. How did I know that what I had seen and experienced was actually for real? I was on a hallucinogen after all! It felt so real to me, but I had to know what others experienced and thought. I needed to sort of verify everything. My research started in the direction of science, but quickly turned toward the world's religions. In *Hallucinogenic Plants*, Dr. Richard Evans Schultes eluded to their religious significance:

> Psychic powers have also been attributed to hallucinogens and have become an integral part of primitive religions. Allover the world hallucinogenic plants are used as holy mediators between man and his gods.

Entheogens, meaning God manifesting, allow you to see a rarely traveled path. They are a shortcut that is usually overlooked, a direct route to the divinity within yourself. Could religions have been created by people that were tripping? Thinking about this made me eager to take another look at

Bible with a fresh perspective. The bible speaks of tongues many times throughout it. However, there are two passages that stuck with me. The first begins in Genesis 11:1:

> And the whole earth was of one language, and of one speech... ...And the Lord said, Behold, the people is one, and they all have one language... ...Go to, let us go down, and there confound their language, that they may not understand one another's speech. So the Lord scattered them abroad from thence upon the face of the earth...

This passage is basically saying that we all began with one language, and then that one language was divided into many separate languages. An all-powerful "God" might have caused it. It also may have been caused by the ice ages and their affect on human evolution; we will never know. Yet the message is still important. We were all one, with one language, until we became separated.

The next passage that I found to be significant started in I Corinthians 12:1:

> Now concerning spiritual gifts, brethren, I would not have you ignorant... ...Now there are diversities of gifts, but the same Spirit... ...For to one is given by the Spirit the word of wisdom; to another the word of knowledge by the same Spirit; to another faith by the same Spirit; to another gifts of healing by the same spirit; to another the working of miracles; to another prophecy; to another discerning of spirits; to another divers kinds of tongues; to another the interpretation of tongues...

This explains that there are many spiritual gifts including the speaking and interpretation of tongues that are all given to us by God. I believe that this is what I experienced. I felt as if *God* was speaking through me. There is no difference between me and god; we are the same thing. Yet it felt like something was coming through me, out of my mouth, which was so divine that it was rarely accessed by my current human incarnation. It was a spiritual gift from the cosmos that was offered to me for comfort and guidance.

The Dead Sea Scrolls of the Gnostics speak of language as well. The Gospel of John, Ch 1 stated:

> In the beginning was the word, and the word was with God, And the word was God. He was in the beginning with god. Through him everything came to be, and without the word nothing came to be. What came to be in him was life, and life was the light of all people. And the light in the darkness shone and the darkness could not apprehend the light.

The Word is God, and through the Word, life is created. I like this passage because it explains that you (God) can create by thinking/speaking. I have discussed this before in other chapters. You really are in control of your reality. Life is like a lucid dream. You only have to wake up during the dream and realize that you are in fact dreaming to gain control. Once you awaken, you will be able to create whatever you wish. Isn't it time, then, for all of us to *wake up*?

I believe that my experience was a combination of all three. I spoke the original unifying language, which was a spiritual gift from the depths of my god/soul. And I was manifesting my divine self through the words by creating what I needed at the time - calm serenity.

I wanted to get a well-rounded, multi-cultural perspective on what I experienced. So I also looked toward the eastern religions for explanation. Bodhipaksa spoke about mantras, or spiritual songs/chants:

> Mantra meditation predates Buddhism, probably by hundreds of years. The origins of mantras go back at least to the Vedic tradition that preceded the Buddha, where mantras were used as incantations to influence or even to control, the gods.

I felt the magical language had the power to control or at least have an effect on reality. It makes sense that this gift originated long ago. The Rg Veda is the oldest text known to man, written in Sanskrit over six thousand years ago. I would go as far as to say that mantras predate the Vedas. The great divine mind always was and is, so therefore any part of it always was and is.

Idries Shah described a possible reason why the tongues or mantras do what they do:

> Mantras create thought-energy waves...
> ...through sound vibration.

Sound is similar to light in the way that it moves through time-space in waves. Vibrations are universal. They can heal and transmit sound. Could this be why the mantras are so powerful?

The Dalai Lama wrote of mantras in his book *The Kalachakra Tantra*:

> Therefore, without depending upon mantra...

98

Buddhahood cannot be attained.

I'm not so sure that this is totally true. I think that every person has his or her own specific key to unlock the door. Some people, like me, may use mantra. Others may dance, sing, clear the mind, go on a walk, or pray. There are many more ways; I'm just listing a few. Be mindful of the fact that religion was created to help us remember our heritage. It is a guide, and we must use it to our advantage. Still, we must only take what is relevant from each source. Learn as much as possible, and always keep open to new possibilities. Everything is always true; it's only the seeker of that truth that changes.

I continued my search and turned toward the indigenous cultures of the Amazon. The ayahuasqueros of the Amazon use *icaros,* or ayahuasca songs, to help structure and modify the visions during ceremonies. A hierarchy exists among the shaman who use them depending on the number and power of the icaros known. The shamans are taught these by each other and most importantly the spirits. Each plant is a spirit-guide and has its own song. The shamans call their icaros their painted songs because they affect the visions so amazingly. They are able to sing a sound that can be visually seen. Was I beginning to learn icaros?

Chapter 14 IS EVERYONE A RAT?

I went to the library to check the recent events about the trial one last time before we left for the cool weather of Seattle. There were several new articles posted on www.freepickard.org. However one in particular, a Topeka Capital Journal article, caught my attention:

> Federal marshals removed William Pickard's handcuffs in court Wednesday just long enough for him to hold his newborn baby before being taken back to the Shawnee county jail...

I had been wondering about Natasha and the baby. I knew she probably delivered it by now. Why didn't they say whether it was a boy or a girl? Todd hadn't allowed me to contact her since Leonard went to prison. He said that I would get into legal trouble if I did. Now that I look back on it, I wish I had ignored Todd and followed my heart.

The Topeka Capital Journal article continued:

> ...Pickard and Apperson were arrested outside Wamego in November after the two attempted to move chemicals and equipment to Colorado in a moving van. According to

court affidavits, electrical surveillance and information from another person led to the arrests...

...Court documents detail an extensive criminal record for Pickard dating back to a 1964 charge of car theft in Georgia. More than 10 incidents, one as recently as 1988, including numerous charges ranging from forgery and false identification charges to arrests for manufacturing controlled substances and carrying a concealed weapon. Apperson reportedly has no criminal history...

The next part was really interesting:

...Pickard has testified, according to court documents, that in the past he has worked as an informant to the DEA in San Francisco, and for two years he was deputy director of the Drug Policy Analysis Program at UCLA...

So Leonard and Todd were both narcs! I started to think back to that file Todd showed me. How deeply was Leonard involved with the CIA? Had he only worked with them on that one operation, or had he worked with them on several?

* * *

"Why were both you and Leonard working for the DEA?" I asked Todd, hoping that he would give some sort of good reason.

"Up at the top, there's no difference between the government and the drug systems." He said this with an air of aristocracy. He loved to be *on top*.

"I don't understand. I thought that people

101

weren't supposed to narc?"

"That is true, to a certain extent. You see, it took a lot of maneuvering to get to where Leonard and I were." He shifted in his seat slightly.

"You're still not answering my question." I was starting to get frustrated. Todd never could answer a question without dancing around it.

"The DEA wouldn't exist if it wasn't for us. And neither would the majority of the prison population. Do you know that 85% of the federal prison population consists of people convicted of non-violent drug crimes?"

"That's a lot."

"Not only does the government make money off the busts, they are able to move money around with drugs. It's a creative form of off the books financing. Do you remember the Ollie North/Iran-Contra scandal? Government officials were smuggling cocaine into the United States and selling it to the American people. Then they used the profits to buy overstocked and outdated weapons from our military. And then they gave these weapons to Iran, so that they could supposedly defend themselves against Saddam Hussein. There have been many other similar scandals in our country involving drug money and narco-terrorism. As you can see, they need us, the chemists, to keep making drugs. So that way their underground cash flow keeps growing. All we have to do is throw them a bone every once on a while so they can save face."

This concept shocked me. It shouldn't have because it made sense. The government is corrupt, nothing new. However I didn't realize the chemists were corrupt as well. All of them couldn't be like that, could they? Some of them had to really stand up for what they believed in. When a person is looking at life in prison as a consequence of their actions, they have to believe in their cause strongly.

Don't they? Aren't there easier ways to make money? Some of the chemists had to be pure. Some had to be there for spirituality instead of money and power. Right?

* * *

Later, upon thinking about this twisted symbiosis, I realized that the chemists, or at least this group, needed the DEA about as much as the DEA needed them. Drugs wouldn't be worth so much money if they were legal and easy to obtain. Thus, the DEA and the drug laws enabled the chemists to make huge profits - like around $3 million per kilo of LSD.

So why is it that these people (both the chemists and the DEA) keep the distribution of the psychedelic sacraments centralized? To me, it seems to be all about the money... Still, I do not see any value in this system whatsoever. The chemists should be thought of no differently than anyone else. And they definitely shouldn't be idolized or looked up to.

Rather than supporting the centralized distribution of psychedelics, I think we should educate each other on the legal indigenous plants that grow freely throughout the world. And we all must remember that we are one. We are all shaman - each of us is just in a different spot along the same path to the divine playground. Therefore, we all must start to be true to our innate self and be our own shaman. Using safe, legal shamanic plants is a much better option than supporting drug networks that have a symbiotic relationship with the DEA.

Chapter 15 ALPHA-O

    I looked out over the city of Seattle from our penthouse on the thirty-second floor of the Metropolitan Tower. It was a beautiful site to see; the sun was setting, and the city lights were turning on. Living in the city had always been a dream of mine. As a teenager, I would watch city life on television sitcoms like Friends and Seinfeld, always hoping that I'd get to be there too one day. Finally arriving really felt good! I loved all the hustle bustle of the people and the sounds from the traffic.

    We were about to try another one of Todd's projects. Alpha-O-DMS. Another name for it is 5-MEO-AMT. I was excited, even though Sasha reported in *Tihkal* that everyone suffered from nausea and/or diarrhea. I tried to prepare for this by controlling my diet, similar to before taking an MAOI. So I avoided caffeine, meat, and dairy products.

    It was an adventure when we tried new structures - especially tryptamines. They seem to be more pure than other substances, somehow. The visions are thicker, with more dimensions, and they are more universal. This might be caused by the fact that the pineal gland makes tryptamines naturally in the body.

    Anyhow, we had an entirely new trip group. The old crew had stayed behind, mostly because there wasn't as much money for everyone. Since Leonard got busted, our cash supply kept dwindling. We were trying to make money by quietly dealing a little MDMA on the side, but we were hot. WE WERE REALLY HOT. The DEA was pretty much monitoring our every move. So what could we do?

It's funny how people are; once they get used to spending thousands of dollars a week, they just don't want to quit. Then they get angry when the cash flow stops. We didn't want to get busted, so the group split up. It was good to see that their true motive was selfish financial gain.

Thinking about peoples' motives, I often wondered what the real reason was behind Todd turning in Leonard. He had said that it was because Leonard had someone associated with narcing out the ET (Ergotamine Tartrate) supplier killed. ET is the main precursor for LSD. They only had one ET source, so they had to protect him. Was this the real reason? Or did Todd befriend Leonard for the sole purpose of bringing him down? Who knows...

I contemplated this question as I walked down to the other penthouse. Our new group was supposed to be meeting there. We were expecting a good size, seven of us total. We met people easily, everyone always wanted to trip. Upon entering the kitchen, I saw Half-pint sitting on top of the countertop beside the scale. She looked like a punk-rock pixie! She was wearing a yellow tutu and black mesh shirt with rainbow-bright knee socks. Shoulder-length dreadlocks fell around her face. The way she dressed always made me smile; she was so cute and shined so bright.

Everyone's attention centered on Todd. "Here, sweetie, take this. You're a little behind." He reached into his pocket and handed me 100mcg ALD-52 tablet.

I ate it immediately. What a pleasant

surprise! "So we're taking ALD first, then Alpha-O?" I was a little confused because the original plan had been to just take the Alpha-O.

"Yes, everyone else took their ALD a half hour ago. I'm weighing out the Alpha-O now. I will give you your dose last, that way the ALD will have time to get into your system."

I could feel the ALD starting to come on as Todd methodically passed out pieces of paper holding the doses. I felt peaceful, yet excited about the trip. My body was starting to tense up slightly which was nothing unusual. LSD and its analogs normally had a cold jittery edge. Uplifting clarity filled my heart as I eagerly awaited the Alpha-O. The anticipation filled me like this every time I dosed. *What would happen? What would it be like?*

I laughed as each person poured a dose in his or her mouth. They made horribly disgusted faces. Could it really be that bad? There were reactions like, "I'm going to throw up!" and "Yuck!" It was hilarious! It couldn't be as bad as MDMA could it? No way, nothing could be that bad!

Eventually, I received my dose. I looked at the off-white crystalline and then said a brief prayer. I hoped to survive the trip without any diarrhea or vomiting. I poured it into my mouth, and it tasted exactly like DMT smelled. POWDERED MOTHBALLS. It was sickening, but it definitely wasn't as bad as MDMA! They were all overreacting, it wasn't *that* bad.

Within ten minutes, I felt warmth surge through my body. My natural power was being awakened. Alive! I felt so incredibly alive! The tension was gone almost immediately. My body felt light, relaxed. Amazing! Colors grew brighter. However, there was little movement and no hallucinations. The world stayed pretty much the same; except it looked like it had been splashed with water. It was reality, just turned up a notch or two.

The group sat in a circle on the floor. As usual, Todd started telling stories. I felt my consciousness start to split up, divide among the group. I felt like an observer, just sitting there, watching what was going on in their minds. They didn't know I was there, at least I don't think they did. I saw their visions and felt their thoughts.

Other people started to tell stories. As they talked, I was able to read between the lines. I could see *why* they were thinking about what they were thinking about. I could see the roots of their thoughts. The anecdotal stories became life histories for me. It was strange. Time really is an illusion. It is all happening now, even the memories.

Half-pint started with her story. She told us about how she liked to hang out with the homeless people around town. "People should respect them more, give them a break. They are people too. So, to help them, I go to stores and steal umbrellas. Then I give them to the homeless people who really need them, but can't afford them." Why? What was the real reason she did this?

As she told her story, I could see what was in the background of her mind. She was motivated by guilt. Why did she feel this way? There was a time when she had teased homeless people with her friends. On one of these occasions, she thought it was funny to take the homeless person's umbrella. Then later, as it started raining, she felt bad. That homeless person might really have needed an umbrella. She felt so sad for doing such a thing that she tried to help them ever since. Ultimately, it was more for her than the homeless. She needed to forgive herself.

The amount of information I was receiving in what seemed like an instant was overwhelming.

There wasn't enough time to process it all. I felt overloaded. What was going on? My heart started to speed up. It was intense and kept getting more intense. It was blowing my mind, being in everyone's mind. More history, faster, faster. I had to leave the room. It was too much. I couldn't breathe. My head was spinning.

I knew chanting would calm me down, yet didn't want to do it in front of everyone. What would they think of me? Would it freak them out? I didn't want them to think I was crazy and laugh at me. So I excused myself and went into the bedroom, closing the door behind me.

My mind could still feel where they were, each of them. It was a little less intense, but I was still in them. Sharing their visions. I could feel Todd also, only in the background. He was watching me watch them. He sent me a feeling of love and safety. He wanted me to know the he was there, keeping me safe.

I sat on the bed in Indian style, which was my natural position for prayer. The chants floated out of me as I rocked my body back and forth with the beat. My heart reached out to the universe. The chants turned into songs and pulled me deeper. They took on a new timeless dimension. They pulled me up and into the divine. I was not I anymore. I was all. I was/am/will be God. We all are God, One Mind. Everyone else just doesn't remember yet!

* * *

Half-pint came into the bedroom in the middle of my meditation. "It sounds beautiful. Don't stop, please keep going. I like it."

I kept singing for a little while. She positioned herself directly in front of me, also in Indian style. At some point, we started to hold hands; our energy felt more connected this way. I usually sang with my eyes closed. However with her, I kept them open the entire time. Her beautiful blue eyes glistened happily with light. A giant grin revealed a full mouth of braces. She was only sixteen, but radiated the knowledge and love of an old woman. I sometimes would call her the little old woman. She even sat slightly hunkered over!

I ended the song and lay back onto the bed to relax. The bed was filled with fluffy pillows and comforters. I took a couple of deep breaths and felt my whole body relax. She curled up facing me under the covers. We gazed at each other for a long time. Every once in a while we scooted a little closer and touched more of each other. I could feel her breath slide across my cheek as I turned to kiss her. I had kissed girls before, but she hadn't.

Love filled our hearts as it slowly progressed to something more sexual, deeper. We felt like we were one flowing soul. I picture it almost like two pools of viscous fluid, slowly combining into one. We retained our own unique qualities for a while, but eventually we were the same. It was beautiful to be that close with another woman. We shared the same softness, the same gentle caress. Women are different than men. They are more intuitive and not as pushy. We shared control and pleased each other with a loving feminine touch.

Somehow the mood started to change. I started to see things again that made me uneasy. I shifted through her memories. At first this was okay. However, when I saw that she was molested at the age of six or seven by a foster parent, I totally freaked. I had no idea that a vision like that would present itself to me. I didn't just see it, though; that is a poor word choice. I felt it. I knew it. I experienced it exactly like she had experienced it. I was in shock.

"Todd, get me out of here. Todd! Todd!" My screams for help were urgent. I couldn't handle any more. It was too painful to see what happened to her.

Todd ran into the room and paid no attention to the fact that we were both naked. He simply grabbed half-pint, put a robe around her, and pushed her out of the room. "What's wrong? I thought you were having fun in here?"

"I was. She's beautiful, and I love her." I started to sob. Deep hard sobs. Tears drenched my face.

"Don't cry, sweetie. What's wrong?" He reached over and wrapped me up in his arms. "It'll be okay. Just tell me what happened."

"I saw her getting molested. She was young." I couldn't control my breathing. The sobs were overpowering me. "It was a foster parent."

"I didn't realize she was a foster child. Wow." He paused for a moment. "Let me go see if she's okay. Will you be alright for a few minutes?"

"Yes." I buried my face in a pillow as he left the room. What had I just experienced? Was it real or only a bad trip? I went over these questions in my mind until he eventually returned. It seemed like I'd spent an eternity in agony.

"I calmed her down and asked her about it. She said that she's adopted and was in foster care until twelve years old. I never asked her about the abuse, it could have made her have a bad trip." He hugged me again, seeing that I was still uptight about the visions.

* * *

The next morning she admitted to me that she was sodomized by her foster Dad for several years and that it really affected her sexuality. This

110

was one of the reasons she was drawn̵ ̵ ̵
sexuality with a woman. I didn't knov
other than cry with her.

INTEGRATION

I was shell-shocked for several weeks. I had
no idea that it was possible to see into another
person's memories. How had I done it? How had I
known about the molestation? Sexuality opened us
up to each other, in this case too far. According to
Rick Strassman, M.D. in *DMT: The Spirit Molecule*:

> Practitioners of Tantra attempt to achieve the
> best of both these worlds. This spiritual
> discipline recognizes that sexual excitation
> and orgasm produce highly ecstatic states,
> and therefore uses sexual intercourse as a
> meditative technique. By combining sex and
> meditation, Tantric practitioners access
> states of consciousness not available with
> either practice alone. Pineal gland DMT
> release, stimulated by both deep meditation
> and intense sexual activity, may then result
> in especially pronounced psychedelic effects.

Not only were we meditating and having sex,
but we were also on a potent tryptamine. These all
must've amplified each other, causing an influx of
DMT in my brain. And this is most likely the reason
I could see so far back into her memories.

My views immediately changed about tripping
and sex. Prior to this event, I would have sex with
whatever girls I wanted while on psychedelics. Todd
was the only man I explored those spaces with,
though.

After this experience, I decided not to go there
with anyone unless I knew and trusted him or her.

during the psychedelic experience is a sacred .ct. It should only be done with your trusted mate.

What is most interesting about Alpha-O is the after effect it had on my sleep and dreaming. I had incredible multi-layered lucid dreams. I had a dream inside a dream inside a dream. So I would be dreaming, and I would wake up and still be dreaming. This was more vivid and real than ever. Since then, I have had much better dreams. However, their intensity decreased after about two weeks.

After the trip, Half-pint and I started to talk about our dreams. The more we told each other the more it seemed as if we were in the same dream. Information was being sent to us by the Cosmos.

There was this little girl who was about four. She was our guide. She led us through time, showing us different spiritual paths. She drew us pictures of spiritual symbols like specific crosses and words written in Sanskrit. She taught us that the original languages and symbols are important; they are more pure, closer to the source. This continued every night for about a week. The interconnectedness of it all! Eventually the dreams stopped, but I think I will always dream differently.

I feel as though Alpha-O somehow changed my brain. It turned on another *new* sense, allowing me to see and feel what others feel. It's just like seeing with my eyes or feeling with my hand, yet it is a new ability. I can perceive what another person is feeling. I just know it, deep inside. I know it in the same way that I know my own emotions. It takes no effort; it's just there, always.

For several years after this trip, my consciousness felt like it was stuck open. I was just floating around freely. And sometimes I couldn't close it off. Often, I'd be walking down the street and suddenly start to see in all time directions. I could see many possible paths into the future in an instant. When this happened, it was difficult to pull myself back to my present time/space incarnation.

My intuitive abilities also became much stronger. I would catch myself finishing other people's sentences for them. I knew/felt when something stressful was going to happen, like a drug bust. One time, I was in the women's bathroom at a movie theatre. And my consciousness split apart into all of the other women's minds. This was without drugs and completely unexpected. I could hardly pull myself back together. Some of the things the women were thinking about while using the restroom were strange! Most of all, they worried too much about little things, like going to the grocery store. It was weird!

Nowadays, these symptoms have resolved themselves. But I still feel like a switch was created in my brain. Whenever I want to be whole and reunite with my God-self, I just flip the switch and shift. The songs help me do this along with meditation. I no longer need to use psychedelics to get there. I can go there on my own!

Chapter 16 STOLEN STEREO EQUIPMENT

It was seven o'clock in the morning when the phone started ringing. I reached over and unplugged it. No one should call that early. Then we heard a, "Boom, Boom, Boom," at the front door. Who was it, and what did they want? "Boom, Boom, Boom." It was so early! Todd got up and hurried to answer the door. I was too tired to even move; I went to sleep only a few hours earlier and had hardly slept for days.

"I'm with the Seattle Police Department. Are you Mr. Gordon Todd Skinner?"

"Yes," Todd answered them sleepily.

"We have a search warrant for your apartment to retrieve a set of stolen stereo speakers. Are those the speakers there, sitting in the living room?"

"These are my speakers, I paid for them. Let me see your warrant."

"Sit down, Mr. Skinner. Over there on the couch. Is there anyone else in the apartment?"

"Yes, my fiancée is in the bedroom asleep." Todd sounded calm and polite. He had been through this kind of thing before and had nerves of steel.

An officer walked into the bedroom, and glared at me huddling under the covers. "Go sit in the living room," he commanded. "And on a different couch than Mr. Skinner."

My whole body was shaking. I hoped they couldn't see it. All I could think about were the bags in the closet. **God, please, please don't let them look in the closet!**

By this time, there were eight officers digging through our apartment. They were emptying out drawers, peeking in cabinets, going through paperwork, and looking at pictures. I was curious why they were snooping around if they already found what they had come for. They had to stop searching the place; it was freaking me out. I needed to get them out of there somehow. "Why are you going through my childhood pictures?" I asked. "Is this really necessary?" I was starting to act a little angry.

"Ma'am sit down and be quiet."

"No, this is my house, and I don't have to. I didn't steal any speakers, and my name isn't on that warrant. I think your warrant's bad." I would rather have their attention on me than on the search. So far they had missed the suitcases in the closet, but they were running out of other places to look.

"Ma'am sit down or you will be under arrest for obstruction of justice!" All of them collected around me, waiting to see what I'd do.

"I just don't understand why you don't simply take the speakers and go. That's what you came for, right?" I sat down and acted a little calmer. It was working. They were no longer searching our place. But how long could I keep this up? I felt like I was walking through a minefield and not knowing where to step.

They didn't answer me; instead, one of them turned to Todd and started reading him his rights. "Mr. Skinner, you are under arrest for felony theft, you have the right to remain silent..."

They handcuffed him and led him out of the room. Then they started to load up the speakers. I hoped it was over!!!

"Ma'am, our van is full so we will be back in about an hour to load up the rest of the speakers. Do not touch any of the pieces to them while we are gone and wait here."

I have never felt so relieved in my whole life! I waited for a few minutes to make sure they were gone, and then went directly to the closet. I couldn't believe it! They never looked inside the suitcases!

Two of our rolling carry-on bags were packed with the largest assortment of psychedelics that I'm sure most people have ever seen. They held kilos of MDMA, MDA, LSD, Mescaline, and DMT. There were smaller amounts of many other rare tryptamines as well. They snooped around everywhere, but totally missed the jackpot. We would've been sitting in jail for life if they'd found them!

By the time the police got back for the second load of speakers, the suitcases had been moved to another, much safer location. Todd was let out on a ten thousand dollar bail the next day, and *thanks to the DEA*, the case eventually went away. Although Todd's charges were dropped, he never got his speakers back.

The Wamego Times wrote an article about the arrest:

> Gordon Todd Skinner, owner of the former Atlas-E Missile Base northwest of Wamego and a principal in the LSD drug bust at the base in November of 2000, was arrested in Seattle, WA. Friday, July 19, on a felony theft warrant from Pottawatomie County. The Pott County warrant was issued July 17, in connection with Skinner's alleged theft of an audio speaker system value at $120,000 and belong to Audio FX, a Sacramento, CA company owned by Chris Malone, who

116

recently filed a quit claim deed claiming ownership of the missile base property...

...Prior to the LSD bust in November of 2000, Skinner had visited Audio FX at Sacramento four or five times, purchasing about $80,000 worth of equipment... ...Malone sent two technicians to Wamego to set up the speaker system at the missile base on a demonstration basis... ...Malone never received any money and he's been to Wamego several times looking for the speakers, which, along with Skinner, disappeared following the drug bust...

During his trips to Kansas, Malone got to know William Leonard Pickard... ...On a recent visit, Pickard revealed to Malone that Skinner, prior to the drug bust, had assigned to him (Pickard) power of attorney over the missile base property. Pickard signed a quit claim deed, transferring ownership of the missile base to Malone...

Leonard and Chris Malone tried to gain control of the ownership of the base through the quitclaim deed. This was a good try on their part, but it didn't end up working. Legally, they just didn't have any legs to stand on.

The Wamego Times article continued:

...This is the second time Wilkerson has filed charges against Skinner in Pottawatomie County. In May of 2001, Wilkerson charged Skinner with involuntary manslaughter in connection with the 1999 death of 41-year old Paul Hulebak of Tulsa, OK from a drug overdose at the missile base. Pott County Magistrate Judge Steven Roth, however, later suppressed the evidence obtained from Skinner and other witnesses in the manslaughter case, ruling that the investigation violated Skinner's agreement of immunity with the U.S. Department of Justice...

This is another example of the *good old DEA* getting Todd out of his problems. Paul Hulebak died from a methadone overdose at Todd's missile base. Todd and Gunnar decided not to take him to the hospital, because they thought that he would make it through the overdose. Needless to say, he didn't. However, Todd had what's called Kastigar (US vs. Kastigar) immunity for the incident.

Todd was a CS (confidential source for the DEA), and legally, a CS is an agent of the federal government. An agent can plea the fifth while being questioned, allowing Kastigar immunity to kick in for everything he or she tells them after that declaration. The CS must be compelled to answer questions after he or she pleas the fifth, but evidently this is a fairly common occurrence within DEA interviews. To put in bluntly, most of the agents were too stupid to realize what they were allowing to happen. Todd realized this and exploited this legal loophole more than anyone thought possible...

The Wamego Times article continued:

...Skinner came to Wamego in 1996 for the purported purpose to establishing a spring manufacturing facility... ...He refurbished the underground facility, ordering thousands of dollars of materials and services from area

contractors and companies, many of who
were never paid...

This article really provided an accurate representation of what kind of man Todd was. He was a scam artist who lied to everyone around him. He only wanted to further himself, yet he was talented at making it appear as if he was helping others and doing good things.

*　*　*

The ten thousand dollar cash bail caused us to almost go broke. The only choice we had was to move to Tulsa. We had no other options.

Moving back to the Midwest was a huge adjustment for me. It was so boring there compared to all the fun places on the west coast. The air was thick, and the sky was gray pretty much all the time. Worst of all, the people talked like stupid rednecks. Did I have that accent when I lived there before? *Yuck!* I had even more trouble relating to them now. I had traveled and lived in the *real* world; they were stuck in their country-bumpkin time warp.

Todd's mother, Kathy, graciously let us stay with her. Her help made the transition a lot easier. She allowed us to live with her for free for nearly a year, and she gave us jobs at her spring corporation. Of course, we kept dealing MDMA on the side too. It was hard to give up the lifestyle we were accustomed to.

All in all, Todd's mom showed me great kindness during that time – almost like a mom would. When I enrolled in biochemistry classes at the University of Tulsa, she even bought a used car for me so I could drive to school.

Chapter 17 THE BLOOD OF CHRIST

Todd knelt down, holding an ornately decorated gold chalice. A magnificent piece to behold, exquisite. It pulsated with energy and spirituality. "Sherom Teleqot Masecot," he began his prayers in ancient Chaldean, and then moved on to a higher prayer. "Ebatone Neahmeh Nohhoaayow..." the language of the gods. Reverent peacefulness engulfed him as the words came forth. He turned to face me and drank several large gulps. Then bowed his head in silence as he passed me the chalice.

"What is it?" I was totally caught by surprise; we had not planned on tripping for a while. Things had been far too crazy lately.

"It's ancient wine. Just try a sip."

"I don't know..." I didn't want to have a bad trip. My mind wasn't as prepared as it should be prior to a journey. Also, I had never seen him this spiritual before a trip. He never prayed or used a chalice any other time. Usually, he would just non-ceremonially weigh out the doses on his lab scale, and then he'd simply pass them out. No ceremony, no prayers. Why the sudden change?

"Just try a small sip. It's time for you to be initiated into the order. You're ready. But I would kneel and say a prayer first if I was you. This one must be taken very seriously." His head bowed slightly, but he still kept eye contact.

I was curious so I knelt down, even though my instincts were telling me not to. What order? The brotherhood maybe? And what was in the chalice? It couldn't really be ancient wine, could it? I examined the liquid; it looked and smelled just like red wine. Why not? I cautiously drank a small sip. It was thinner than normal wine, and it had a woody taste. The most interesting part was the way it tingled as it went down. A warming sensation filled my throat and stomach.

"Okay, I drank some, now what is it?"

"It's ergot wine." He smiled slyly, knowing he had gotten one over on me.

"ERGOT WINE! Oh my God!" I was in shock. "Ergot can kill people. I wouldn't have taken it if I had known what it was. It's St. Anthony's fire! It can make you lose body parts if you touch it! Oh, my God!" My head was spinning. *How could he have not warned me?*

"I knew you would react like this. That's why I just told you to drink it. You get so afraid sometimes. There is no need to be; you are safe." A slight giggle escaped from his lungs.

"Are you sure it's safe? Where did you get it?"

My heart was racing.

"I made it when I was younger. I did an alcohol wash of the ergot fungus with the wine. Then I corked the bottles up and stored them. The ergot fungus fed on the sugars in the wine, giving it the woody taste. I let them age for about ten years. It is best to wait a little longer, but I felt it was an appropriate time to open one anyway. Every year it ages, it will become a little less potent and easier to control the dose."

"How do you know what a safe dose is?" I asked, looking at him skeptically.

"Ergot is a fungus and a precursor for LSD. Ergot is interesting because we really don't know what happens to the alkaloid concentration over time. It moves around, changes. So the dose is guesswork."

"Isn't ergot what Socrates used to take at Eleusis?" I thought it was kind of cool to be taking something that the founders of the idea of democracy used to take, but that our current democracy has made illegal.

"Yes, except for he did a water infusion of the ergot, instead of alcohol."

"I can feel it already." I took a deep breath but couldn't ease my anxiety. "My chest feels tight, and my heart is racing." My heart had never beaten that fast. "My hands feel like they're going numb. Are you sure I'm going to be okay?"

I lay down onto the floor to relax; yet my chest became tighter, heavy. I started coughing and gasping for air. Time passed. I don't know how much.

"Here take a Valium. You will be alright, just breathe sweetie." He handed me the pill. Then picked up the chalice again and kneeled down beside me. He took several large gulps. After it was empty, he turned it upside down to show me that there wasn't any left. "See it's safe. You only drank a sip! Look how much I took!"

"But you can handle a lot more than me; you are three times my size!" I weighed about 110 pounds and stood 5'8". Todd, on the other hand, was a giant at 6'5", and he weighed somewhere around 275 pounds.

"Come on, let's go lie down on the bed where it is more comfortable." He reached down and grabbed my hand, helping me up off the floor.

The visuals were really starting to kick in now. They were thick and heavy like my breath. Dark colors, red, purple, and blue. They overtook me; I could no longer see my hand when I held it up in front of my face. A different world existed inside of me. A liquid oceanic playground for the mind. Would I come back from this space? Spiraling thoughts that made no sense. Fear of the unknown. Would I be okay?

My chest still felt heavy, but I sat upright. This seemed to make it a little better. My heart started to throb slightly. Every few breaths, I felt a sharp twinge along with the throb. Was the ergot causing the chest pain or was I? Was I having an anxiety attack? How could I tell the difference between a real pain and one that I manifested with my mind?

Instinctually, I started to chant my calming mantra, "Telelelelah-luu Letetwah," over and over again. I rocked with the words. "Telelelelah-luu Letetwah." I held my hands up, palms facing each other in prayer. The L's rolled off my tongue and took on new depth. They sounded like the echo of a thousand birds flapping their wings in the air. The mantra held me and kept me safe, like when a mother holds a child. I was going home to safe territory.

I began to sing songs from my soul, rooted

deep within the divine. The songs carried me away with them, teaching me about the universe. At one point, I saw the double helixes of DNA swirling out of my mouth along with the words. Language gave birth to being. That's how I interpreted it anyway. Time was dilating. How long had I been floating on the breath of the universe?

Todd came into the room as I was floating back. "Oh, don't stop sweetie. It's beautiful."

I was unsure about singing in front of him, so I backed off a bit. I chanted for a while, trying not to make a fool out of myself. I had to sound like a crazed lunatic, singing gibberish! Every now and then I would look over at him to try to gauge his reaction. He was sitting up, facing me, and getting very into it. He was actually enjoying it! When I'd stop he'd look up disappointed, and think 'start again' or 'keep going'. This went on for a while as time slowed.

I started to see holographic symbols floating in a circle around Todd's head. I had never seen symbols before in a trip. They were translucent almost like glass. Empty space had taken on a form. They constantly rotated, allowing me to see all of their sides. A few of them looked like symbols from the zodiac. Others looked like Sanskrit or Arabic. Some of them can't readily be compared to anything. Where did they come from? What did they mean?

Events started to become circular. "I feel like am singing, seeing, and going to the same places over and over again."

"Oh, you're stuck in the loop! It will just keep going, and eventually you'll come out of it." He lay back and closed his eyes.

Around and around I went, time moved in a circle.

Over and over and over again.

Over and over and over again.
Over and over and over again.
Over and over and over again.
Over and over and over again.
Over and over and over again.

Finally I popped out the other side. It felt like eons had passed. I lay down beside Todd, cuddling up close to him. He and I were one, one body, one mind. We no longer needed to speak; linguistic devices were a hindrance to us now. We knew each other's thoughts as we thought them. We could feel the depth of each other's love. It's an incredible gift from the universe to feel existence with no boundaries or doubts. One soul, at home once again.

We felt as if we knew everything; all the knowledge of the universe was at our fingertips. We were at the top of the cosmos, the simultaneous beginning and end, the eternal godhead. We could see in all directions at once.

I came to the realization that my future and past were somehow connected to my dreams. I started having unusual dreams around the age of eight. These dreams would reveal a sequence of events in my future. They were easy to distinguish from normal dreams, because they had a different texture. More real. However, I never could tell when in the future they would occur. It could be in one month or two years. Whenever the event sequence did happen, though, it always felt like a déjà vu. I could see that this phenomenon was me remembering who I am. Me remembering who and what we all are - divine co-creators.

Then the loop happened again.
Around and around and around I went.
Over and over and over again.
Over and over and over again.
Over and over and over again.

Again I came out the other side. This little voice in the back of my head, kept saying, "your heart isn't beating right." It was strange. I felt as if my heart would sort of stop, and I would roll out, far out into the ocean of the divine. Then I would feel and hear a loud bang, and it would start beating again, really fast this time. I would in turn surf back in on the same wave that took me out. This whole sensation happened several times. I rolled in and out with the waves of universal consciousness.

It turns out that Todd actually was beating on my chest. But he didn't tell me about it until I came down. I guess my heart really was stopping or at least slowing down! I think this was the closest I've ever been to death.

There was safety in death. Total security. I saw that death is nothing more than a shift of cosmic life energy. Fear filled me, and then I eventually let go. I sort of release myself to it. My new/old form, the god within all of us, overtook me. Love and happiness held me tight. It was almost like a caterpillar hatching out of its cocoon and turning into a butterfly. Or perhaps *returning* to a butterfly...

"Here, sweetie, chew this up. It's another Valium. Your heart is beating way to fast. You need to calm down. Try to take deep breaths."

"Okay." I couldn't really talk; I was too high. I tried to breathe, deep and slow. It seemed to help a little. I was afraid of overdosing. "It feels like my heart is stopping."

"You're okay, just breathe. And drink some of this juice to keep your blood sugar up." He handed me a glass and watched to make sure I didn't drop it.

I drank some of the juice and cuddled up next to him again. How long had we been tripping for? I felt like I was ancient, floating on the cosmic time/space folds. Right then, I understood that time

126

and space are illusions; they're only here for our amusement. I saw that, at the base of all Being, we are one evolving consciousness. And we are all incarnations of that same self-reflecting divinity.

Chapter 18 TRANSUBSTANTIATION

Out of all my journeys, ergot was my most difficult. It was also one of my most productive trips, and therefore, it was one of my best. I had gone on trips before that, which seemed like near death experiences. But during my ergot trip, I *really* felt like I died. When Todd was pounding on my chest, it really felt like my heart was stopping. Despite the fear that my brush with death aroused in me, it brought me a sense of calmness. I knew what death felt like! And it wasn't bad at all!

The chalice and prayers heightened my curiosity. Why had he been so ceremonial during the ergot trip and none of the others? What was the meaning of it all? He was so careful with his words, his humble demeanor, and even how he held the chalice as he drank. I had seen communion in church before and knew symbolically this is what he had meant by it all.

Still, I wanted to see what others thought and started to research the major religions more thoroughly. I knew that they could give me the answers I needed. I found a text on Catholicism that seemed to help. According to F. R. Montgomery Hitchcock in *Transubstantiation*:

Transubstantiation means the change of one

substance into another substan
special sense of Roman divines, it ı
on the *pronouncing of the f*
consecration by the priest, the su ̲ ̲ ̲ ̲ ̲ ̲ ̲ ̲ ̲ ̲ ̲ oɪ
the bread and wine cease to be, and are
replaced by the substance of the Body and
Blood of Christ...

To me, this passage means that a prayer can change a substance into God. Todd blessed the wine before we drank it. Could this have had an effect on our trip? I believe that a prayer that comes purely from the heart can do anything...

A few months later, Todd explained more to me about how transubstantiation related to psychedelic chemistry. He had said, "You must pray over each batch as you make it. You channel divinity through you and into the sacrament. This is essential. You must sing light into it, bless it, and bless all who will consume it." This was the most spiritually valuable thing Todd ever taught me.

Leonard also spoke of prayer in a Rolling Stone Magazine article:

> ...When the subject of the Brotherhood of Eternal Love came up one day in the Shawnee County Jail, Pickard stopped short of admitting any contact with the group, but did speak of their activities with a certain knowing reverence: 'I understand there have been a few LSD chemists that would never make a batch of LSD ever, ever, without offering prayers for the safety of the people that might use it. And should it act as good medicine throughout the world. So I'm told.'

* * *

Could Entheogens be at the root of most of the major religions? This question led me to reexamine Christianity and its link to the ergot infestation of bread. In Luke 22:19-20, the Holy Supper was described:

> And he took the bread, and gave thanks, and brake it, and gave it unto them, saying, This is my body which is given for you; this do in remembrance of me. Likewise also the cup after supper, saying, This cup is the new testament in my blood, which is shed for you.

The bread and wine could have been infested with the ergot fungus. St. Anthony's fire, named that after the patron saint of the priests who took care of the sick, has created awareness of the history behind ergot poisoning. All through the middle ages small villages would have outbreaks. In the book *St. Anthony's Fire,* John Fuller explained what some of the people felt like during the poisoning:

> He eventually excused himself from the group, returned to his room, and lay down on the bed in a futile attempt to get to sleep. It was impossible. His mind kept inexplicably turning to the thought of potatoes, potatoes of every size and shape. He was amused at this thought at first-why should he be thinking of potatoes in the middle of the night, or rather just before dawn?

This definitely sounds like coming down off an LSD trip to me! I've lain there many times with my brain racing and just not been able to sleep. More descriptions of the symptoms were included in the book:

130

...the fifth day after the illness first
the dominant symptom was insomi

As the symptoms developed, the doctors slowly realized that the ergot theory-the poisoning from mold forming on certain grains-was becoming a more logical possibility...

Psychic disturbance, a definitive symptom of ergotism, was certainly in evidence now...

Ergot has also been used as a sacrament historically. In fact, it's a significant part of our country's heritage. The underlying concept of our democracy rests at the feet of Socrates. Interestingly, Socrates was heavily involved in the Eleusinian mysteries. Initiates worshipped the goddess Demeter by pilgrimaging to Eleusis once a year. Once there, they would take part in a special ceremony that consisted of consuming kykeon, which was most likely an infusion of ergot in water. In *The Road to Eleusis*, R. Gordon Wasson, Carl Ruck, and Albert Hofmann described kykeon's effects:

There were physical symptoms, moreover, that accompanied the vision: fear and a trembling in the limbs, vertigo, nausea, and a cold sweat. Then there came the vision, a sight amidst an aura of brilliant light that suddenly flickered through the darkened chamber. Eyes had never before seen the like, and apart from the formal prohibition against telling of what had happened, the experience itself was incommunicable, for there are no words adequate to the task. Even a poet

131

could only say that he had seen the beginning and the end of life and known that they were one, something given by god. The division between earth and sky melted into a pillar of light.

Clearly, ergot is likely the psychotropic ingredient in the Eleusinian brew.

* * *

The Rig Veda is the oldest known religious text, and it is the basis of Hinduism. It is estimated to be around 6000 years old. Throughout the Rig Veda the God Soma, most likely an Amanita muscaria mushroom, is worshiped. They explained how to prepare it by pounding its flesh and getting it to excrete a juice. Then they described combining it with milk before drinking it. This was how they worshipped their god - they drank him and then became him.

Hymn VI from the Rig Veda stated:

1. SOMA, flow on with pleasant stream, a Bull devoted to the Gods, our friend, unto the woolen sieve.
2. Pour hitherward, as Indra's self, Indu, that gladdening stream of thine, and send us courses full of strength.
3. Flow to the filter hitherward, pouring that ancient gladdening juice, streaming forth power and high renown.
4. Hither the sparkling drops have flowed, like waters down a steep descent they have reached Indra purified.
5. Whom, having passed the filter, ten dames cleanse, as 'twere a vigorous steed, while he disports

him in the wood.

6. The steer-strong juice with milk pour forth, for feast and service of the Gods, to him who bears away the draught.

7. Effused, the God flows onward with his stream to Indra, to the God, so that his milk may strengthen him.

8. Soul of the sacrifice, the juice effused flows quickly on: he keeps his ancient wisdom of a Sage.

9. So pouring forth, as Indra's Friend, strong drink, best Gladdener! For the feast, thou, even in secret, storest hymns.

Doesn't this seem a little like the communion of Christianity? Could it be possible that through time people have forgotten or lost touch with the true meaning of communion?

To me, it makes more sense to actually become God in order to remember who you are than to just take it on faith. All the visions in the bible make perfect sense if you read them with the mindset that the people were tripping and writing about their trips. Try reading the bible this way; you will learn a lot.

* * *

Entheogens are not the only way to God. There are many other paths to choose from; some just get you there a little quicker than others. These other paths include yoga, dance, meditation, singing, prayer, and sexuality. Still, entheogens are like riding an elevator to the top of the building versus taking a lifetime of stairs. Both travelers get there eventually. One traveler simply saves a little time.

Also, you must walk many paths in life to become truly fulfilled and enlightened. The more rigorous methods of consciousness alteration, like meditation, prepare the traveler to *launch*. It is like they are the *pad* that prepares you for it all. Daily practice centers you and allows space for an optimal experience. It sort of helps you have a good set and setting within your own soul.

All in all, I've found that set and setting are really important. If you pray, meditate, fast, or do some yoga before a trip, you will be headed in a much more spiritual direction than you would be if you're at a party and you just carelessly drop some acid with your friends. You can have a good trip anywhere; however, the right music, lighting, people, and surroundings really can nudge a trip in the right direction from the beginning.

Chapter 19 THE TRIAL

"Can you believe that we've gotten subpoenaed by both of them?" Todd paused to laugh and then continued. "The prosecution and defense?"

"It's pretty crazy. Why do they both need to serve us?" Their tactics were confusing.

"Well, you see sweetie; they can get each of us on the stand twice now. This gives them more time to prepare." The tone in his voice turned serious. He loved to be *the teacher.*

"Whatever, I hope they don't actually call me up there. Isn't their list of people to take the stand long?" My heart picked up pace as the conversation progressed.

"Of course, and you really don't have much to say. I mean you weren't there or anything." He pushed his eyebrows down slightly as he pushed his glasses back up onto his nose.

"What am I going to do if I have to go up there? What if the defense attorney Billy Rork asks me questions that incriminate me? Like about our MDMA dealing and the stuff Karl covered up for us?" If they put me on the stand, I would get shredded. *I knew it.*

"It's okay, calm down. All you have to do is plea the fifth like I'm going to do, and they will give you what's called judicial immunity. You see, I already have an immunity agreement that was issued by the Department of Justice before L got busted. I also have Kastigar immunity from the DEA interviews. Regardless, I'll still plea the fifth on the stand so that the judge is forced to issue me a third form of immunity. We have to cover ourselves; we are the only ones that will." His foot started to tap, like it always did when he thought deeply about something. "If the judge gives you immunity, you have to spill everything. Anything and everything that you've done in the last four years that you even suspect of being illegal. Because once it's issued, you are immune federally and in every state for everything you say."

"Should I tell them about Karl sweeping everything under the rug?" My stomach was in my throat. I didn't want to go up there either way.

"Really sweetie, I don't see why you are getting so uptight. I took the stand for six days during the Boris Olarte trial. It isn't that bad." He lay back onto the cheap hotel bed that the Federal Marshals had provided for us. "Come here and cuddle with me. It will be okay. You'll survive, I promise."

* * *

Everyday local newspapers published an article updating readers on the events at the trial. It was the biggest thing to hit Kansas in a long time. The Topeka Capital Journal reported that:

> After two and one-half days of jury selection, prosecution and defense attorneys on Wednesday finally settled on eight men and four women... ... the trial is expected to last six to eight weeks.

136

Background on Skinner

In 1989, in Cherry Hill, New Jersey, Todd got busted with forty-two pounds of weed and was charged with kingpin charges. This wasn't his only load to go to Cherry Hill; he was flying in around 1,000 lbs per week from Tucson. That's right, *flying.* Back then, they didn't check luggage. He would load up eight to ten suitcases, take a limo to the airport, and simply fly out without a hitch! One of his customers got hot and sloppy, though, which drew heat to Todd.

Todd waited for a year to go to trial. All the while, he was looking at life in prison. Somewhere in the midst of waiting, he made a deal and began (or possibly continued) to work as a CS for the DEA.

Todd began working closely with his stepfather; Gary was an agent with the criminal enforcement division of the IRS and also an agent with the Organized Crime Drug Enforcement Task Force in Oklahoma. This is most likely Todd's original DEA connection and who trained him as a CS. Todd worked closely with a law enforcement group out of Florida to bring down a top member of the Columbian Medellin Cartel, Boris Olarte. After which, Todd was quickly let out of prison in exchange for his help.

The Rolling Stone Magazine reported that:

> ...He [Todd] developed a nose for trouble. After leasing a seventy-eight foot oil-field utility vessel for use off the coast of Louisiana, Skinner installed fancy electronic gear on the boat, then wrecked the craft, which he had failed to insure, off the coast of Jamaica in a hurricane. Customs officials in

the Cayman Islands boarded the boat and
gave Skinner an hour to leave the country...

Todd told me that he used this ship to
smuggle fuel into Jamaica and skip paying tariffs.
His partner there, John Morgan, owned all of the
gas stations on the island. John also was growing
most of the marijuana. When Todd realized this,
they quickly became partners on both projects.
Whenever John had weed that was left over or not
good enough to sell, Todd would turn it into hash
oil. Then he'd smuggle it into Canada for sale. As a
trusted partner, Todd ended up meeting the other
business partners of John's - the Medellin Cartel.
The question that still rests in my mind is: Did Todd
plan the Olarte bust *before* he got into trouble in
New Jersey? I wish I knew.

Skinner Testifies for the Prosecution

The Topeka Capital Journal reported that:

> Gordon Todd Skinner, the conspirator turned
> prosecution witness... ...testified Tuesday
> that William Leonard Pickard's role in the
> conspiracy was to get the chemicals and
> make the drug... ...Skinner told jurors
> Pickard was a member of the Brotherhood of
> Eternal Love, a group from the late 1960s or
> early 1970s that produced marijuana,
> hashish and psychedelic drugs. He decided to
> cooperate with federal drug investigators,
> Skinner said, because he thought someone
> associated with the man who provided ET, a
> chemical essential to making LSD, had been
> slain. 'I fought with him (Pickard) extensively
> on this issue,' Skinner said, adding that the
> associate had cooperated with law

enforcement officers in Oregon or Washington, leading to the imprisonment of several people and making it more difficult to get ET. Skinner said Pickard had tried unsuccessfully for three years to convince him to kidnap or drug the person then take the victim to Guatemala.

It turns out that the source for the ET went to Afghanistan at some point after Sept. 11, 2001. While visiting, he was executed because of being an American. There is no proof of anyone working under him ever working for the Feds or having been killed.

The Topeka Capital Journal reported that:

> Skinner said he sought immunity for himself from federal prosecutors in Washington D.C., telling them, 'I have what I believe is the world's largest LSD laboratory.' He wasn't believed at first, Skinner said. But on Oct. 19, 2000, he finally signed an agreement in which the Department of Justice granted him immunity from prosecution in exchange for evidence in the LSD lab case...

Todd received immunity by going to the head of the Department of Justice in Washington D.C. They gave him total immunity for production and distribution before he ever told them one piece of real, hard evidence. They took him on his word. This makes me think that he had worked with them many times before. Otherwise, why would they trust him like that? Originally he was only going to give them the lab. However, somewhere along the line this plan changed into also busting Leonard and Clyde. The DEA knew the location of the lab for three weeks before they decided to bust it. They conveniently waited until Leonard and Clyde came to move it to its new location in Colorado.

The Topeka Capital Journal reported that:

> Skinner told jurors of his checkered past, including that he had been convicted of a federal misdemeanor linked to an Interpol identification badge, represented himself as a doctor in June 2000 and prescribed unscheduled drugs, has a pending theft case in Pottawatomie County and has used aliases...

The "Good Dr. Skinner" was also in residence in Seattle during the speaker incident. You see, that is how we convinced the managers of the penthouse to rent to us. Todd told them that he was a 64-year-old doctor from England. He supposedly was here in the United States on sabbatical from the university in which he usually taught! I know this sounds unreal, but they all believed him. The bigger the lie he told, the more likely he was to pull it off. He claimed to invent an HIV vaccine that was in animal test studies. He offered to give people IV's as treatment for their illnesses and prescribed medicines for everyone in the building!

The Topeka Capital Journal reported that:

> Skinner, who owned the silo site, said Apperson's role was to set up and take down the LSD lab. Apperson received $100,000 for a major lab set-up and $50,000 to take it down if a landlord was coming through. Apperson also handled the lab's mechanical functions and may have laundered money...

His own roles, Skinner said, were to launder drug money, find locations for the lab, deal with the public, make communications decisions, handle security issues and distribute LSD in Kansas. Skinner also testified that: Pickard and Apperson wanted to move the lab to Kansas because it would be remote and easier to determine whether they were being followed. The lab had been moved from Aspen, Colorado, to Santa Fe, New Mexico, then to the silo site...

Todd always bragged that the lab was his and that he was in charge of the whole operation. He told me he synthesized the type of LSD that went by the street name of "white fluff". Todd also said he gave it away for free. On the other hand, Leonard made what was called "lavender", and he sold it for around $3 million a kilo. Todd believed that people should never sell psychedelics, because they're sacraments. Of course, Leonard didn't agree.

Still, Todd's stance was a bit of a con, like most of the things in his life. He would sell MDMA, and justify his actions by claiming that MDMA was an entactogen rather than an entheogen. And Todd was perfectly alright with selling entactogens. Also, Todd was willing to profit from the LSD lab if he did something else for the money too. Therefore, when he helped launder the money, he'd reward himself with a chunk of it for his efforts. He would also use lab profits for day-to-day operating costs. So, if you get right down to it, Todd profited from the sale of LSD too.

The Topeka Capital Journal reported that:

The witness, Gordon Todd Skinner, testified

141

.. ...illegal drug money would enter Las
s casinos as Dutch currency and emerge
American greenbacks... ...How drug
money is laundered into clean money: LSD in
manufactured in the United States, goes to
Petaluma Al, goes to Europe, where it is sold,
money including Dutch guilders returns to
Petaluma, California, and then is paid to LSD
conspirators. The conspirators then take
guilders to Las Vegas casinos, pay guilders
into casino, gamble a while, and then cash in
remaining money, including winnings or
losses, and either wire it to a location, receive
American currency or get it in money orders.

We made many trips to Las Vegas, and all of
them were as exciting as the first. It was fun to see
Todd and Leonard in action; they were both smooth
talkers and very good at what they did. Our whole
group paraded around the casinos like we owned
the place.

We were even decked out in expensive clothes
to look the part – Armani and Gucci. On our second
visit, Todd took me to the Armani store in the
Bellagio, where we were staying at the time. He
bought me two suits and a beautiful dress. I had
always dreamed of having expensive clothes. The
material felt better against my skin. Plus, after that
shopping trip, I was usually the best-dressed person
around. Instead of people looking at me like I was a
weird Goth girl, they looked at me with respect, like
I was somebody important. *I was, I had the clothes,
right?*

I remember one occasion when Todd and
Leonard went to play French Roulette. We were
staying at the Paris in their best rooms, so all we
had to do was take the elevator downstairs. Todd
started playing with a large stack of plaques. They

ranged in value from $1,000-$10,000. He started throwing them down across the board, as if they were pennies. After an hour of play, he was up $64,000 and decided to stop. It was amazing! Afterward, we all went over to the Bellagio for beluga caviar and wine, costing only a measly $4000!

The Topeka Capital Journal reported that:

> ...This afternoon, William Rork, defense attorney representing Pickard, started the cross examination of Skinner. 'This isn't the first case you've been a confidential informant, is it?' Rork asked for his first question. Before Skinner could answer, Assistant U.S. Attorney Greg Hough objected, and after a long conference between prosecution and defense attorneys and U.S. District Judge Richard Rogers, Rork started another line of questions, asking Skinner about his schooling and personal drug use.

Skinner's Education

The Topeka Capital Journal reported that:

> Skinner graduated fro⌐   ⌐hool in 1982 in Tulsa, Oklahoma, ⌐   ⌐or Gardner Spring Company, ⌐   ⌐ed by his mother. Skinner   ⌐ege level [classes], includ⌐   ⌐nd the like. Skinner   ⌐d in mathematics   ⌐e⌐   ⌐d by the time h⌐   ⌐re⌐   ⌐hing he could f⌐
>
> Accord⌐   ⌐Todd started to produce sma⌐   ⌐tamines at age

sixteen, but he was not very good at chemistry until he got a little more practice. Todd told me that his father taught him how to extract mescaline from peyote when he was nineteen. Then a physicist who worked for NASA supposedly taught him how to incorporate light into tryptamine chemistry in his early twenties. Todd was probably a self-taught LSD chemist, but no one really knows.

The Topeka Capital Journal reported that:

> Skinner testified he first used nitrous oxide (laughing gas) and mescaline, then referred to a list of drugs that he earlier admitted he used, including LSD, peyote, marijuana, PCP and more than 15 other drugs. Skinner said he used LSD and mescaline as 'sacraments,' not as recreational drugs... ...Skinner testified he experimented on himself by taking measured amounts of drugs... ...Through word-of-mouth and magazines, he learned of conferences and attended them where he met 'a small community' of other people doing the same thing, some for a long time...

The Rolling Stone reported that:

> ...though he never earned a college degree, he says he studied for awhile at the University of Heidelberg, in Germany. 'There is no way for me to describe the depth of Todd's knowledge,' says Moise Seligman, a retired Army major general... ...'I have never met anyone who could sit in the same room with Todd Skinner, as far as brain power is concerned.'

144

Pickard's Education

The Rolling Stone reported that Leonard:

> ...spent the summer of 1962 interning at the Argonne National Laboratory in Illinois. A year later, at the age of seventeen he won a Westing House Talent Search, on of forty teenagers recognized as the top science students in the United States. Twenty-two scholarship offers rolled in unsolicited. Pickard chose Princeton. The temptations of Greenwich Village jazz clubs, a brief train ride away, distracted him, and after lass than a year, he dropped out...

> In 1974, Pickard formerly returned to school, enrolling at Foothills College, in Los Altos Hills, to study biology and chemistry. Then he was off to San Jose State, from 1976 through 1978, to study organic chemistry and neurophysiology.

> By 1987... ...he turned up at San Francisco State University and fell under the influence of the legendary drug researcher Alexander Shulgin [Sasha]...

> Pickard received his Master's Degree in Public Policy from the Kennedy School of Government in 1997." Finally he moved on to UCLA, where he worked on drug-policy research.

Leonard came across as a very educated man. From the beginning, he started to teach me about interacting with people at different level than I was used to in Kansas. One time, we were at a

Kinko's in Las Vegas standing in line to make some copies. He looked over at me and stood very straight and tall. "Baby," he said. The whole group used to call me that, because I was half everyone else's age. "Your back is like a beautiful string of pearls. You must start with your head and stand very tall, allowing the pearls to dangle there, nice and straight. Stand with pride."

His suggestion stuck with me. After this conversation, I was always mindful of slouching.

Some of Pickard's Criminal History

The Rolling Stone reported that Leonard:

Has a rap sheet stretching back to his teens and has served two prison terms for manufacturing drugs, including LSD and the rarely seen synthetic mescaline... ...Pickard was arrested twice in Alabama in 1964 for forging checks. The following January, he was arrested for stealing a car...

Leonard was busted in 1977, in Redwood City, California, with am MDA lab. Then he was busted again, in 1988 in Mountain View, California, but this time he was busted with an LSD and mescaline lab. As you can see, Leonard had been at it for a long time!

Pickard Reveals Government Connections

The Wamego Times reported that as a Harvard student:

He researched drug trafficking in Kansas, Afghanistan and the former Soviet Union in an attempt to stem the proliferation of drugs

146

in the United States...

Pickard said his research took him to Moscow, where he met with government officials about drug use, and to Northern Afghanistan where he posed as a drug trafficker to infiltrate a heroin trafficking ring run by an Afghan warlord who became the Deputy Minister of Defense following the fall of the Taliban government. To lend credibility to his testimony, Pickard dropped the names of some heavy hitters in the U.S. Government, including Robert Bonner, commissioner of the U.S. Customs Service and former director of the Drug Enforcement Administration, and Robert Gelbard, assistant secretary of state and ambassador to Indonesia during the Clinton Administration...

Robert Bonner, commissioner of the United States Customs Service, testified last Wednesday... ...Bonner answers directly to Tom Ridge, recently appointed director of Homeland Security for the United States, Bonner is also a former director of the DEA and a former U.S. District Court Judge in LA.

Bonner received a call from Pickard, saying he had knowledge of fentanyl manufacturing in Russia. He recommended that Pickard go to the DEA immediately, and contacted Donnie Marshal, head of criminal operations at the DEA. Bonner gave Marshal Pickard's phone number, and then he stayed out of it once he had passed the information on.

Marquardt's Lab

The Wamego Times reported that:

> He [Leonard] received an appointment as a research fellow at Harvard Medical School and began researching the outbreak of fentanyl use in the United States, thought to have been caused by the clandestine lab of George Marquardt, a self-taught chemist tracked by the DEA from Boston to Goddard, Kansas, where, in 1993, he was busted and later imprisoned...

> With the knowledge of the Harvard faculty and DEA Senior Chemist Roger Ely, Pickard said he corresponded with Marquardt in an Oregon prison and received responses...

The most interesting response was when Marquardt told Leonard that the DEA hadn't seized a large portion of his lab. This led to Leonard's defense team making the claim in court that Todd might've somehow gotten control of the unseized portion of Marquardt's lab and that Todd could've been producing fentanyl in Kansas also. *Of course, the prosecution didn't like this very much!* Ultimately, though, the court ruled that the claim was hearsay and that it was inadmissible.

Research in Russia

The Wamego Times reported that:

> ...he prepared a 'briefing paper' for the US State Department entitled 'What Should the State Department Do About the Drug Problem In Russia?' Assistant Secretary of

State Robert Gelbard was his sponsor for the project... ...Pickard's research for the paper twice took him to Russia where he met with Russia's head forensic chemist and the head of the MVB (the Russian version of the FBI) to discuss the 'explosive outbreak' of fentanyl use by students in Moscow...

...Pickard said he sent the briefing paper to Gelbard and communicated his findings by e-mail to the DEA's Roger Ely, who testified last Tuesday. Ely said he learned of Pickard through Dr. Alexander 'Sasha' Shulgin, a toxicologist-pharmacologist, who e-mailed Ely and asked if it would be okay for a Harvard student working on a project to contact him. Shulgin has invented dozens of mind-altering drugs and is often referred to as 'The Godfather of Ecstasy'... ...Ely said he became cautious about dealing with Pickard after Shulgin told him Pickard, in 1988, had been arrested at an LSD laboratory at Mountain View, California. Pickard was later convicted of possession of mescaline and possession and manufacture of LSD.

Operation Infrared

The Wamego Times reported that:

Following his 1988 arrest and subsequent conviction, Pickard was imprisoned in the US Federal Correction Facility at Terminal Island, California, where he met Mohammed Akbar, an Afghan national serving a 12-year sentence for heroin importation. Several years later, as a student at Harvard's JFK School of Government, Pickard said he tried

149

to broker a deal to retrieve four stinger missiles in the hands of an Afghan warlord in exchange for Akbar's early release. He said he was also instructed by the US Customs officials to arrange for a large shipment of heroin from Afghanistan to the United States to try to uncover the smugglers' distribution system. Pickard said that at the direction of US Customs, he traveled to Afghanistan and represented himself as a drug trafficker to Akbar's family and friends, and he met with Abdul Rashid Dostum, the Northern Alliance warlord in charge of the heroin ring who is now Deputy Defense Minister of Afghanistan...

In testimony earlier in the week, U. S. Customs special Agent Peter Louie said he had been contacted by Pickard's family and Pickard provided serial numbers for several Stinger missiles, and the numbers were 'credible,' Louie replied. The Customs Service passed the missile information to an unnamed federal agency, but that agency didn't do anything with the information and the missiles-for-release trade never took place. Pickard said the Stinger deal fell through because the CIA did not want to participate...

This made me wonder if they were really being truthful about the outcome of Operation Infrared. When I looked at the file, it had said that the mission had been completed. It was very clear. I wonder if they did in fact do the trade, and because of the heroin importation, they didn't want to admit it. Was this an example of the "off the books financing" that Todd mentioned earlier? *Sounded exactly like the corrupt U. S. government to me...*

Pickard and Skinner's First Meeting

The Wamego Times reported that:

Pickard said he first met Skinner in February of 1998, at a conference of the American Academy of Forensic Scientists at San Francisco... ...Although Skinner testified earlier he had met Pickard in 1997 at an ethnobotony conference at San Francisco...

Pickard described Skinner as a 'fascinating person' who showed an expertise on chemical compounds and who talked freely about his 'ayahuasca' experiences (ayahuasca is a hallucinogenic tea brewed from rain forest plants). 'Mr. Skinner talks and everybody else listens,' Pickard said. Following the forensic science conference, Pickard said, the two talked often by phone, and some months later, Skinner invited Pickard, to Kansas to see his refurbished missile base. 'He said it was one of five he owned in Kansas, and he also owned one in Colorado- a former NORAD headquarters,' Pickard testified. 'He was incredibly generous. I'd never seen anything like it. I assumed his funding was legitimate. I was delighted to make a new and interesting friend.'

Government Misconduct

The defense decided to recall Todd as a witness with the hope that they might gain some new information that would help their case. The Wamego Times reported that:

...under direct questioning by Pickard's defense attorney William Rork, Skinner made the following claims: On October 27, 2000- during a walk-through of the missile base by DEA agents- Special Agent Karl opened and swabbed the inside of a can of ET found inside the base. The alleged incident occurred prior to the DEA executing a search warrant at the base October 31, 2000. On the October 27 walk-through, John 'Zach' Zajak, with DEA headquarters at Washington D.C., made a personal video of the missile base which was never entered into evidence by the prosecution.

Of course, later in the hearing, the DEA agents refuted the claim of having opened the ET. Karl said that he didn't open the canister. As a forensic chemist, he knew it could cause convulsions. They did, however, release a copy of the video to the defense. *Whatever happened to not withholding evidence?*

Throughout the entire trial, an unnamed individual would call the defense and explain to them what was happening on the prosecution's side. The person would give the defense questions to ask in order to make the trial turn to their favor. This person called almost every day and gave Billy Rork pages of questions. Despite this person's efforts, the trial went in the wrong direction anyway...

* * *

The evening after the trial was finished, as we were waiting for the verdict, Todd started to cry. At first, I thought it was about Leonard and Clyde. Upon questioning him, though, he told me that it was about Karl. "Karl has been my friend and confidant for almost three years. I haven't done anything without consulting him. It's hard to say good-bye to a friend."

"Are you crazy? That man isn't your friend. What about L and C? They were your friends!" I was furious. *Was he really that foolish and stupid?*

As I watched tears roll down his cheeks, I let out a sigh of relief. It was actually over. And I never had to testify. I went up there and pled the fifth. The judge refused to give me immunity for my testimony, so I was finished.

"Why can't you just be happy that we get to go home and sleep in a good bed?" I eventually asked, trying to bring around a positive change in him.

"Oh, I am sweetie. It's just going to be much more difficult now, without Karl's help." He wiped off his face, trying to stop his emotions.

"We'll be better off without him. I hate the DEA. They have ruined our life, not helped us. We'll be okay. You'll see."

The Verdict-Guilty

The Topeka Capital Journal shared the news of the verdict:

> Six hours after they began deliberating, federal jurors on Monday convicted two California men of LSD trafficking charges... ...Monday was the first day of the 12th week of the trial... ...The defendants, first Apperson followed by Pickard, were stone-faced as the verdicts were read. Within minutes of the verdicts, Apperson, who had been free on bond pending trial, was handcuffed and taken into custody. Pickard has been in

custody since Nov. 7, 2000. Pickard portrayed himself as an academic conducting research with high-level contacts in federal law enforcement circles, the U.S. State Department, Russia and Afghanistan. He told jurors he was en route to destroy an LSD lab Nov. 6, 2000, when Kansas Highway Patrol troopers stopped his vehicle...

Scott Lowry, the presiding juror, said jurors 'found that the evidence was clear and convincing. It was a pretty easy verdict to come to.' That jurors needed only six hours to reach the guilty verdicts following a long trial was indicative of how jurors felt about the evidence... ...Another juror, Jim Mason, said audio tapes I which jurors heard the defendants' voices use the words 'my' and 'our' when referring to an LSD chemical they wanted returned to them was important evidence...

William Rork, Pickard's defense attorney, said the trial 'was one of the toughest cases I've ever defended in trying to get all of the facts before the jury to consider.' Rork complained that the defendants had to 'play hide-and-seek' with the government to get the evidence about the case...

* * *

After weeks of bouncing from hotel to hotel, we finally went home to Tulsa. I was drained from it all. The press was always snooping around, everyone stared at us, and it felt like we were being watched twenty-four hours a day. I'm sure they had our rooms bugged, and they might've even had them on video. *I was so glad it was all over.*

GORDON TODD SKINNER'S CHEMICAL USAGE
(Given to court for immunity)

1. N, N-DIETHYLTRYPTAMINE
2. 5-MEO-ALPHA-MT
3. N, N-DIMETHYLTRYPTAMINE
4. 2-ALPHA-DIMETHYLTRYPTAMINE
5. ALPHA, N-DIMETHYLTRYPTAMINE
6. N, N-DIPROPYLTRYPTAMINE
7. ALPHA-ETHYLTRYPTAMINE
8. 3, 4-DIHYDRO-7-METHOXY-1-METHYL-b-CARBOLINE
9. 7-METHOXY-b-CARBOLINE
10. D-LYSERGIC ACID DIETHYLAMIDE
11. MELATONIN
12. 5-METHOXY-N,N-DIETHYLTRYPTAMINE
13. 5-METHOXY-N,N-DIISOPROPYLTRYPTAMINE
14. 5-METHOXY-N,N-DIMETHYLTRYPTAMINE
15. NOR-5-MEO-DMT
16. 1, 2, 3, 4-TETRAHYDRO-b-CARBOLINE
17. ALPHA-METHYLTRYPTTAMINE
18. N-ETHYLTRYPTAMINE
19. N-METHYLTRYPTAMINE
20. 6-PROPYL-NOR-LSD
21. TRYPTAMINE
22. TETRAHYDROHARMINE
23. ALPHA, N,O-TRIMETHYLSEROTONIN
24. PSILOCIN
25. PSILOCYBIN
26. CEY-19
27. ALD-52
28. BOL-148
29. ERGONOVINE
30. METHERGINE
31. ANY AND ALL ISOMERS OF LSD
32. COLD WATER WASH OF ERGOT
33. WARM WATER WASH OF ERGOT
34. WINE (ETHANOL) WASH OF ERGOT
35. ANY COMBINATION OF 32-34.

36. 5-FLUORO-ALPHA-METHYLTRYPTAMINE
37. 6-FLUORO-ALPHA-METHYLTRYPTAMINE
38. BANISTERIOPSIS CAAPI
39. PEGANUM HARMALA
40. 6-METHOXY-HARMINE
41. GLAND SECRETIONS OF BUFO ALVARIUS
(SONORAN DESERT TOAD)
42. MIMOSACEAE ANADENANTHERA, COLD WATER,
WARM WATER, AND ETHANOL EXTRACTIONS
43. THE FRACTIONS OF THE ABOVE EXTRACTIONS
44. ACACIA SP. (AS MANY AS COULD BE FOUND)
45. DESMANTHUS ILLINOENSIS
46. MIMOSA HOSTILIS
47. COLD WATER, WARM WATER, AND ETHANOL
EXTRACTIONS OF 44-46
48. THE FRACTIONS OF THE ABOVE EXTRACTIONS
49. 5-MEO-DMT AND DMT DISSOLVED INTO BUTTER
50. VIROLA CALOPHYLLA
51. PHALARIS AQUATICA
52. PHALARIS ARUNDINACEA
53. PHRAGMITES AUSTRALIS
54. ARUNDO DONAX
55. PSYCHOTRIA VIRIDIS
56. PSILOCYBE CUBENSIS AND OTHER VARIETIES
57. PANAEOLUS SUBBALTEATUS
58. PSILOCYBE AZYRESCENS AND OTHER VARIETIES
59. COLD WATER, WARM WATER, AND ETHANOL
EXTRACTIONS OF 50-58
60. THE FRACTIONS OF THE ABOVE EXTRACTIONS
61. 50-60 WERE TRIED WITH MONO AMINE OXIDE
ENZIME INHIBITORS (IRREVERSABLE AND
REVERSABLE, SHORT AND LONG LASTING, MAO (A)
AND MAO (A&B))
62. PARNATE
63. MOCLOBEMIDE
64. NARDIL
65. L-TRYPTOPHAN (EFFECTIVELY BANNED BY THE
FDA)
66. D-TRYPTOPHAN
67. DL-TRYPTOPHAN
68. 5-HYDROXY-L-TRYPTOPHAN

69. 2C-B
70. 2C-I
71. DOB
72. 2, 5-DIMETHOXY-4-METHYLAMPHETAMINE
73. 3-METHOXY-4, 5-
METHYLENEDIOXYPHENETHYLAMINE
74. MDA
75. MDMA AND VARIOUS ISOMERS AND ANALOGS
76. TMA
77. TMA-2
78. MESCALINE
79. ESCALINE
80. PEYOTE AND ITS EXTRACTIONS AND TEAS
81. SAN PEDRO AND ITS EXTRACTIONS AND TEAS
82. CAFFEINE
83. THEOBROMINE (FROM CHOCOLATE
84. MYRISTICIN
85. KETAMINE
86. NITROUS OXIDE
87. SALVINORIN A
88. SALVIA DIVINORUM
89. SALVINORIN C (DITERPENE)
90. IBOTENIC ACID
91. AMANITA MUSCARIA, ALL KNOWN VARIATIONS
92. MUSCIMOL
93. AMANITA PANTHERINA
94. ALL EXTRACTIONS, PREPARATIONS, AND
TREATMENTS KNOWN AT THE TIME OF #92-93
95. VALIUM
96. MEPERIDINE
97. SUBLIMES
98. DOLOPHINE
99. MORPHINE
100. HYDROMORPHONE
101. NUMORPHAN
102. CODEINE
103. HYDROCODONE
104. OPIUM, ALL TEAS AND EXTRACTIONS THEREOF
105. ALPRAZOLAM
106. TEMAZEPAM
107. SECONAL

108. CARISOPRODOL
109. OXYCODONE
110. MORNING GLORY SEEDS, TEAS AND EXTRACTS THEREOF
111. BABY HAWAIIAN WOODROSE SEEDS, TEAS AND EXTRACTS THEREOF
112. GHB AND ALL ISOMERS AND ANOLOGS THEREOF
113. TMFPP
114. DXM
115. METHOXYSAFROLE
116. PROCAINE
117. LIDOCAINE
118. CARBOCAINE
119. NIPHEDIPINE
120. NORVASC
121. 7-METHYLTRYPTAMINE
122. 5-METHYLTRYPTAMINE
123. RESERPINE (INDIAN SNAKEROOT), AND OTHER EXTRACTS
124. PSEUDOEPHEDRINE
125. BENZOCAINE
126. ACETYLSALICYLIC ACID
127. FUROSEMIDE
128. ALL FORMS OF ANTIBIOTICS
129. NYSTATIN
130. FLUCONAZOLE
131. IBUPROFIN
132. ZOLPIDEM TARTRATE
133. SILDENAFIL CITRATE
134. FLUNITRAZEPAM
135. BETA-BUNGAROTOXIN
136. SODIUM PENTATHOL (USED TO REMOVE WISDOM TEETH)
137. ALL AMINO ACIDS, THEIR DERIVATIVES AND METABOLITES, IV AND ORAL
138. MAGNESIUM SULFATE IV
139. VITAMINS AND MINERALS IV, IM, AND ORAL
140. EDETATE SODIUM IV
141. ALPHA LIPOIC ACID, IV, IM, AND ORAL
142. DEXTROSE, IV AND ORAL
143. SOD IV

144. ALL KNOWN BETA-CARBOLINES
145. ALCOHOL
146. CANNABIS (ONLY USED SIX TIMES IN LIFE)
147. L-DEPRENYL
148. BETEL NUT
149. VANADIUM I.V.
150. KAWAIN
151. METHYSTICIN
152. YANGONIN
153. KAVALACTONES
154. 1, 3, 7 -TRIMETHYLXANTHINE
155. VETALAR
156. YOHIMBE
157. HYDERGINE
158. VASOPRESSIN
159. DEHYDROEPIANDROSTRONE
160. 2-DIMETHYLAMINOETHANOL
161. VOLCAGNA
162. LA-111; LSA; MORNING GLORY AND EXTRACTS
163. 4-PHOSPHORYLOXY-N-METHYLTRYPTAMINE

Chapter 20 FOXY

Todd was holding up a glass pie pan with partially crystallized brownish goo covering the bottom. "It's 4-Acetoxy-DIPT. I know it looks like crap, but I don't have the chemicals or equipment I need to fully crystallize it. Do you want to try some with me anyway?" A childish grin and a tapping foot gave away his eagerness.

"Not really. I have a summer class starting tomorrow and I don't want to miss it." I had been going to the University of Tulsa for the last year, trying desperately to get my life in order. No more partying, just school. Since the trial took up so much of my time the previous semester, I was trying to make it up in the summer.

"Okay, well I'm going to try it." He got a knife out of the drawer and scraped up some of the crystallized goo. He probably took 10-20 mg. "Look at how crystallized it got without pulling a vacuum!"

The crystals were wide, spread out. What did they feel like? The temptation was overwhelming, so I ran my finger along the top of them. I knew instantaneously that it was a bad idea. There was some of the goo stuck on my forefinger. I rubbed it in with my thumb. It tingled that magic tingle. And that's all it took - I was dosed. I really hoped I wouldn't miss class over this. *Why had I touched it? Why?* I was so stupid sometimes. I washed my hands, but I knew it wouldn't help.

"I think I'm dosed," I eventually admitted.

Todd smiled happily. "Let's go for a drive."

"Okay, but are you sure you're going to be able to drive?" The whole car idea made me nervous; driving and tripping don't mix.

"Of course, this is going to be a really weak trip. Foxy is light, similar to MDMA. If the ravers take it, I can drive on it." He was already walking out the door, ready for an adventure.

We got into the C-4 Porsche. It was a sunny day so we put the top down. It was fun; we drove with the music cranked up as loud as it would go. Todd loved to drive fast, so we headed out of town where there was more space and less traffic. We ended up at a nearby lake.

It was such a beautiful day. I had been stressing out too much since we'd moved to Tulsa. Growing up and being in the real world sucked! That's about when I realized I had to go to the bathroom. So we stopped at one of the nasty public restrooms.

The effects hit me extremely hard. The tiles in the bathroom floor began to move. It was as if they lifted up out of the floor and started to line dance. The once drab colors became metallic pastels. The tiles radiated a multitude of bouncing light prisms. I felt incredible; a very warm and sensual fuzzy feeling came over me. I felt like cuddling.

The intensity kept increasing. It was coming on quickly, a little too quickly. What was the peak going to be like? I wondered if Todd really made Foxy, or was it something else? Foxy was supposed to have an active dose of 20mg. I knew I didn't absorb 20mg through my finger. But whatever it was, it was fantastic!

I barely made it back to the car. "What's wrong, sweetie?" Todd was laughing, obviously amused by the expression on my face.

"I'm getting really high. It's coming on so fast. How will I make it to class tomorrow?" I took a few deep breaths. The rush was incredible.

"Sweetie, just enjoy it. You'll make it to class tomorrow, I promise. I will take you there myself." He shifted the car into first gear and took off.

"Do you think we should be driving when we're tripping this hard? If I feel like this from my small dose, then you must be *really* high."

"You're tripping that hard, sweetie? Wow. I'm coming on, but I'm not too high to drive. I'll head back into town, though, just to be safe."

Later:

Todd and I were lying on the bed, looking up at the ceiling. Grateful dead bears danced across it. Millions of them were dancing and laughing. I could feel their joy. The bright neon joking bears eventually morphed into piece signs. They grew into three-dimensional holograms and glided through space. Tie-dye patterns started to crawl around in the background. It was like a screensaver on a computer, only with depth and emotion.

Somehow I connected with the headspace of the people who made the symbols the center of the 1960's. I wondered if they saw them when they were tripping too. Could this have been why they used them to symbolize their views? Could tripping have helped them see that peace and love are the best options our society has? If so, then why are entheogens illegal? I could see what times were like back then, so similar to the present. Still, in today's world, we're at war with ourselves, and there are fewer protesters.

My field of vision started to flash like a strobe light. My whole consciousness pulsed along with it, uncomfortably. It felt like listening to a person run their fingers across a chalkboard. It made me cringe as it grated on my nerves. I felt as though I might start seizing like an epileptic. It was strange, and I wanted it to stop.

My first instinct was to start chanting. The chants quickly turned into intricately textured songs. The songs, or mantras, were a multi-dimensional language that transcended time and space. There were subtleties in them that were not in normal language. They were different, more beautiful than anything I had ever heard. They lifted me up and made me strong. The words were a part of me, sort of like my arms but different. They were my cosmic arms reaching up to grab the ladder to the divine. And my heart was in it completely. **Love, then light, then language.**

The strobe light was still in my head, but I could transcend it. I would just put it to the back of my mind and let the songs work their magic. I started to move my hands, weaving them through the air. They would go into specific positions alongside certain phrases in my songs. I could see in all directions, into any time. I could sense the others who'd used them in the past. *Were these the mudras they spoke of in Hinduism?*

I felt the divine unity of the mantras with the mudras. This was how it was supposed to be done; I knew it. My soul was filled with more loving emotion than ever. This was how I was supposed to worship. This was how I was supposed to get back, to reunite with the godhead.

INTEGRATION

I noticed several perceptual changes after this experience. I saw the world in what seemed like permanent Technicolor. This was fun at first, but it

163

eventually started to make me nervous. At night when I went to sleep, strobe lights kept flashing behind my eyelids. It made sleeping incredibly difficult. Did I somehow change my brain? How long would this last?

Eventually, both of these effects went away. Still, for years after this trip, rainbow light prisms would bounce off car headlights at night making it difficult for me to drive. It was kind of cool; yet, it sometimes made me wonder what had happened to my neurons. In hindsight, I was most likely suffering from HPPD, or hallucinogen persisting perception disorder.

Anyhow, after this trip, I also realized my mantras and mudras could create a path to the spiritual part of myself, even when I wasn't on a psychedelic. *They help me remember the way.*

Remembering is easy when my heart is in it - really in it. Purity and the heart are so interconnected that they're almost the same thing. However, purity is guided by the heart. If my motives are pure, I can go anywhere and do anything. If my spirituality is pure, I can remember quickly and easily. I simply go home. I do not try. I just go. No effort. Only a smooth divine shift.

* * *

Most of the statues meant to represent Hindu and Buddhist deities have their hands positioned in mudras. The position of each finger is said to change the meaning, since each finger represents a different energy system. Achaarya Keshav Deo stated:

If a human body is a machine, the mudras are the controlling switches of this machine.

164

Dr. Dale M. Schusterman wrote in his book *Sign Language of the Soul*:

> Practitioners of yoga use mudras to focus energy in certain ways during the postures (asanas), and especially during meditation. Each mudra has a mantra or Sanskrit power phrase associated with it, and the two often function together.
>
> The Polynesians use special hand positions in their dance rituals. They are used as a non-verbal narrative tool that expresses the story they are telling.
>
> Paintings and engravings depict Jesus, angels, saints, and other biblical personalities with their hands showing specific mudras.
>
> Kabalistic literature includes many diagrams of the hands with Hebrew letters on the different joints, and modern rabbis continue to use the blessing mudra of the Levite priests.
>
> It is not uncommon for people in deep meditation to have their hands unconsciously form specific mudras. The hands can, and do, reflect deep inner states of consciousness.

The realization that I was not the only one to experience this divine gift was comforting. My connection to humankind, my brethren, was stronger. To me, the information I learned while tripping felt extremely true - the truest of all truths. However, it still felt good to verify what I'd learned in my journeys through historical, philosophical, and religious texts!

Chapter 21 RETIREMENT PLAN B

Todd always joked about what he referred to as retirement plan B. Retirement plan A consisted of his few strategic business investments. Plan B was a jail cell paid for by the Feds. He would always joke about it, like it would never happen to him. Well, the three of them, Todd, Leonard, and Clyde ended up in jail by the time it was all said and done. The Topeka Capital Journal reported that:

> The primary prosecution witness against two men convicted in March of LSD trafficking has been charged in Oklahoma and Nevada with kidnapping and drug charges. A Nevada federal grand jury in early September charged Gordon Todd Skinner with one count of possession with intent to distribute about 341 grams of a substance containing ecstasy... ...Later that month, Skinner and two other people were charged with conspiracy to commit kidnapping, kidnapping and assault and battery with a dangerous weapon...

* * *

Todd ended up accepting a plea bargain for

three and a half years on the MDMA charge. This guaranteed him a short vacation rather than the ten years he could have gotten if he lost in court. And believe me, he would have lost.

The MDMA bust happened at the Burning Man festival of 2003. He was out of control and brought way too much product to the festival. Everyone was talking about the chemist in the RV who was handing out free psychedelics. He knew he was hot and gave most of his *library* to a friend to store for him. When the BLM authorities knocked on the RV door, he eagerly invited them in. He thought the place was clean, so why not? But somehow they found a 341 gram bag of MDMA with Todd's fingerprints all over it. Luckily, I was able to get out of there before the bust went down.

However, during the month prior to Burning Man, Todd manipulated me, physically and sexually assaulted me, and drugged me against my will. *It was the most terrifying experience of my life.*

It all started with us having relationship issues and breaking up. I wanted to go legal, but Todd would never conform to that sort of lifestyle. Todd was also starting to behave strangely, unpredictably. He'd get really angry with me, and I'd see hints of a violent side to him I'd never seen before.

Consequently, Todd and I broke up shortly after the trial. We got back together around the time of the foxy trip, but then we parted ways again right after. Due to these break-ups, I got my own place. I also started dating Brad. Brad was 18, and I was 21. I enjoyed being with someone closer to my age. Plus, Brad wasn't anything like Todd. He wasn't controlling, bossy, or ready to fly off the handle at any moment.

Still, Todd wanted me back, and he was willing to do whatever it took to make that happen.

So Todd started threatening Brad and me. To screw with my head, Todd dosed my house with some sort of mystery psychedelic that made me trip for three days. While this was going on, he told all my friends that I was perma-fried, messed up psychologically from taking too many psychedelics. Todd also assaulted me at one point, giving me bruises on my neck and arm.

Out of fear for our lives, Brad and I went to the local police. They took photos of my bruises, and we gave written statements about what had been going on. We ended up getting temporary restraining orders, but this didn't help. Todd just became more mean and out of control.

So we went to the DEA. We both told them about Todd's violence and his MDMA dealing in Tulsa. Of course, involving the Feds did nothing to improve the situation. Looking back, it actually made things worse.

Somehow Todd found out that we went to the DEA. Neither of us told anyone about it. Going to the DEA, even if it's necessary to save your life, isn't something you want to tell people about... I've always wondered if one of Todd's DEA contacts told him we made statements against him. *I suppose I'll never know.*

So, with tensions rising, Todd convinced me to meet him alone in his hotel room. He threatened to turn the tables on me; he said he'd go to the DEA against me if I didn't meet with him. After seeing what he did to Leonard and Clyde, I believed him. *And I was scared.*

Immediately when I got to his hotel room, Todd overpowered me and used a needle to drug me with numerous substances (I'm still not sure what they were). For three days, I drifted in and out of consciousness. At one point, I smelled the distinctive plastic-mothball-like odor of DMT being cooked up in the hotel room's coffee pot. I only have a few other brief glimpses of those three days. Todd eventually stopped drugging me and let me go, though, because we'd *supposedly* worked out a truce.

Now, I'm sure you're wondering, why didn't I head straight to the cops when he let me go? Well, like I explained earlier, I'd already tried going to the local police and the DEA prior to this incident. Since they didn't help me before, I assumed they wouldn't help me if I went to them again.

Instead, I simply went back to the apartment I shared with Brad (I'd moved out of my house after Todd dosed it). More events transpired over the next week that, to be honest, are just too painful for me to talk about in detail. However, to sum up a very long story, Brad and I ended up deciding to go talk with Todd at his hotel (a different hotel than where he first tortured me). Todd had claimed that he wanted to make a truce with Brad too. He'd said he wanted us all to put our differences behind us. *But Todd had no intention of setting things right.*

Todd got a friend (William Hoch) to help him, and he proceeded to drug me again. After which, he drugged and tortured Brad in front of me. Todd was pissed that we went to the DEA, and he wanted us to pay for it. He was also angry that Brad and I had fallen in love.

After nine days, Todd finally decided to release Brad. I tried to convince Todd to take him to the hospital, but Todd thought it was best to drop Brad off in a field. So that is what went down. And Brad found his own way to the hospital a few hours later. He was in intensive care for several days, but he survived.

What happened to me? Well, my nightmare continued. Todd drugged and manipulated me into staying with him for another month. He dosed me just about every day. After a couple weeks on whatever he was giving me, my skin began to turn yellow from jaundice. This sign of liver damage seemed to worry Todd, and it caused him to slow down on the drugging.

Even so, he filled its place with psychological abuse and manipulation. He convinced me I was being watched at all times by a team of his government contacts. And my mind wasn't working properly after all the trauma. I was a mess. I couldn't see through his lies and threats. By the end of that month, I was a shell of a human being. A zombie.

Since we were running low on money, Todd decided that we needed to sell some MDMA. So, he rented an RV and drove us to Burning Man. And that brings us up to the MDMA charges and his consequent imprisonment.

Sadly, I ended up getting charged with kidnapping along with Todd. I was never convicted of it, though; my kidnapping charge was eventually amended to accessory after the fact. I ended up pleading no contest and received a diversion (no felony on my record) and a $52,000 fine for restitution.

Still, I never should have been charged with any of it in the first place. I was under extreme duress and basically kidnapped too. But the Tulsa authorities never believed my side of the story, even after I begged them for years to give me a lie detector test.

Todd ended up getting a life sentence for kidnapping Brad. But he was never charged for the horrible things he did to me.

* * *

As for Leonard and Clyde, the Topeka Capital

Journal reported that:

> William Leonard Pickard, 58, Mill Valley, California, was sentenced to two concurrent life terms in prison without parole, and Clyde Apperson, 48, Sunnyvale, California, was sentenced to two 30-years sentences without parole... ... [they] requested that each be incarcerated at a federal prison facility at Lompoc, California, because their families live in California... ...[they], each with his legs shackled and wearing the orange coveralls of a federal prisoner, sat side by side during the sentencing. As he was sentenced, Pickard leaned his head on two fingers, his face flushed and his chin quivered. Apperson was expressionless while he was being sentenced. Neither man had any supporters in the courtroom when he was sentenced...

> Before he was sentenced, Pickard made a lengthy statement to Rogers, saying he had authority from the federal government to communicate with drug traffickers and manufacturers in 1997 and that his job description in the state of California specifically included interviewing drug manufacturers and traffickers. Pickard said that he told a DEA special agent and an assistant U.S. Attorney that Gordon Todd Skinner was concealing a chemist and a laboratory tied to the drug ecstasy... ...Federal officials didn't take action with the information...

Chapter 22 AT THE END OF THE RAINBOW

I traveled to the 2004 Toward a Science of Consciousness Convention in Tucson, Arizona for two reasons. The first was closure, and the second was to move on. Life had been spiraling out of control for the last year.

Once people heard that Todd got busted, they started to feast. They knew I was in a vulnerable position. Our storage units got broken into and everything of value, including all of my clothes, was stolen. A *friend* that was storing some of my luggage threw it all away in fear of a DEA raid. Another *friend* of ours filed for a lost title on the C-4 Porsche, which had recently been signed over into my name, and sold it out from under me. They kept the money for themselves, of course!

My life was a total wreck. Fighting the kidnapping case was really stressful. It was also painful being separated from Todd. I know this may be surprising, since he'd abused me so much during the months prior to Burning Man. But even after all that, a part of me still loved him.

Trying to understand why Todd had become violent at the end of our relationship was so confusing for me. When he was abusive, he didn't seem like himself anymore. Then the anger would subside, and he'd seem more like himself again.

His behavior caused me to keep attempting to break all ties with him; yet, I never seemed to totally succeed. I kept hoping that he'd change back into that beautifully spiritual person I first met. He'd promise he would, and I'd let him back in my life again. *Why had he turned violent all of a sudden? Why had he hurt me? How could a spiritual teacher, mate, best friend, and brother do such horrible things?*

All in all, I've found that life doesn't just hand you a perfectly balanced yin-yang. You must balance it yourself. In reality, life is more like a lopsided yin-yang. The good must be accompanied by the bad for either to exist. The good times are sprinkled throughout life and so are the bad times. *The bad ones just seem to occur in slightly larger portions and more often.*

I try to hold onto the good memories. I wrap myself up with them like a blanket, a comfort blanket. This way the bad can't sink in too far, and it sort of balances out the lopsidedness.

So I was glad to be back in Tucson, the city where I've often felt most at home. The people living there seem to be on a different vibration. They have culture, texture, and spirituality. I think the primary reason for this may be drug trafficking. The whole economy of Tucson profits from the multi-million dollar industry, and because of it, many people live outside the system. They have no time schedule and lots of cash flow. The artistic and spiritual sides of a person can flourish when it is not beaten down by a forty-hour workweek and hours of television.

I knew I desperately needed to find a truly spiritual community. I prayed for something to happen, and right on cue, the universe provided an answer.

As I took the sugar cubes, the sun was just

beginning to set over the desert. I was a little nervous about the challenges this experience might hold for me. I hadn't tripped since Todd had been arrested. I was trying to forget about the pain by blocking it all out of my mind. With this much emotional baggage, I knew it was possible for me to have a difficult trip. Yet, I felt it was time. I needed to work through it to become stronger.

I could feel the LSD send energy shivering up and down my spine. My whole body felt it coming. I sat on a porch swing that overlooked the entire city. The sky was dark and the city lights put off a warm glow. The traffic moved along the freeway in the distance, commuters driving home. Pulsating energy surged through me and increased by the minute.

Mary arrived somewhere around this time. She looked beautiful and was smiling, like always. "It's so good to see you!" Her voice sounded light and happy as she gave me a big hug.

"It's good to see you too." I returned her hug appreciatively. "It's been a long time." I wasn't tripping yet; it was just coming on, so we could still hold a coherent conversation. I figured it would be good to integrate on that level before I got too high.

"Yeah, almost two years. I thought I might never see you again. Joe and I waited around forever, but you guys never called."

"Things got weird after Seattle. You were lucky you weren't around, believe me. Would you like to dose with me? I've got a few more hits."

"No, I can't. I have to work tomorrow at the hospital." She paused and then continued. "I am also afraid of tripping for three days like last time. It was scary. Since then, I've only tripped a few times. Each time I get slammed no matter how much I take. I can take the smallest dose and be the highest one there."

"That happens to me too. I think it's because

once the pathway is created in the brain, our headspace goes back to the farthest point every time. It's sort of like learning how to read. Once you know how to put the letters together to make words and put the words together to make sentences, you no longer need to sound out each letter."

"That makes sense." She bit down on her lip slightly as she pondered it all.

"Are you still going to the University of Arizona to be a nurse?" I asked.

"Yes, in fact, I graduate next month. Can you believe it?" Her smile got bigger than I had ever seen it.

"I'm so proud of you. It makes me happy to see that somebody actually made it. Somebody actually succeeded. Most of the people I know are either in jail or hooked to some sort of heavy drug."

"Oh, I know. Joe and I aren't together anymore because after you guys left, he started using cocaine. Now he's a total junkie. It's sad." Her smile left as quickly as it came. "If he would have had psychedelics to use, he probably never would've touched the stuff."

"I have seen so much of that. And it is sad. I pray that the laws will change, and that the powers that be realize what they are doing." It was good to see an old friend and spiritual companion. Mary had really accomplished a lot since I last saw her. It was good to see her success.

My legs started to shake and shiver. Then the sensation spread throughout my body. I wasn't cold; I was just shaking. It gave me an uneasy feeling. I'd had the shakes before, but not this bad from this small of a dose. I was always afraid of getting a bad drug, and to have it somehow damage my body, brain, or worse kill me. I knew this was probably not going to happen, but it still was in the back of my mind. So I tried asking myself, "What is death anyway?" or "Is death really so bad?" And this made me laugh at myself. There wasn't anything to worry about; death was just a shift in consciousness.

I wondered if the tremors were psychological and caused by my anxiety, or if they were real and a side effect of the drug. It all could have been in my head. I was working through a lot of pain and fear. Yet somehow it felt out of my control. Changing my breathing did absolutely nothing. Changing my headspace through conversation didn't help either. So I tried to ignore it for a while. *Why was it happening?*

Mary suggested that we go for a drive up to Starr Pass to look at the stars. I thought it sounded like a great idea, anything to get my mind off of my trembling body! I had rented a convertible, so we drove with the top down the whole way. It was truly beautiful. The trip was finally starting to come on very nicely, except for the shaking.

I drank some juice along the way, but that only eased the tension a small amount. I tried to calm my body while taking my mind to another, very peaceful place. I didn't allow the fear and anxiety to take over, even though they could have very easily. Again, I tried to control the tremors with my breath. Calm and even. However, chanting was my cure all. So if it didn't stop soon, I would just chant them away.

We got to the top of the mountain. It was amazing. I could see the city far below, off in the distance. The stars were bright and almost three-dimensional. We both lay down side-by-side on the asphalt pullout. The ground was still warm from the sunlight hitting it all day. I was in awe as I felt myself expand and become one with the earth. I could see the stars as the earth saw them, light in motion. "I am the world!"

Mary just laughed. I guess I did sound sort of

strange! Awake, remembering my heritage. We talked for what seemed to me like millennia, but in reality it was only a few hours. We talked about life, love, and the nature of reality. At one point, I was explaining that I was held under different rules than *normal* people and Mary interrupted me by adding, "The oldest soul." Her comment caught me off guard; I am still pondering it...

But back to what I was saying about being held under a different set of rules. Once I gained a glimpse of the divine knowledge, it changed me forever. I *know*, so therefore must rise to the occasion and live up to that knowledge. I cannot just *get by* any longer. I must spread the comfort of peace and happiness, and I must show others through myself. Not only by being an example of purity, but also by shining love and light into the world. Light is contagious, almost like an infectious giggle. The giggle just spreads; it takes no effort and cannot be stopped once it gets started. In this way, we must nudge each other in the right direction - always spreading the love and light.

The tremors finally stopped!!! What had taken so long? The visuals were mild, even though I could feel I was peaking. I felt so happy and at home. Enlightened and in love with the universe. I was glad that I didn't have an anxiety attack; I was safe, one with all.

If you look at a trip starting at one shoulder, peaking at the head, and coming down at the other shoulder, then my most difficult spots were the shoulders. I always ended up at the godhead eventually; however, it was the beginning and ending leap that were sometimes difficult.

We drove back to the house, listening to some ambient techno. I wanted to hear music that would take me deeper, farther in or out. I danced in my seat, gliding my hands threw the air in their familiar mudras. The mudras, or hand positions, seemed to take me away as I swam through the ocean of the universal mind. I navigated the headspace with them; power surged through me as I moved. I connected with people in my past and future, as we drove with the wind in our hair. Floating timeless in the breeze.

When we arrived back at the house, the evening was quieting down. Maria looked incredibly tired. She had to go home and get some sleep, so she could work the next day.

"I wish I could stay for longer. I'm so glad I got to see you. My life has been so flat spiritually since you guys haven't been around." A few tears oozed out of her eyes as she said this. She quickly wiped them away, not wanting me to see them.

I was sad to see her leave. "We can always be together in our memories of the headspaces. We can meet each other at those common memory folds during our present meditations. This way we can be together, now and always. I hope you understand that. Think about it and you will."

Before she left, we gave each other a big hug. Neither of us knew when we would see each other again. It had been two years since our last visit. But what is time to Cosmic Family anyway?

I was coming down very smoothly. My back hurt from lying on the asphalt for hours, but otherwise I was in good shape. I started to think about Todd, my so-called spiritual companion and teacher. Why had he hurt me in so many ways? How could he have done those things to me, when he KNEW? What led him astray? Did he get too stressed out from the trial and everything? Did he experiment with the wrong chemical structure? *Who knows...*

Everyone is made of dark and light. The dark must be acknowledged, yet the light must remain in control. Both are part of the whole, holy self. Why does darkness taint so many souls? Why did it gain control of Todd? Every person struggles with darkness in their own way, I suppose.

I believe that following my heart and remaining pure will keep me on course. *I forgive you my brother, and I hope to see spirituality in you soon.* This thought comforted me and brought peace to my heart. *I thank the universe for allowing me the experience.*

PART 2: TODD'S LETTERS FROM PRISON

Chapter 1 INTRODUCTION

I will let the letters fill in Todd's perspective on things. He wrote them from 2003 to 2005 while he was awaiting trial for the possession of MDMA charge in Nevada and then the kidnapping case in Oklahoma. I have transcribed the letters exactly as he wrote them. They are complete with typos, secret chemistry codes, notes on synthesizing different entheogens, and pictures of his drawings.

I haven't been able to decipher some of his codes, and they were written so that I would be able to understand them. So have fun and read carefully! Who knows what they'll lead you to? At one point, I thought it might have been instructions on how to access a numbered bank account or even a GPS location of one of his libraries. I honestly don't know.

I omitted full names and sections that were redundant. I also changed names to protect certain people's identities. As well, I placed text [inside brackets] to fill in some of the back-story pertaining to what Todd was writing about.

Chapter 2 THE CHEMISTRY LETTERS

October 2003 (County Jail – Reno, Nevada)

Oct. 3, 2003

Dearest Krystle,

I find myself writing you, in the most strange and dark of circumstances. My tremor is getting worse. The left side of my body is numb most of the time. If I drink caffeine I feel improved; yet, I pay for the respite three hours later. The tenacious tremor is of some concern, I confess – I wait for some sign of abatement, six weeks is the time to give. I stopped "Benzo's" [Valium and Clonopin] on September 4th, 2003; therefore October 19th is maximum date for turn around. It is hard for me to maintain a high level of hygiene. I try to take two showers a day. I only get one change of clothes a week – the smell of the clothes at seven days is horrendous. The food is mostly synthetic – I truly marvel that it is legal to feed anything this. Yet, I know freedom is a state of mind – and I know I am free. The center of my soul is solid, and my heart remains steadfast – in light and love. Even in this deplorable state – I am glad to be alive. I have voted on the side of Life. The Doctor has increased my Dilantin to 400mg, he is perplexed by my condition – it is not following "Benzo" detox standard norms. I have been waiting for your Kansas address. I go back to the timeless moment in the sand in Mendocino, California; and I am free of this place, full of hatred and obtuseness. To grab eternity in an instant and hold it forever. I have moments that are sinking in form – a deep sadness, a loud worry throughout my peripheral – it may be withdrawal. I Love You with all my heart. To have been in love with you is worth this. I love you enough to let you go in grace...

You can send a letter with someone's return address – and give me an idea of your statement [to the Tulsa police in regards to the Oklahoma felony kidnapping charges]. Did you get a copy? Do you have a strategy for me? I have had a very good hour now this is why I wrote you now. We will see how long it lasts. Stop at 3:58pm – dinner is here. Back at 4:26pm – the food was real turkey and gravy. No grievance from me. Now that I remove myself from this morass – and dive into this letter – which is an escape a form of an etymology – a look into the "Logos." My mind and body seem strong for now. As I cast off the manacles of this place – I ascend into the mansion of thought. I read in a book sent to me that Hebrew was not spoken for 1800 years and was artificially revived recently. Just a note. How is work at BD's? Six days in a row – that is hard...Are you losing or gaining weight? I can see no windfalls for us. I wonder how we can placate the Gods.

My pencils are becoming dull. I will try to write more. I may have to stop in order to sharpen them during something called tier-time – when we go to general population out of our cells. I go out for about four hours a day – it is really in, to the inside of the pod. I think about you all the time. Been out on any dates? Love my wuv. You have by far been my greatest love. I think this situation will break our love. I hope not. Try to write me a short letter everyday and a long one once a week. You are my "why." A man can bare any "how" if he has a "why."

The charges in Tulsa are vociferous or as Aston [one of Todd's Oklahoma lawyers] says, "inflammatory." I wonder how far the gods will go on this one; I think more shoes are going to drop. My mother says you got arrested in Dewey, Oklahoma [for failure to appear and pay a speeding ticket].

I thought you were going to give that up. I am going to close this so I can sharpen pencils and 4 pages may be max for $.37 can send. Love you, Todd

Oct. 4, 2003

Dearest Krystle,

I will use a running letter form. I will keep an open letter for you. Please send your mailing address. Did you get letter from Ed? It is faster if I send it to Ed's instead of my Mother's. In your next letter – what do you think will happen to us? Any insights into the situation? My pencils are too dull... My mind has given me a good 6 hour run here. Chess game is still poor. Now that I am 3 days into 400mg of Dilantin – the Doctor may need to push me up to 500mg. Blood level of Dilantin has been too low not taken into account my size [6'5" and about 225 lbs]. I will have blood drawn in 5 days.

Love you very much. I wonder if I am going to sleep tonight?? My Mother is really mad at me. I do not think she is sending money. If you would please send $30 as soon as possible. I am going to need $200 to file a motion; the Feds may pick the cost up. I go to court on Monday 6th of October [the Federal felony possession of MDMA charge from when Todd was busted at Burning Man]; I think that is the date... I really need a law library. I am going to bed now...

Next Morning, 11:05am, Bad morning, digestive disorders, headache, blurry vision (just started I have not had that problem in here before) No tremor – the Dilantin may be working now. You go to court in Tulsa on the 24th [the kidnapping case] of October? Will you stay at my Mothers? Please answer my questions in a letter. It is much harder to write than yesterday. I hope you are at my Mother's on the 24th of October so I can call you...

Chess game is still poor longest period of weak chess in my life. Numb on left side. Temperature is getting cooler outside. Before you buy your air tickets [to possibly visit him in Reno, Nevada] I need to be on an up trend – and much better. I do not want you to see me like this. Got a haircut from a guy named Edward. He is from the Bay Area. Brilliant mind, fun to talk to. Lunch will be ready soon. The food is always the same for lunch. Guards and inmates have nicknamed it catfish food. I understand why. And to quote Vonnegut "it makes me want to laugh." Still have no address for you. Ask your lawyer if Oklahoma will try to bring me in for Preliminary of Hoch [also charged with kidnapping along with Todd and myself].

Love you with all my heart. I am at a loss without you. Hoch is out of his mind. He wanted to kill you when he found out you had gone to the DEA [I've discussed some of this before, but I went to the DEA and told them about Todd's activities before the kidnapping. Todd was out of control; he had set up a lab and was putting out a really bad form of "black tar" LSD that gave everyone that tried it seizures. I tried to reason with him, but his behavior only got worse. Beyond sending multiple people to the hospital, he had been injecting me with psychedelics and sedatives against my will. He did this during one of my many failed attempts at

186

breaking up with him; he tried everything within his power to convince me to be back with him. Drugging me into submission was a last ditch effort. I honestly thought he might kill me by accident or kill someone else with the bad acid. Walking in to that DEA office was the hardest thing I have ever done. I brought Brad with me; he was selling MDMA for Todd and could verify that what I was telling the DEA was the truth. Of course, within days somehow Todd found out that we had gone in. They never ended up doing anything to stop Todd. If the DEA had listened to my warnings, Brad never would have gotten kidnapped. And I never would have been drugged/forced/manipulated into being there while Todd did all those horrible things to him.] I told him he was nuts and asked him why he was so bitter in life. He said Skippy life in the last 6 years has been rough. I think we need to go interview his ex-wife [omitted name]. I can barely write, sorry – I miss you.

The other inmates call me Professor Lechtor (Hannibal Lechtor of Silence of the Lambs – great – no peace of mind). I am bigger than all of the other inmates I have seen, that is strange. It is 30% Black, 30% White, 30% Mexican, and 9% other races – 120 men to a pod. Maybe? Shaking again – strong tremor. I need to stop writing until this improves. It pulses in strong waves, erratic in trying to figure out pattern. You are distant on the phone. I hope that changes. Letters help me – please write and ask others to do so - like [omitted names]. Out for now.

Went to Doctor – the nurse told me that they think the tremor has nothing to do with "benzo" withdrawal. The nurse said the tremor is not bad, but is evidence of problems they cannot see (i.e. slow thought, pulsing waves, micro-twitching). She said she hopes it all stops 30 days after Dilantin stops. The blurred vision is from Dilantin. They are going to double the time to take me off Dilantin – they are taking me a lot more serious now. My sleeping time is a little better. My chess game is still bad – in fact it is the second worse it has been since my arrest. I have a good chance of moving jails in the next two months. I believe I go to court on 10-6-03, not positive. I am going to file two motions at court time. I am going to ask for a new bail hearing [they denied him bail the first time] and change of location, and maybe motion for reciprocal discovery. I have seen no lawyer since 9-9-03, I fired in writing to the Judge the Lovelock attorney [Lovelock was the city jail he was in first, directly following his arrest at Burning Man with the MDMA]. I hope I get concurrent, and only two sentences otherwise I am looking at more than 10 years, a very hard and long time. I do not know how you are going to stay in love with me through this.

The main goal now is to move to a place I can have staying power at. My Fed point level is 26 points. It will lower to under 22 points if I work my case right. 26 points is very good – one felony, one misdemeanor. At 22 points I will be at 70 months max. They should offer 35 months. That's if I was someone else. Please give me as much info about Oklahoma as you can. As you can see above, the tremor is strong now...

The case [Fed MDMA charge] is not real clean and easy case. I think they will offer me about 5 years Fed time, which I need to finish 85% of 5 years. The problem is any other charges breaks the back of my time. Oklahoma may win in getting over ten years which I will have to bring in 70% of violent state time. Arizona fed charges [he never ended up getting charged for impersonating a Treasury Agent in order to scam free generators for Burning Man] are soft and make the battle more complicated for

Feds and Oklahoma. What hurts me the mo
other state charges, none related cases.
seven years is about the max, and above that it may
be in effect, life. At my age, 39, and build and
health, I should be able to handle 10 years Fed
time. 5 years state time would be about the most.

I am losing weight again. I need to build my
body up. I need to over the next two years get ready
for prison. For some reason I think I am going to get
and do seven years. I do not know why that number
keeps coming back with a seven year sentence. I will
be in a halfway house less than five years. Maybe we
can last for five years. In Fed prison I can have long
visits and a lot of free time with you. All visits with
family are contact [This means people can hug and
kiss once at the beginning and end of visit, and they
can hold hands throughout visit.], up to four hours
at a time. I qualify for Lompoc Fed... Unless I have
special circumstances – I am western Fed location –
and that is good. Is Sunday 10-05-03 your last day
in the six day run [He was referring to my job. With
no other options, I had started to work as a stripper
again to pay for my escalating legal bills.]? I figure
you are feeling rough by now. Hope you can stand
six days... Sorry for such long letters, I wish I had
your address so I could send the letter to you faster.
Give me the logic of what you plan to do. Tell me
what is going through your head. Send me a long
letter. I miss you a lot. I am not very hopeful about
either criminal charge either Reno or Tulsa; both are
hard cases to win in total. I have been stressing a
lot the last two days... I have yet to learn pinochle. I
do not feel like playing cards.

This pod which now holds 112 men – had a
gang problem. The Mexicans have two major gangs,
one is called 13, IIIX, or border brothers the other is
called Sardino – the Southern group. Above both
gangs, is Mexican Mafia – We had the luck of having

members from all three groups in our pod. The three do not get along. A special force of police and sheriffs came in to handle the problem, I still have no idea what went on. I am learning a lot of strange things. I need your help in the next four months – I need money to get these motions filed and to make it through this place [Everything in prison costs money, toothpaste, shampoo, stamps, pencils, paper, envelopes, doctor visits, extra food, etc.]. I hope to relocate into a Fed place. I hope we can live close by. I have a real hard time being away from you. Please write the longest letter you can. I need a lot of communication from you. I need to move to Fed place for health reasons. I need real food.

I'm sorry my letter was so unfocused. The juxtaposition of thoughts is not a strong point of mine right now. Have you ever eaten a Kumquat?? That is what Fruit you get in a Laissez faire system. My soul misses your soul. Did you sit in jail a second time? Up in Dewey [for failure to appear and pay speeding ticket]? I think you will probably be arrested some more over the next six months. Do not take 5 years probation it is too much, you will get fouled or violated. It is tough for most people. I had no problem on probation out of Woodbury, New Jersey. Most fail probation. Can you buy me two books – one dictionary and one non-fiction that you think I would like? I have read one book since I have been here *Ten Thousand Lovers*, written by Edeet Ravel. The book hit me hard. When you come I am going to release my property to you. When I move places my property will be locked out and I will not be able to use any property at all. What are you going to do with pawned items – the pawn stubs are gone [Todd pawned the wedding ring he gave me to finance the trip to Burning Man]? The pawn stubs had to go because it shows where the $2100 in cash came from. Can you give Bill my address? One more

190

page and I will be finished. I think 14 legal pages is the max 2 stamps will pay for. Be glad to see my luv. What do you think Hoch is going to get? Have you asked your lawyer? My left arm is very numb. The back of my left hand has no feeling. These are not good symptoms. But I still hope part of it is "Benzo" withdrawal...

Love you very much – I know that you are the only mate I can ever love like this. Hope you still feel the same way. You seem so different on the phone. Please write and tell me your heart. Do no become hard – there is always hope. "Change is King" a quote of Thales. Hope and Light are not that far off. My mind is coming back. Love you, love your heart, love you forever. My other half. I have paid a lot for this relationship – it was worth it. Love you, Todd

Oct. 5, 2003

Dear Krystle,

I love you very much. I sent a letter to Lovelock lawyer 2 weeks ago – I sent duplicate letter to the court. Last night I got an order from the Magistrate Valerie Cooke that says "Defendant is ordered to cease all ex parte [on his own without an attorney] communication with the court. Any concerns that the defendant has concerning his case should be directed to his counsel of record only." I am being refused access to any attorney now and now have an order from the court. I spoke to my mother last night – she said you spoke to her that day – she said you want to know why I haven't written. I have written three long letters to Ed's house or PO Box. My chess game is still poor. I seem to be frozen up in certain mental functions. But the twitching or small tremors "seem" to be improving. I just wish my cognitive process was better. I wonder what will happen when I come off Dilantin.

I need a place to send my legal papers. Last time I was in serious trouble – when I was in New Jersey – I had no girlfriend or wife. It is much harder when your love is away. I am so in love with you. I am not complete without you. This withdrawal is much worse than I thought it could ever be. My cellmate is difficult. He does not have good hygiene – in fact it is terrible. He has a childish personality. He has not had an address or home in 5 years, he is 41 years old. Enough about him. Could you send me a soft back dictionary? For about 25 days I had a strobe effect going on with my visual field. I have had so much neurological chatter in the last 30 days, I feel like I am coming out of this. I sweat every night and I freeze every night. The television plays from 6:00am to 1:00am most days [Todd always hated television]. I have landed in special hell, designed just for me. I drink hot water all day, it helps calm my nerves.

I wish I could see you. I am to call my Mother today. I am still trying to lose weight. Please send a picture of yourself it would mean a lot. Please, please, please. The numbness is going away slowly. But the trend is good. I went through a bad nausea period – it is gone. I have more pictures of Liv [Todd's youngest daughter] than anyone else. I am still writing with a 1.5" pencil. I'm glad to be off of "Benzo's" just a little rough way to do it. Need your help. I have had to become so humble around you; it is hard to lose my life in this way. In many ways you got a bad deal. Sorry I have been so weak. I need a place to send my legal papers – could you help? I am in a better mood now. The "Benzo's" really messed my life up. I hope to walk on a beach with you – again. It is sad not getting letters from you. My roommate/cellmate has a bad temper. He tried to get in a fight with me over nothing. Good thing I could wipe him out. Size is important in this place [Todd is 6'5"]. He is such a low life. I cannot even begin to tell you his low life history. Don't forget about me – I love you with all my heart. As I come off all these drugs – "Benzo's," Phenobarbital, Dilantin, I am returning to my base self. I have been so stressed out in the last five years. I promise, I will be more stable in the future. Do not lose hope in us. I am going to try to do everything I can to win my freedom to be with you. Stop.

11:05am, 10-6-03, No tremors for 12 hours, and I played chess, game is a little improved. Sleeping better – still sweat heavily (profusely) have a better feeling inside. The neuro-chatter is down. The no tremors could be the higher dose of Dilantin. When I drink caffeine I feel better?? I thought I was to go to court today.

All my 1.5in pencils are dull. Running out of stamps. Please send money, my Mother sent none. Even $30 would help. After this Sunday I will only have money for a few stamps. Still no letters from you – one letter in one month. The nurse told me when I come off of Dilantin – just coming off could send me into seizures...

My Mother gave me your address. I will have to trade some stool items for stamps and envelopes. I may not use your new address. I think I can send 9 pages in this letter. Need your help. My Mother asked me why I did not get a job – there are no jobs here, this is a detention center – and because of Oklahoma charges I am in Maximum Security. I am not eligible for any work program. Kidnapping is considered a very violent crime and assault with a deadly weapon is a very violent, the two combined even though they are floating (not convicted) are as bad as anything but murder. Another violent charge and I will be seg out, that means I will be in permanent segregation. I am now classed as very dangerous (no fights since I was 12 years old and never pointed a gun at anyone).

Took 4 x 100mg of Dilantin last night – vision went very blurry within one hour. Federal Marshals have special note on me – has used large amount of LSD – therefore, I have to be in chains even when I am locked up behind bars at the Courthouse. No one can tell me why I did not go to court. I choked all night I do not know why. Things seem to be improving. I have brief times when I am happy.

Please send: picture of yourself, money, book (dictionary) ask Mom how, letters – as many as you can, send blank pages if you can writing paper is scarce... I am effectively "Pro Se" [representing himself without an attorney]. I am glad to have not sent in any motions. Fill the motion I am sending you. Love you, Todd

Oct. 6, 2003

Dear Krystle,

I live in a cell that is 7.5' x 10' two bunk beds, one sink and one toilet. All the lights are fluorescent slow cycle – they strobe at 60 cycle. Because of my tremors and such they have to put me in lower bunk bottom tier. I can eat breakfast at 4:30am – I almost never eat breakfast. Breakfast is usually oatmeal (6 tablespoons) and canned fruit, dried milk is the drink. Lunch is always the same cat food sandwich (still trying to figure out the food it is made from) pasta salad and real fruit. Dinner changes greatly. Small tremor has come back in last one hour. This is the last stamp I have I will have to trade for more. I am growing my beard back. Once I come off of Dilantin (if I can) I will start losing weight as fast as possible. They have a new mail time 9:00pm Mon-Fri. Deadline for mail is 9:00pm at night. My energy is up. I hope to lose 35lbs. How is your weight? Hope to get a letter at 5:00pm tonight from you I will leave this letter open until 8:45pm tonight or 10:00am tomorrow morning...

My IQ dropped a lot under the reign of valium. Physics is out now. I hope the brain makes a comeback. It is so hard to write with these pencils. I am trying to get ready for approximately a seven year stay. Consciousness is a negative state of entropy. Since I moved to Unit 7, on 9-11-03, I have been teaching chess. The inmates are very happy to learn formal chess. Many of their games have improved greatly. One 19 year old, who sold MDMA for a living, after two lessons was beating most other players. Against the best players I am losing 50% of the time. I went fifteen years without losing. My cognitive skills are way down. Tried to visualize a 3d molecular structure could not come close. Numbness still going away. Utopia what a strange concept. As you can see my mind drifts a lot. I think you will be amazed at my old personality coming back – you have never known the old Todd. Maybe I was a marionette – and Valium was the puppet master. Too much stress last five years. Please write flow of consciousness to me.

Someone needs to remove the art lights red, blue, and such 3ft area around them need to be cleaned up.

Music I miss music. I miss driving – and taking you to the coffee shop. I miss going to the movies.

One man's prison is another man's monastery. Here I am in the monastic life (sans fun). What is life about – just being. I am too large for this cell. Hope you can read these letters. Life is a book without words unless in love we write. Is this a dance from tomb to womb and that is it?? What is the point? What is life about? I remember – but what does that mean? Time the old prankster of being. And I wonder. Is it really cut and dry. And I see a reflection of my soul – and it makes me want to laugh.

Your hair length and hair color? How is your health? It is 10:00pm and no mail from you – no mail at all. I am going to bed. Love you.

10-07-03, 11:10am, woke up at 4:25am went out ate breakfast – got a call to go out – thought I was going to court – instead I went to infirmary to have blood drawn (Dilantin levels). I sleep hard from 11:30pm till 4:30am – cannot sleep anymore after that – although today I went back to sleep after 6:00am, slept till 10:30am. Less sweats in night time. Last night a younger man fell and hurt himself the guards brought in a stretcher to take out of the pod and my cell mate almost got us a 3 day lockdown. He tries to get in a fight with me every other day. I will get a new cell mate soon. Hope to get a second letter from you today.

My Mother says things to me over the phone and I can not even defend myself, because it could hurt you. Try to ease up on what you say to my Mother. I am I a real box here – I am loyal to the end with you – and I ask very little in return from you...

Oct. 9, 2003

Dear Krystle,

Hey, sweetie – How are you doing? Sine on Pumpkin – Love you. Found this page dated 10-07-03 – sent it to you. What is you schedule form October 15th to October 24th work and such?? How is work? How much are you making?? Made any friends? Can you fill me in on what Chris [omitted last name] is up to? What do you do for fun? Any chance you will move to Reno, NV once I know how long I am going to be here? Or where ever I will be.

Try to keep a legal file for me and phone #'s written down. [Omitted list of legal phone numbers] Keep this information as every time I move I lose access to info. Please call Bill and ask him to write me. How did the [storage] unit move in Tulsa go?

If you move close to me, and help me, I can get through this better. I am going to write 3 motions over the weekend. Ask my Mother to send November calendar to me – thanks. If I could talk to you every other day and you could look up cases – I could bury them with motions – a few have to stick and those that do not may make a good appeal. When one is down the other needs to help – mates – are in up time and down times. I really need your energy and help. Motions for weekend: rewrite bail motion, motion to dismiss legal counsel, motion for access to law library.

You know I am writing these motions without forms, dictionary, legalese, law books, and such – with a 1.5in pencil because I am dangerous – oh – well. Love, Todd

Oct. 9, 2003

Dear Krystle,

It looks as though I am not going to get library access IAP says Federal Law only addresses convicted Federal inmates.

My chess is coming back, won every game for 2 days, moving fast and can see three to four moves ahead. Having daily problems with my cell mate. No tremors for two days...

I stand a chance of a facility change. My nervous system needs a change. If I get a change I have more staying power. Be careful what you say to anybody. Think through life problems. As I improve I hope my letters will become more legible it has been twenty years since I had to write letters. I make a genuine apology for any transgressions that have hurt you – from me. Namaste. I bow to your soul. I ask forgiveness – from you. Your benevolence towards me – is not lost on a hollow soul. Thank you for being there, when all others left. Again, thanks for the letter you sent me...

My bed is rough to sleep in. Most of the inmates are con-artists on a small scale. I do not think they have a modicum of intelligence. We (inmate) do not eat salubrious food – not even close – the fruit juice is totally artificial – a synthetic blend of swine sweat. I have seen the ingredients. At least I am over the insomnia – I have taken a big hit here – sorry for all the problems. I now get three changes of clothes. I know the magic words to get new clothes...

Oct. 10, 2003

Dear Krystle,

My Mother was really hard on me today – she said Mary from Garder asked Brad why he did not pay for the rent and he said "I was till Todd cut my dick off" – what is Brad trying to do? [Brad had items stored in my storage unit in which he never contributed to the monthly payment. He got a court order to enter the unit and take his items out. I couldn't be there so Mary, Todd's mom's employee, was there on my behalf. After Brad went through the unit many of my personal items were missing including my childhood photos, college diploma, stereo components, and artwork. Later, he actually came into the court room and bragged about having my stereo.] My Mother said Chris [omitted last name] is claiming the stereo system is his – what is all this greed – I am sitting here and you are my wife you should have gotten the car, the stereo system, and any other assets. I am sorry for the problems you are having...

Oct. 11, 2003

Dear Krystle,

I have a plan to turn on a telephone in Reno that will call forward to any number of yours. We can talk on Sunday 10-12-03 about it. I got your letter in which you talk about Sherin dying (sorry about the loss) [my childhood cat, she was 17yrs old]. It was not fair that Brad was able to go through the units – his stuff was all in one place. Brad is already EMBELLISHING and out right lying, he told Mary that I "Cut his dick off" – Mary is past 70 years old. It goes to show you about his low life ways...

I stopped worrying about my situation – I just go minute to minute. This is a tough pit stop. I now get peanut butter at night and some nights cheese and crackers...

10-13-03, after I spoke to you I took a hot shower for 30 minutes the shaking stopped and my mind cleared up. I cannot handle any pressure on the phone. I am beyond my wits end. Hearing your voice helped. I want to have children with you – I wish things were different...

I am trying to survive this hell hole. You have no idea how bad this place is. When I was in New Jersey, it was humane. I mailed a test mail; my mail is being sorted some odd way...

Ask my Mother where the title to the car is. After Billy stole the car – I now wish I would have done things different. Billy is a very under handed person. Do whatever you have to recoup the loss. [After Brad was released Todd and I went to Arkansas to stay with Billy and her husband. Her husband had been keeping Todd's C-4 Porsche in his name to help Todd hide assets. While we were there, the title to the car was signed over into my name. We left after about nine days and went on to Burning Man, without getting the title formally sent through the state and the car registered in my name. All I had as proof I owned the car was that title. It got seized at Burning Man. For some reason they mailed it to Todd's mother instead of me. I never have seen it since. Billy and her husband took possession of the car and subsequently sold it. They made at least a $40,000 profit; I never saw a dime.] On the rings [Todd pawned my wedding rings to finance the trip to Burning Man] the yellow diamond should get between $5000 and $10,000. The pink should get about $2000 to $4500. I am less sure of the pink – it is so small... [I never could afford to get them out of pawn. But after all that happened, I really didn't want them anyway.]

Oct. 19, 2003

Dear Krystle,

I did not know where to send letters so you will have a gap. Thanks for the $20. I have good lawyers – you do not have to spend money on that. I reduced my meds and things improved. Three days ago I felt like my old self. I have more hope, I will return to solid nervous state. Since I never know if I am going to talk to you – I will write all info on what is going on.

1st: If you pick up a felony (I think you will in Oklahoma) you cannot see me for sometime – unless you stay married to me. I cannot get visits or when I am released (supervised release 1-3 years Fed Oklahoma, I do not know) I cannot meet with any Felon exception my wife or other family members.

2nd: Met with Lawyers – info that is important. My Felony in New Jersey is over 10 years old – it is called stale and does not count against

200

me. That leaves me with a misdemeanor which is a criminal history of one. The MDMA amount was a gross weight of 341 grams, they weighed the container with it – my lawyers said this would drop my points. My points are 26 points... Lawyers say I have no chance of moving out of this facility. No reason will get me moved out...

I love you but I love you enough to let you go. I do not want to stop your life. My Mother said she is going to give Projector and Stereo system back to you. Sell these items, the money is yours.

Oct. 20, 2003

Dear Krystle,

I want you to know I will love you, for all of my being. You will go a path away from mine. I am letting go. I read what you want from your letters or none letters – and what you say. Life is so short to be hung up with my problems. I hope you keep in touch but understand if you do not. Do not worry; I will not bother you when I get out. Go free of worry about me...

So when will our eyes meet again? Blues eyes – I love blue eyes. You I love the most. When we first kissed on Shattuck in Berkley. Our hand meet – a moment I will never forget. The host was blank. The Eucharist was an ordinary piece of bread. 5HPT and sleep. I stopped counting at 8, 50mg. The communion was a placebo. Remember, "Let's go to Church" – and that contemptuous look. Lack of THC and too much 5-Hydroxy-tryptamin (real 5-HPT). When off the THC regressed to a very young age. His mind was formed with the THC molecule, wrapped into the cortex was this neuro-modulator [He is referring to Brad, the victim in the Oklahoma Kidnapping and Assault with a Deadly Weapon Case].

Breathe [omit Sanskrit and symbols]. Enlightenment is to let go in this moment and not grasp anything. And the old man said, "My children's, children's, children and this mountain shall be moved." To love and not love is to live and die – to live and love is to live and live and live.

May un i verse – one thought – uni verse – one vibration – learn to see into its heart. Look change in the eye and smile – who was that old Scribe of the Order of Roses – anyway. The old inkwell and pen moving about the page...

Oct. 21, 2003

Dear Krystle,

Spoke with my Mother tonight, she asked Ed to find you. She cursed me out because I told her that the car [Billy and her husband] took was yours – she said she had nothing to do with it. I was told by her that she told them to key it [the keys were lost also]. She says this is not true...

10-27-03, I stopped writing, my Mother said you are angry at me and hearing from me causes you problems. I will write less than one a week... I have a great cell mate – moved in five days ago. He is 47 years old and he is very smart – his name is Ferrill [omitted last name]. He is here on many complicated charges involving money transaction – at worst, he is looking at 20 years. He is also both a Fed inmate and a State detainee. I have watched two movies since I have been here – I cannot handle stress in movies for some reason. My nerves are still in grate, hyper mode. Guards have been difficult for days now. I go outside two times a day now. We can see nothing but the sky. My beard is full. If I read, I read a book a day. Read ten books since I have been here. Hygiene is way up – take 30min hot, hot shower once a day. I pay off workers to get extra clothes to change into. The vegetarian diet is good...

November 2003 (County Jail – Reno, Nevada)

Nov. 4, 2003

Dear Krystle,

I do not even know if you get or read these letters. I read part of the evidence on the Tulsa case. Brad [omitted last name] in a sworn statement supported by Tulsa police state "teen [18 yrs old] was sexually assaulted so police would think he was gay and was injected with chemicals so authorities would refuse to believe him." Brad said he was not gay. Brad said he only smokes pot – in small amounts and for only two years.

I wonder how we can live in a system that allows such a skewed legal system. If Brad says it, it is true.

1) Brad came back to the hotel after I asked both of you to leave.

2) Brad was pushy that night.

3) Christy acted strange early that night. [Todd's girlfriend at the time. She was there during the first half of Brad's kidnapping. She also testified against Todd at his trial.]

If enough force is applied in court you will see some other patterns forming. Why did [omitted first name] Hoch come out of nowhere?? [Todd hadn't seen him for eight years, and then he just showed up two weeks before Brad was kidnapped. Todd introduced him to me as an old Defense Intelligence Agency (DIA) buddy that worked for him as a part time hit man. Todd explained to me that I had never met him before because he was only brought in, in case of an emergency. I was scared to death of Hoch. His emotionless demeanor totally freaked me out. He carried a gun that had a metal military seal on the side of it, so I tried to stay out of his way.] Why did Hoch want to kill Brad? Why did Brad switch from trying to be your friend to trying to be my friend? What was Brad up to? Some of Chris's [a friend of Brad's who was selling ecstasy pills for Todd] stories were true. Now I am left with all this to deal with – And I was physically sick during this time [Todd had been taking prescription fat blocker pills which caused him to have nosebleeds because of a blood platelet problem. He had to go to the hospital several times during and immediately prior to Brad's kidnapping]. Again, what God did I piss off??

Today I got locked down for my 3 hours that I have tier time for being late to take my optional Tylenol. The Tylenol was to help the headaches from the Dilantin. So I get in a bunch of trouble – not allowed to explain – I was to see Doctor but refused. And so on. Fifteen minutes later guards came into my cell and say "Skinner you have a visit – you are only locked down for 30 minutes – your Doctor meeting is on – you have lawyers here. The guards then talked to me about what happened and said it was a misunderstanding...

Nov. 7, 2003

Dear Krystle,

Today I woke up and the unit was getting ready to have an inspection. My cell passed, thirty minutes later two guards went into the room and took three sheets from me, and this list: two pairs of underwear, two pairs of socks, four pencils, two pairs of pants – because I had extras I was locked down for a day – No Big Deal because in real time it meant I lost one hour and thirty minutes of tier-time. The problem was losing the pencils; it took me a month to get those one inch pencils.

I have not taken Dilantin for almost three days. Any sentient would have refused poisoning in perpetuity by my captors.

I hope this ephemeral in mind time, this less than Fed retirement plan B, I am in now. Now that I have been conscripted to Reno monastery, enjoying the monotonous discomfort one instant at a time – so I can pay my debt to civilization. This fine house of hell, in which its affairs are ran harum-scarum on a good day, is just what I need at age 39. Not for one moment am I showing in gratitude for life's gift here – it is just wonder WHY I am locked down – when I am in Maximum Security...

I called my Mother and asked her to call you, to find out your plans. She told me she has not spoke to you in over a week...I have been taken off of vegetarian diet because I ordered a shrimp Ramen Noodle Soup. The medical group now wants me to take 400mg of Dilantin or I cannot take any. This place for some reason wants to keep me on high doses of Dilantin. I will not take more than 200mg of Dilantin a day and that dose for only two more weeks. I need to come off of Dilantin to check where my nervous system is at. When my doses get up to 400mg my eyes start to cross...

This place has had a lot of problems over the last four days. Outside detectives have been doing some sort of investigation into the inmates. We have been under tight controls. I am in Maximum Security holding now, because of Oklahoma. Still have same roommate/cellmate – that is the one break I get. Easiest roommate I have ever had. Very smart, glad to have a clean, smart, well mannered cellmate. Tensions between black, whites, and Mexicans are running high. There has been a lot of shuffling in the Max holding...

Could you send me a soft cover book on English and grammar? I have not written letters in over twelve years. It is best to send two books at a time. If you cannot send me books, then I will ask my Aunt Betty to send them. Again, I look forward to going to Federal Prison. I can have as many books on religion as I want in my cell; please send some my way. You would not like Reno weather...

Called Mother again today to talk to children they were not there. She told me I need to tell children what is going on. Which is what I have wanted to do all along. I do not know why I even call – it bothers me so much. I want to stay away from all those problems. I am persecuted because of my religion (spiritualism) by the US Government and by many who do not understand – because they are asleep. I am blamed for many things I cannot control or change. This Brad [omitted last name] thing has been spun to completely destroy my persona. This cast over my being is one of perpetuity. Yet I must endure. I must remain and become more pious towards the so-called enemy, a really hard one, love your enemies and forgive them. When one has won, bow and surrender, when you win you lose, when you lose you win – if you know both sides of the same coin – you have balance. It is easy to be susceptible to hatred or anger... A soul must overcome the lemon in life – look at being through a different lens.

A broad spectrum of introspective views on any given reality is how one dances in life. It is not the easy way that yields the great Dance.

Just received your letter dated 11-1-03 – you asked me to drag out time before I go to Oklahoma – Well even if I wanted to go back soon – I could not, even if Oklahoma and I wanted me to go back soon – it would not happen. I have waived my speedy trial rights up here – even though it was done without my consent. If I plea out it takes till January 13, 2004 to get that before a Federal Judge, then I have to wait a minimum of ninety days to be sentenced then thirty days to go to Federal Prison. That's the fast track. There is no way to move faster even if a Federal Judge wanted to. Next that is an unreal timeline. It never happens that fast. If I go to trial, a year minimum till all is finished. Oklahoma can do all it wants but here is a real timeline – I have studied this completely...

Send me a letter on why you think they [Oklahoma] have such a good case on me. What kind of evidence do they have – take a deep breath and write a letter. Each witness has a large problem to overcome. What I nee to know is what are the sentence structures like. After Aston [one of Todd's Oklahoma attorneys] looked up guidelines – he was shocked at how little time they carried; 10 years kidnapping and conspiracy of kidnapping, and 5 years assault with a deadly weapon. He said I was looking at a plea out of five years. The cost of case in trial and problems does not yield enough time. I do not know. I have little hope of concurrent time. So I have little to worry about as I run Federal time up. The case in Oklahoma is not as strong as you think, the legal elements to the case could be a weak point for DA.

After your letter I know I am going to be here longer than sooner, so please help by sending books. I also need money. I need you to send $50 as soon as possible. I need two books a week. If we are going to strap in for the long haul, I need your help...

Nov. 18, 2003

Dear Krystle,

207

Vito and I spoke for a long time today – he believes he will be granted a "Global Resolution" by Oklahoma and Federal US Attorneys. I know very little about "Global" agreements, yet I find it hard to believe Oklahoma would go along. Vito says the main reason is this: Oklahoma does not want the cost of housing me, 2nd Oklahoma without an agreement will have a hard time getting me there, 3rd Oklahoma can avoid embarrassing points on this case, 4th DA will save an enormous amount of time (i.e. does not have to file writs and such).

Weight on MDMA down to 251 grams (90 gram reduction) [from when they first weighed it]. We may go for a purity test, depends on how long – if it is 80% pure or less I am down to two years. I wonder how that overweighed the MDMA by 90 grams...

Nov. 22, 2003

Dear Krystle,
This is going to be a letter not filled with good news.

1) My Mother was in the Hospital until this morning.
2) Kally [Todd's first wife] told the children I am in Jail.
3) The children are mad at my Mother and not talking to her.

About Oklahoma case, as you know I met with Vito. I read file on early evidence of Oklahoma case. Hoch went to DEA on the 14th of July and called them from Morgan City, LA. DEA picked him up from bus stop in Tulsa. He refers to two agents, Doug and Rick. Oklahoma case is a boiled down and filtered Federal case. The interview is a farce and a fraction of info Hoch has – for example Hoch claims he does not know Christy's last name. Many holes in Hoch's statements. You need to read it, Hoch says terrible things about you.

Brad's statements change from Houston hospital to Tulsa interview. He blames his condition on Hoch. This gets more convoluted. Note: I know who got info to FBI in 1992 – I am sure Hoch was source. Ask cat; Ask him what went on in 1992. Big operation of Feds.

Hoch in Tulsa interview said I trafficked in Lortabs, Quaaludes, and other drugs. I have never given Lortabs away much less sold them, next I have never given Quaaludes away or sold them or even held one in my hand. The USA banned them in the 1970's.

Why Lortabs – because Brad was busted with them. [Three months before Brad was kidnapped, Brad was arrested with Lortabs and a small amount of pot with intent to sell. He pled out to the pot charge and got probation].

Brad says in his interviews that he used only Pot in last year to two years – and only drugs I gave him.

By the way, Hoch claims liquid morphine was also brought over the border.

In my entire life I never talked about lortab until I met Brad. Tulsa police are going to try and dump his drug dealing on me.

Hoch implicates you when it works for his story and takes you out when he needs to. Is Hoch really in Tulsa county jail? He worked with Tulsa police and he worked with DEA and yet his bail is still $200,000 [after one month, they lowered his bond to $20,000 so he could afford to get out]. Did you see Hoch in the courtroom? What was he wearing??

There is nothing you can say about me that would hurt me – Hoch has lied so much that anything you say is going to clear up timeline. As long as you tell the truth you can say anything. Do not lie – Hoch did and look what happened. Krystle I do not mind you trying to help yourself out on this case, what I am trying to say is – make sure you have a real deal in hand...

I am so cold in this place the heat is out again. My cellmate and I have become heating engineers, we tap into utilities and generate heat – most of the inmates are very cold we are just cold. Ferill (my cellmate) has lost 10 counts in the last week, he is looking at 80 years – he has more trials to come...

Do you remember me saying something about Hoch planting something under Porsche car seat?? [There was a pair of pliers with hair and blood on them under Todd's seat. I found them when I was cleaning the trash out of the car and subsequently threw them away.]

Sunday, 11-23-03, woke up room was below 60 degrees – I was shaking until I ate. This is getting to be ridiculous – everyone is very cold – outside temp at night is 20 degrees. I must be hypoglycemic because I do not shake after I eat. This shaking and withdrawal shaking are different. My room is so cold I do not know how much longer I can write.

You should call my mother and make sure she is alright. Maybe you could go help her for a few days. I hope she lives through all of this.

Only thing I can figure is Christy – gets asked by DEA on Friday [she got caught up in a small pot bust days earlier, right around the same time Brad was released] she talks to Hoch, he thinks he is going to get hit with Kidnapping; he calls DEA from Morgan City and goes from there...

Nov. 25, 2003

Dear Krystle,

I received three letters from you today. Thanks – by the way the old you seems to be coming back. I want you to know I love you from the core of my soul. When I am away from you my heart is broken. I love and loved you more than anyone or anything. I bow to you in disgrace for anything I have wringed you with.

I am very limited in what I can say. You are all that kept me intact in the last four years.

I have many higher court rulings that will help you with your case in Oklahoma. I will send them to you.

I am sorry about anything that has done to you to harm you – I never wanted you harmed and I believe you are not. I am sorry to my core about any negative from me to you. We tore each other apart – we always should stand as one. I was very weak in the last six months, the fat blocker made me so very weak. The move from Valium to Clonopin was a mess.

I also want you to know Brad did not love you. He was so hard on you when we told him about you being married. He winked at me as he made you cry. He tried to become buddies with me – at your expense. I love you from a different spot in life. My soul is broken without you. Your songs are a high order event. You have great gifts. I wish you would still call me your mate and mean it. I know you are having a very hard time – I will always defend you and say positive and good things about you. You are above all things my cosmic friend – my cosmic mate – and my love...

I am not worried about you taking the stand – that it will hurt me. I want you to be ok. Again, I have a strong defense for you. Hoch lied so much is

211

his interview – also, DEA and police rigged his statements in order to get elements of kidnapping. You are right, you are innocent.

I miss your soul. I would never want any part of you in jail. I love all of you. I always will.

Is it wise for your lawyer to contact Hoch's lawyer? Ask your lawyer?? Do not pay him one more dime – you need to be careful. Lawyers are scam artists...

Nov. 27, 2003

Dear Krystle,

Thanksgiving Day, I send my love. I worry about you piggybacking letters for "L" to me. Have another person in Kansas receive piggy's and send them again. Do not trust "L" – and calls from him are very risky – his calls are tracked. You cannot afford to piss off DOJ!! Think about what you do. Do not talk about Topeka case with him – it is very risky. My Federal discovery indicates we are all on a thread. Do not make waves. You can listen to anything he says but do not add info. The Feds are behind Tulsa Case – do not shake the cart.

Hoch's statement to Tulsa Police was carefully orchestrated – you should read transcript. It is what Hoch didn't say that shows what DEA is worried about. Brad on the other hand said too much.

Read both transcripts!!! Why did they not use Christy's? Or Dana's at storage unit? [Someone had tried to break into my storage unit to try to get Brad's possessions. This is before he got the court order that allowed him to enter my unit. Dana, the Storage unit manager, took photocopies of their IDs and got the whole thing on videotape. I decided not to press charges against them.]

Side note: On the case (Federal) my discovery shows that Nevada state drug cops added evidence one reason Feds cannot use all evidence – someone added cut or something that was dark brown to white MDMA to get weight up. So I stand a chance of going below 200 grams – I have no idea?? MDMA goes back for 4th weighing and is going for a % purity test. Net weight with cut 251 grams at 10% cut I get 200 grams. Who knows.

Remember lawyers are only there to extract money. Do not trust your lawyer. Anyone who says you have an agreement with DA and it does not come can not be trusted. Your lawyer is playing old game with you. Start making plans – make sure you get on Medicine so you can eat in bad environment [I suffered from anorexia that was made worse by stressful situations. It was hard for me to eat in public places; I would always feel like I couldn't swallow and would choke on food. After Todd's arrest, it completely cleared up]...

Joyce sent me a photo of the Arizona house backyard. People like to mooch off of me. Mike and Gunnar [Todd's employees and entourage] took a little too much. Do you remember Mike wanted a split in the money for the last three months. I would have been better off leaving Mendocino, CA without staff. I spent $80,000 in Arizona 1st four months (that included move). I think it was a mistake to go and get house in Mendo. If I would have had a smaller place in California and moved to a smaller place in Arizona things would have been better. Mendo after bust was problem. A lot of people – Petaluma Al and ET man all wanted me gone. Mike and Shana [entourage] were not very loyal. Emma [Todd's second wife] sure caused a lot of problems – not deep.

Please call my Mother it would make her feel better. She helped you when others could not.

213

Dec. 1, 2003

Dear Krystle,

Hope this letter finds you smiling. Vito told me today that only reason he wants to weigh MDMA again is to buy time. This week he talks to Tulsa DA about case – if that does not go well he will get a reweigh.

US Attorney will cut me a good plea, but it has to be done in a timely manner. Again please read hospital report and mini-discovery report!!

I guess you have moved to [omitted name] house. We will call you a Trogalite (ask Bill). In fact no letter from Bill.

If you go to Tulsa please send some more books (please ask them to send them two and two no more than two at once) Thank you.

I may have a blood sugar problem. It would be nice if I could find out if you read my letters, so in a letter tell me you read my letters.

Sweetheart, sweetheart, I want you to know how much I love and loved you.

Sometime six months or longer we got in a fight over the cell phone you had that was new in style. You grabbed the wheel of the car and we fought, you through the cell phone out the window – do you remember this?? You looked over at me and said I poked your eye [I think Todd actually combined two stories here. One is when I through my cell phone out the window because I was tired of him taking it from me and running up my bill. The second was sometime later, when he pinned me down on the bed by my neck and threatened to poke my left eye out with his thumb while he was in a rage. I still don't know why he did this to me. It

214

seemed like during the last six months of knowing Todd anything would set him off.] – The look you gave me was one of – I betrayed you at a basic level – this look stays with me. I am sorry from the bottom of my heart. One should always be graceful with the one they love. I was having a classic "Benzo" problem that is why I was trying to get off of them. I was also becoming hypoglycemic – that I did not know till I got here.

I know that our future is not with each other. You have made that clear. I have no proof you even read my letters. I know you would become un-married soon if not for legal reasons. My blood sugar problem is bad. The Dilantin was only part of the problem – 2 hours after I took it my blood sugar would drop. I have to eat small amounts in order to avoid problem. I get cold and stay cold. I have many rough days. The letters you write bring the most joy I get. When you write a negative one it really hurts. One reason I love you so much is you stood by me in the worst phase of my life. No one else stood by me. You were my little person who I loved so much. I know I snapped at you many times in last 2 years – and it got worse – but from July 5th on it stopped [That's actually not true. He drugged me against my will, in Arkansas, for a nine-day period after Brad was released. At the time, he had me convinced that I accidentally got dosed with something at the older couple's house we were staying at. He said that the woman must have been trying to kill her senile husband with the drug. Todd actually convinced me to go tell the old man's children that I was drugged by her and that she was trying to kill her husband.] – I knew that I loved you beyond that, when you left with Hoch in the car behind his car I worried more about you then than ever [when Hoch and I let Brad go] – I was really afraid he would hurt you. You both took so long to get back – I was terrified that he had

215

hurt you. I am so glad you are alive and well. Hoch wanted to kill you for some reason. He said Skippy she went to the DEA, she's got to go. And when I said, "What the Fuck are you talking about – she is my wife and I love her more than anything." He was shocked. I love you enough to bow and let you go. I smile at your soul. Please grow in peace and love. I want you to do better than you ever could. I pray for your best light to shine forth. I want you to do so well in life. I wish only the best for you.

I am shaking from the cold right now so – I know my penmanship is very, very bad. Love to your life – I will make sure you are protected in the Tulsa Case – if DA and Police have a heart and soul of any type...

The large tank truck from Arizona was really a mess when it started to slip back it just kept moving it was very dangerous on that hill – very bad experience... [Todd scammed a company in Tucson to give him a large water truck, water tank, and two large generators to take to Burning Man. He told me that he had impersonated an IRS agent, and the IRS was going to pick up the bill. The water truck died on a hill just outside Phoenix.]

Joyce sent me an article on Leonard and Clyde – Clyde's sentence was a little harsh. Why did they get 2 sentences each concurrent – maybe one was for conspiracy and one was for possession – and if one is overturned the other will stick. Clyde should have taken seven year deal no testifying.

Hope to get a letter from you soon. Stopped shaking about two hours ago. Love you a whole bunch, and wish you much happiness. Sing a song for me – when and if you feel like it. Do try to keep in touch over the years.

Did you see where Leonard went to DEA on me about MDMA – what was that about and when did he go?? In 1997 he went to some official about MDMA didn't know my name was in it.

I am not going to Lompoc. I can tell you both of them are going to California prisons...

Dec. 7, 2003

Dear Krystle,

Thanks for the long phone calls – I will always love you. I am glad to have met you in this life. I think about you all the time. Today's calls lifted my spirits.

12-08-03, Hey Sweeti, How are you doing? I kiss your soul and bow to your divine spirit... You have no idea how much it helped me to talk to you. Do not worry I will not take SSRIs. I know the long term problems – I am the one who was down on them first. I had the first really hot shower in over three weeks. I am much better. What happened in court? This is Monday morning and I am to talk to Vito today. Be careful with who you talk to about your legal defense or problems, you do not want them taking stand against you.

My cellmate, Ferill, went to court today – he goes about twice a week now. He has so many legal battles. He has about 12 civil lawsuits going and four criminal lawsuits. What do you think about Dean working for the DEA? Maybe Jerry should be told. Is it true Rachel was in a very bad car wreck? My Mother said she got two calls about it. Anything one says on the phone to Dean may be recorded.

I wonder why Lovelock [Burning Man] Sheriffs told Tulsa police you were around there.

Do you have any idea how long I will be in Tulsa jail for – six months – one year?

You need to get you weight up to over 120lbs so you can handle being sick better – you need to follow a blood sugar diet.

[The following is Todd's reply to what I accused him of over the phone. I said that I thought he drugged me every day through out our relationship. I never had an eating disorder until meeting Todd, and then as soon as I was away from him for good – it disappeared as fast as it came. Also, I felt like I was withdrawing from something for at least a month after he went to jail. I always had what Todd would call a "hypoglycemia problem", and yet again when he was out of my life – it stopped.] The problem with any drug that would work in the tryptamine path way over a long time would be subject to tolerance without MAOI. And the down regulation in the brain would negate any long term change.

Even 5-HTP (5-hydroxy-L-tryptophan) becomes down regulated – that is why one must cycle even base building items as fundamental as L-Tryptophan are subject to heavy tolerance rules. Even simple L-Dopa channels are subject to tolerance.

By the way you should take some sort of 5-HTP food supplement. Be careful with large doses of alpha-lipoic acid for blood sugar, even 200mg can cause a wave.

The next problem with long term tryptamine use is how did you get it in your system and how was it kept stable. The cycle is short on tryptamines unless they have MAOIs on board. Even with heavy front ends 5-fluoro-alpha or 6-fluoro-alpha (18hrs) they become a MAIO into themselves. Even single front ends methyl become MAOI in large amounts; remember chocolate at Double Tree (alpha-MT). And large 3d structures make for problems.

Even beta-6-methoxy-N, N-DMT cannot be given with ease. If one changes backend to "DMS" the strength will decrease. Alpha-5-methoxy-DMT has less transfer than 5-methoxy-DMT and 5-

methoxy-DMS is too large while 5-fluoro-alpha-methyl-tryptamine is potent but a powerful MAOI. Effective in doses of 25mg but instable – storage of temperature less that 0°C. Alpha-O structures have MAOI type properties. Alpha-O-DMT is structure platices [sp?] in form of Guart [sp?] count.

So tryptamines are troublesome to work with for long term use, three days or more.

You said you had withdrawal for thirty days – even OCs [Oxycontin] are over within 14 days max – most problems finish with in 5 days. I see some people with opiate addiction here. And very many people have meth, rock, speed problems here. 75% of all the drug problems.

6-Fluoro-alpha-methyl-DMS has extreme legs (48 hours but cycles up and down and is unstable to light and temp) the structure starts to produce many metabolites, post cursors of alpha, beta, and upper difintis-claus-form [sp?].

Plus brain would have an affinity for "DMS" over food causing downstream effects.

Enough for now. I am getting weak right now and don't know why. I love you with all my heart. I really need to get to federal prison – this place weakens me so much.

Dec. 15, 2003

Dear Krystle,

Thanks so very much for the beach card. Anything you send me brings sunshine to me. You will never know how much you mean to me...

Ferill and I moved to a new warmer cell, much warmer – after one night I got moved out. Because of whatever problem I have – I must be bottom bunk bottom tier – I was moved in with a man from Korea. He has more charges than anyone I have seen here. The federal agencies that are after him. Secret Service comes once a week to talk to him – listen to this, one of his friends figured a way to make credit cards and bypass the Visa central computer and a team of Koreans hit the casinos for 1-2 million a month (3 guys) – I do not even know how to say this guys name – he is on a $750,000 bail. He thinks he is getting out in a few months – he has never even seen a lawyer. Somehow I don't think he is getting out in a few months...

Dec. 17, 2003

Hello Sweetheart,
I have finished my morning shower my handwriting should be better.
The beach without time.
Waves were lapping on the sand. The blue sky sported a few lazy cumulous clouds. There was a series of rocks, irregularly spaced a little back from the waters edge. The rocks were very massive. The sun was at high noon, yellow-orange in its hue. A faint aroma was in the air; salt, seaweed, and clean ocean air. We had been to the beach before – a timeless beach. The breeze stirred, the waves folded in time, we were one with this spot. The breaking of the surf generated a soft white noise that reminded us of our atemporal nature. The sun was past the zenith, over the ocean now. A crab scuttled by, sidewise, dexterous, its eyes swiveling on their stalks. We could see drifting seaweed; kelp was beached to our left. Time froze as if in a surrealistic painting. The sky, weather, ocean, geology, and indigenous life was perfect. Almost an extravagance, if not for the fact that it would define a moment without time.
A few seagulls were in the distance to our extreme right. We looked out and around at a long sweep of brown sandy beach. We were at the

enigmatic door of no time. A universal port, meeting spot for the timeless beings – the atemporal souls of existence, home away from time. The tide was coming in ever so slow. We looked out into the deep blue horizon. The inexhaustible waves from the ocean ebbed in a symphony. Phantom moments, like in a dream, the gaps in time we found. A flawless frozen moment. You and I were at the interstellar spot to see each other and know beyond anything who we were/are. The normal limitations imposed by causality – do not apply to our beach without time. We ran our hands through the sand – as if to see if we were dreaming. We were our ancestors, space-time travelers. The sun was warm; the breeze was cool. The top layer of sand around us was dry – they deeper down, the wetter the sand. We had eternity in an instant. We unbound time. The Baraka of now – no more clocks of shadows. We cast off the old monster called time.

No time, just us for as far as we could project – symmetry of thought, interdimensional looks at each other. Change vanished, polite as it may be – change took heart and left us to our solitude. We had moved across the threshold of an instant – we fell into an invisible space between instants. No longer concerned for our survival – But loving the now. The breeze stirred up, tousling our hair – and we smiled. We know how much we loved each other and how rare this animated discourse would be. And we were One – and we are One – and we will be One. On that clear day – we could see forever through time – through space. The shackles were broken – we became unbound. I love your smiles. We bowed to each other. To our atemporal divinity we knelled. Brave Helios was our witness. We spoke in a common Logos. The sand had a dust-like quality – and when dry sparkled in the sun light.

The pulverulent sand changed colors in a dance. The real sacrament of life is LOVE...

I wish to show you a word: <u>Quaternion</u> – in math it is an element of a system. It is one of the components of four-dimensional vectors – these vectors behave somewhat like complex numbers...

Dec. 22, 2003

Dear Krystle,

Again Merry Christmas. And I send you a Happy New Year wish. Sorry letter #29 was so bad I just had really hard time with it. The guards had us take our blankets to be washed today – now we have no blankets for a day. The inmate next to me refused to hand in blanket – because he was cold – they took him to the "hole" isolation – this place is unbelievable. Mean people. The unit #7 is having shower problems. The guards are really difficult right now. I do not know why they are so hard on us. Fifty percent of the unit moved out to other places in the last three days. Many new faces. Ink pen is running out...

I never want to be cold again! In order to warm my feet up, I pour warm water into the cell sink and lift my leg up to place my foot in sink to warm foot up. This is so absurd. I am shaking right now...

Dec. 23, 2003

Dear Krystle,

1) Why did Hoch want to Kill Brad last day in Texas? Why did Hoch want to kill Brad in Tulsa?
2) Why did Hoch start planting evidence in Tulsa?

222

3) Why did Hoch tie up Brad in Texas?
4) Hoch claims that I injected Brad in Texas the night he said we arrived – yet Hoch's syringe was damaged from Hoch using it too hard on Brad. There was no working syringe. Hoch also has wrong time of us going to Houston, claims we were there by 6:00-8:00pm, not true. We were in Tulsa at 4:00pm.
5) Hoch wanted to control Brad during this time.
6) Why does medical report say blood on Brad's wrist?
7) Hoch's timelines are off – why I realize he can dump things on me but some sort of these can be proven.
8) Just like he claims he was in Yukon, Oklahoma when he was on his way to Pryor.
9) He has story on flat tire and getting new room in Texas, look at what he claims it is created for some reason. [When Hoch and I let Brad go it was getting dark outside. My night vision isn't very good, plus I was freaked out and scared to death by what had been done to Brad. I drove over the median while getting onto the highway, and we got a flat tire. The next day, Hoch took the Porsche to a tire shop and got it fixed. So that way the car would make in to Louisiana where Todd was scheduled to look at and possibly buy a ship.]
10) Why did Hoch beat Brad up in the car [Hoch drove Brad from Tulsa to Houston while Brad was passed out] – what really happened?
11) Did Hoch beat up Brad in Hotel in Texas?
12) All I can figure is that Hoch got carried away – then figured Brad was going to finger him – Hoch got scared by talking to Christy and called DEA and dumped most on me.

13) What does not fit is Hoch placed wire cutters under seat in the Porsche. Also, why did Hoch want to control Brad? What was Hoch up to? I had not heard from Hoch since 1999, I am sure of it. Why did Hoch dislike you so much?

14) Why was Brad nude? [When we got down to Houston and first saw him in the Hotel room with Hoch; he was lying on the bed completely undressed. There were ties for his arms and legs on the four legs of the bed he was in; they were made out of what looked like a ripped up sheet.]

15) Why did Hoch have such a strange collection of items with him – when he showed up in Tulsa – Did you check out his possessions that he had? One does not travel with that stuff.

16) It was like Hoch was homeless or had nothing.

17) When he first got to Tulsa – all he could talk about was going to bed with Christy and how much he did not like you. Brad and Hoch talked a long time – I wonder what was said.

18) Hoch was mad about Brad and you going to the DEA – He said that it put him at risk – why? I even asked him that – I said what the hell difference does it make to you.

19) He was mad at me for allowing Brad and you to go to the DEA and not doing anything about it – I told him it did not affect him and I told him what you two said – He claims Brad had a different story.

20) Do you remember Hoch laughing at Brad? Do you remember story about Brad peeing in bathroom?

21) Hoch wanted to keep you away from Brad – when he laid him down – why??

22) What was this torture shit in Texas?? What do you think Hoch did to Brad down in Texas?

23) What happened to the clothes Brad was wearing last day in Tulsa.

24) Because Zima has such a low alcohol content Hoch must have give Brad a lot of shots. The medical report shows a bunch in Brad's shoulders and in crotch area. [Todd had given Brad a shot of valium and clonopin prior to his trip with Hoch to Houston. Todd gave Hoch a needle and syringe; then told him to stop at a liquor store on the way to buy some alcohol. Then he instructed Hoch to give Brad a shot of the alcohol, no more than 3cc, every time Brad started to wake up. Todd said that the combination of alcohol, valium, and clonopin was supposed to keep him asleep.]

25) You said to me Brad was poorly treated by Hoch in Hoch's room [in Tulsa] – something about Hoch left him on his stomach and Brad was choking – what was Hoch trying to do? It was like Hoch wanted Brad to die – why? [This happened several times. I would leave, then come back and Brad would be lying in a bad position, lips blue, wheezing, gurgling, and barely breathing. I would then sit him up, pat on his back, and try to make him wake up and breathe.] Why would Tulsa DA be sympathetic to Hoch – without Hoch there would have been no kidnapping – nor would Brad have been beaten.

26) Notice that Hoch never mentions – the fact that he injected Brad – yet, he told me and I saw many injection spots. Plus, Hoch broke the syringe he had.

27) DEA was on case too fast. Brad was found 9:00am approx. Christy was dealing with DEA in Pryor by 1:00pm – How can DEA have moved so fast?? Remember it is an hour drive to Pryor. And do you think Texas police first call is to Tulsa DEA. No – it does not make sense. DEA was already involved before 9:00 morning time.

28) Why are there no statements from Christy??

29) Why did Christy leave that night in Brad's car and come back, what was she up to?

30) Who was working with DEA before that night?

31) Brad says he did not know we were married – there is a legal reason for that.

32) Hoch is the one who wanted to drive Brad asap – Hoch wanted out of hotel as fast as possible – why?

33) Hoch also wanted him room paid for, for one more night

34) Hoch insists to Police I had a room on the 8th floor, on top of a 14th floor and 15th floor.

35) Why were we not arrested on trip though Tulsa – when Hoch met us in Broken Arrow parking lot. DEA must have wanted a bust of some sorts. [After a few days in Louisiana, Hoch went to Tulsa to the DEA. Todd and I went to Arkansas for nine days, where Todd kept me heavily drugged most of the time. Then we headed back through Tulsa. After a few days in Tulsa, we were on our way in a rental RV to Arizona, and then finally to Burning Man. I didn't try to get away from Todd because I felt like there was no point in it. I had lost all will to struggle against him. The only thing I could think of was to keep my head down and try to survive somehow. I mean, I tried to go to the DEA and get them

to help me; it did nothing but make my situation worse. I also tried to go to the local Tulsa police and get temporary restraining orders; that didn't work either. If I went to go stay with a friend or family member, then Todd would follow me there. I didn't want more people to be hurt by this out of control situation.]

36) Hoch threatened Chris. Wonder how police are going to deal with that??

Dec. 25, 2003

Dear Sweeti,

The Oklahoma legal system is like its Hog Farms; reminds me of the way they used to weigh Hogs in Oklahoma. They would get a long plank, put it over a cross-bar, and somehow tie the hog on one end of the plank. They'd search all around until they found a stone that would balance the weight of the hog and they'd put that on the other end of the plank. Then they'd guess the weight of the stone. What is it with these pig stories?!? You never know.

Is this some sort of red neck version of logic – an inverse Occum's razor of function – the goat roper hog farmer thinks Occum is a hillbilly...

Dec. 27, 2003

Dear Krystle,

Hello, sweet heart, the pen is still going. I am having a blood sugar low – I just drank a large amount of Tang. It is really an off brand called Okeef Breakfast Drink. I am not well – my bio-system is having problems. I am shaking hard right now. Please pray for me. Thank you.

Hare, hare – Krishna, Krishna

Hare Krishna, Hare Krishna
Rama, Rama
Rama Krishna
My Sweet Lord...

Remember the fun we had at Ali Baba's Middle Eastern food. You loved to eat there... We sure have been to a lot of Sushi Bars in the last four years. Whenever one of us would get up from bed to go to the restroom the other one would follow. You used to get every cold, flu, sickness anyone was carrying – you germ bag – you. My sweet pumpkins. The fish tank in Mendo was a battle field we would go in there to see the aftermath of many battles. Do you remember when we flooded the room with tank water – 50 gallon went onto the floor. I love you so very much. You got mad at me about the rave you were going to throw (have). Pig farm was a low point – do you remember Joe's rave – a pig farm – what is it with pigs – that was one strange place, really strange. [Joe and Mary threw a rave at an actual pig farm in the Arizona desert. We didn't know it was a pig farm when Todd took mescaline and I took LSD. After we started to feel the effects we also started to smell the pigs. It was dusty, disgusting, smelly place.] Do you still wish to go overseas?? Live in a different country...

Dec. 29, 2003

Dear Krystle,
Happy New Year! Wish you the best. Hope you have much fun. Remember our 2001 New Year – we were one. Love and light – it was wonderful – I love you so very much – pumpkins. Hard to write with one inch pencil. This will not be a long letter. Please send me a letter – tell me what you did on New Year's Eve...

228

Adam Tiggly the former World Kick Boxing Champion is here – for real – he got busted with less than 1/8 ounce of pot – two year sentence. He is three cells down from me – I will write a letter about him. I miss you and love you very much. Love, Todd
January 2004 (County Jail – Reno, Nevada)

Jan. 13, 2004

Dear Krystle,

Did you go to Tulsa to buy storage unit [one of our units was being auctioned off]? Bill sent me a letter and said he has your snapshot/photo albums – Tell him god job on code work in letter. He says he cannot get a hold of you. Send him a letter or phone him and have him mail your photos to Ed's house. I thought you would be happy to hear he has your photos – when you get them tell me what is missing. I assume your classes have started. I got a card with a dog on it and $25 money order. Thank you. Hope your leg/knee gets better. Tell everyone I said hello. Wish you the best; hang in there, have fun. Short letters, I have no pencils other than this less than one inch pencil. I remain, Todd

February, 2004 (County Jail - Reno, NV)

Feb. 02, 2004

Dear Pumpkins,

We are locked down for the night, you asked about TV's, only on about 6 hours a day and only one TV, and yes we get DVD players. We get about two movies a week. I do not watch TV. The sound is not a problem. We have about 30 people on PC [Protective Custody] – Blues. I can take as many showers as I want a day; this unit has plenty of very hot water. I try to take two 30 minute showers a day. I am cleaner than anyone I have met here.

...If I go to a camp like Nellis Air Force Base we can see each other every day, no supervision. If I go there or similar camp I will be very free; Vito is trying hard. My work with the Feds helps a lot. Nellis is in Las Vegas, Nevada. There are three camps that are on Air Force Bases out west. Air Force Camps have no fence or walls.

...I should have taken Fed offer to go to the Florida Region – but I was tired. I am worn out playing with the Feds. And that is over for life, because of sworn statements on Court proceedings.

We will be able to look debonair and powerful once again. We can make what we want out of life – we can make it glamorous – we can have adventure – and plenty of action. I WILL NEVER HURT YOU AGAIN – you are my light and love... ...We will make it. We are strong and we are different, unique.

Feb. 04, 2004

Dear Pumpkins,

I was glad to see your understanding of ascending spirituality as you go up you must become purer. And you are expected to behave different – this is my understanding... ...Be circumspect when telling people about ascending into the Godhead – it is a bit much for most. One spoon at a time Sweet Jesus. Time is a fun thought.

It is important to go get *Waking Life*, the cartoon we watched in Arizona – You will understand it better – You will get it now. A beautiful piece. The time-space concept is a tricky one, much care grasshopper!

The letter you sent was well written – Thanks... "Speak it into being" is what "we" are all about. The more perfect "Logos" of Philo Judeas. If the mind you are talking to is not ready you must wait to send it into a deeper level of transcendence. Go slow. Most that use entheogens cannot remember the "Godhead" much less work with it. The trick is to flow – the non-trick is to be able to go to the "Godhead" with out the use of an entheogen.

Do not push this on others; we are unique. Beings able to go to the "Godhead" and remember are rare. Being able to go and work with it is even rarer. Do not show off in this area. Be quiet about this. To be able to do this is to open a door in the deepest and most intimate sanctum of your soul. This is the door to "non-time" – a door to a soul far beyond what a conscious ego would ever reach. You are very much in a "Buddha – Watts" headspace – "Buddha Nature is not everlasting and death defying; it is rather timeless and transcendent" – Grasshopper. I still want to write the letter to you on transcendental numbers, it will help.

Remember when I wrote you this – Being is what the BRAHMINS express in that sacred, mystic formula which is yet really so simple and clear. "Tat Tvam Asi" – this is you!

Could the solution to the dilemma of indeterminism be a universe in which all possible outcomes of an experiment actually occur? Time-waves.

I am making the newspaper again. I will send you and Ed the articles. Joy, happy, joy!

Being a person includes both a celestial self (face of Godhead, one of the many masks of the Great Face) and its negation, forgetting you ever dreamed (ascended). Like Cinderella returning from an enchanted evening (entheogens) you leave your Magic Shoes, abandoning your whole self to work like hell trying to survive the hastiness of everyday life. You go back to cleaning what seems like someone else's ashes, and struggle to succeed in the confines of consensual reality... ...If we do not have solid footing in Magical spaces, we seek protection in the Impermanence of everyday reality. Uncertainty and sometimes loneliness make us tremble. While battling to survive and accomplish something, we lose ourselves in the details. Subtly longing for a message (truth) about some infinite task or reassurance that in this world, there will be justice and Freedom from suffering. Maybe I will call you Alice instead of Grasshopper – Now you see.

"Tat Tvam Asi" – or your last letter ended as "Ebatone Neahmeh Diodeseh" – I get part of the formulaic work, could you help with "Diohdoseh"?? I know the first two parts.

These trances, formulas and "acts of power" were a form of space-time expression, common ground for all who were present. The experiences took place in hyperspace, (4d), in a magical and unifying atmosphere. To quote you from your last letter dated 1-27-04, "Time and space exist for oddity or uniqueness to manifest itself" – a central thought of Taoist in form. This realization is the beginning of a new world-view, the modern shamanism that senses the interconnected nature of our "separate" realities.

Cinderella, Namaste, yes off to the Emerald City at Night. Mythology is so important – to transcend reality. I doubt this being of existence is "Ex Nihilo" (out of nothing.) You know how I hate the big bang. It just does not feel right. SYNCHRONICITY is part, in all, a reflection of a human-like universe.

Lord Byron and 50 A.D. to 99A.D, Niner, Niner, Alpha, Delta. The circle of time –see movie and solve puzzle. Every move you make, every thought you have – I am there.

Keep pushing your mind – learn a new word everyday. I am trying to expand my vocabulary. I am thinking about new exotic structures in chemistry.

...You wrote "every breath is an incredible spiritual event" – the theme of the movie *Baraka*.

Sorry I did not connect the dots – I leave that for you Grasshopper.

I meet with Vito tomorrow – we lay out a defense plan with Tulsa. He should talk with Tulsa D.A. in next seven days. Let us hope for the best.

...The book is a major downer – why did my Mother send it? I am not fond of Russian books. I just had dinner and low I am shaking. I cannot explain how this stuff works. My pencil is getting short and dull. I am not able to recall what I have read that well. Some of these trash novels from here I barely remember reading, not that I want to. The better books I can recall, somewhat – all physics and philosophy books I can remember.

Hope to see you soon. At Federal Prison, I cannot get mail from inmates or felons. I have sent to letters and got them back. One needs to file a form to write someone in prison. I would be very sad not to get mail from you. "L" is going to have a hard time being "Max" at Lompoc, CA. Good, I do not want his negative mail. Sorry my writing is bad now. I feel better when I write you. I have not seen the sun or sunlight for three weeks.

...Only send money if it is from your heart – I hope Aunt Betty remembers to send the $100 check. Please send a letter on what Monroe and Kramer said about Oklahoma case...

...Freedom Is A State of Mind. "Build thee more stately mansions of the soul, as the swift seasons roll. Leave thy low vaulted past. Create new orders and temples, each nobler than the last, oh forlorn child of the stars". Each line is changed, a little poetic fun.

233

Nisi dictum haud refiecendum – If it ain't broke don't fix it.

Book that helped me, read it years from now – you will not like it until much time has passed. *Tractatus Logico-Philosophicus* by Ludwig Wittgenstein. Study Georg Friedrich Bernhard Ricmann – Curvature Mathematics. It is a beautiful and powerful story of math.

...I have never given you the ship scam complete story – it was classic, fooled coast guard, oil companies, Bill G., whole bunch of oil ship assholes – it was a classic. One of the better scams, the deal was I had no scam in mind. It was a fun time, even K.I. had fun. You know the shoe string no fund scam. It was a blast of the first order. Bill G. actually won, the bastard, over $150,000 in that boat – Ivo took $50,000 hit, it was a ball. But, I got a fortune out of cash flow. All in all you would have loved it. Classic fun. Moise [a two-star General] even made a little on the deal.

The FINEX Deal was even better. It happened in the 1984-86 time period, my Mother is still pissed – truth is I got screwed – but I let another underwrite it. I have had a lot of fun in my life. Money has flowed for so long that I forget how hard it is for most people. Life is a blast – let me tell you – it is a true blast. Just wait a little bit and you will be dying for action. I know you, a true partner in crime. Do you know how much debt I have shucked since you met me – TONS. I sloughed off a lot in Arizona. Steve lost his ass with me – how about Pepper – I think over $100,000. Blaze lost, and Boudry took the normal hit, Gas Company, and Mantis, and such. You have to laugh. Just wait, the show is not over yet.

"L" was around for some of the best – "L" used to love the game – He would always bet I could not pull it off. I won all the bets.

Should have gone to Han's city or close by. Next, chapter is that. Once I am well and free – the game is a foot.

...My roommate is to leave tomorrow; his nickname is "Wolf." He is 21 years old and sleeps 20 hours a day. Bush submitted a $2.4 trillion budget. He is slashing/cutting prison funds; he may sign a sentence reduction bill, 65% instead of 85% time served. That would be a big break. Let us hope and pray. I can remember when the whole G.D.P. was not $2.4 trillion, now that is the federal part alone.

Math:

<a+ b> is a function its conjugate a – b

<a + ib> is the form of a complex number
$\qquad$ A complex has a real part <a>
$\qquad$ And an imaginary part <ib>

$\sqrt{-4}$ = is an imaginary number in complex form.

-2i = $\sqrt{-4}$
-2i · -2i = 4 · (-1) $\qquad$ i² = -1
= -4
= $\sqrt{-4}$

The full complex number of $\sqrt{-4}$ is:

{0 + (-2i)} or (0, -2i)
Also
{0 + 2i} or (0, 2i)

Complex numbers are VERY important. It is how we solve complicated problems. If you multiply a complex number by its conjugate you get a real number solution.
$\qquad$ As this:

a + ib multiply by its conjugate

$(a + ib) \cdot (a - ib) =$

$a^2 - iab + iab - i^2b^2 =$

$a^2 - i^2b^2 =$ because $i^2 = -1$

$a^2 + b^2 =$ real number

This is a powerful conversion, learn it. It will allow you many avenues to solve real world problems. A powerful Tool. It is beyond this though...

I know you are not liking the Math, Please hang in there, it is so very important. This world is run by math – please hang in there!!! You need to lay the foundation right. The next letter I will try to write on the rigors of Quantum Mechanics.

Ψ is the wave amplitude, this ties in with Mind. With Light – Fiat Lux.

There will come a day when you will know why we have walked the Roads we have. It is so important to build a Structure of Thought – the rigor is so critical. Please work on your Algebra, it is so important. Are you proving the Theory of Calculus?

"EMANCIPATE yourself from mental slavery, only the mind can set itself free, oh happy day" – Bob M.

Feb. 05, 2004

Sweeti,

Back to complex numbers; do not confuse conjugation with squaring. Mathematically, the process of conjugation is similar to squaring but just a bit different. Squaring complex numbers produces more such numbers, where as conjugating

236

and getting the absolute value gives us real numbers. Conjugation is a form or means lucid dreaming.

We will learn how to do polar to rectangular conversions. Complex numbers are one way to map conscience. Complex numbers are used throughout all of real applied math. Algebra allows for different tricks to be used to get better solutions and understanding.

In your last two letters you bring up the free will topic. The language of some aboriginal peoples, such as Hopi, does not contain the words for time, the past or the future. There is no movement in creation from past to future, but only a passage from dreaming to waking reality and back again (*Waking Life* brings up the Hopi.) Hopi speak of "that which is beginning to manifest", corresponding approximately to our consensual and non-consensual realities. For the Hopi, real objects are part of the past – they have manifested.

What physical image will we form in the future? I am writing about actual garb, clothes we wear. By the time I am out, 28-41 months, or five years. I plan to be at 200lbs. plus built up. My grey is going away in my beard – that is strange and my hair is getting much darker. 5:08 pm, mail came, Vito did not. He had to change days; I will know soon when he is coming.

My Mother sent pictures of "polar" [her dog] and Christmas dinner – Sweeti, please eat more – you need to eat better – I know you. Stress is working on you in a different way now. You must get more sun and better nutrition. Kansas is hard on you. I am worried about you; your heart looked sad. We will make it through this. We are strong – do not let the sleeping men of the USA affect you, hollow souls of no light. Take very good care of yourself. I realize you are scared – fear nothing... ...I need to cuddle you up and make you safe. My little sleeping partner – I laugh at how we used to get up in the middle of the night to go to the bathroom together. I send my love to comfort you and be with you. Do not fear me. ...We will dance on the wings of time once again...

I finished my second shower of the day. I am working on getting my mind back into higher math, having a hard time.

You can express the geometry of complex numbers in trigonometric fashion that is in terms of angles (θ).

θ is the angle between R and x.

$\tan(\theta) = y/x$, $x = R\cos(\theta)$, $y = R\sin(\theta)$

as is complex number Z can be converted in terms of angles:

$Z = R[\cos(\theta) + i\sin(\theta)]$

Mathematicians call $[\cos(\theta) + i\sin(\theta)]$ the "angulas Factos"

The above is important; I will expand on it in other letters. Do not become bored.

The concept of "Pure" is tricky. Why do you use it? And what underlying precepts are working with such nomenclature. Is 5-HTP a drug? Is DMT a drug? At what point is the item food? Do not blindly embrace Buddhism. No man is an Island unto Himself. As one goes up the Ladder the Rules do Change. Do not jump from Thesis to Thesis. One is not a Rock... Grasshopper! Rigor, Rigor. Try to find fault with Buddhism – Question the Form of syntax. It is hard for me to write plus I can't spell anything – I am hitting some real blanks. I have tried to write many papers to you and have been unable. My Mother said you wanted to go to Law School. Another impulse – write me about it.

I know you are getting bored.

Are you working on Limit Theory? And f(x)...
and such? What is now, the topic in Philosophy?
Write me about Noble Truths, thanks. "Wise Man
sees similarities, Fool sees differences" – So Alice,
which side of the toadstool eat from today? You are
my family – love you. Do not hide from yourself. And
dampen the ego a wee bit.

Feb. 06, 2004

Pumpkins,

I am trying to see of I can send seven legal
size pages with only $.37. I think I have done it in
the past. I stay warm most of the time. I eat a small
amount of food at 4:30 a.m. everyday now. I had a
bad cold for the last ten days. I am getting better
now. My cellmate, "Wolf", did not go to State prison
yet. He got 2-5 years instead of 20 years.

Conjugation is like taking complex number
and multiplying by its Reflection – Best way to say
it. $(a + ib)$ and its reflection $(a - ib)$; therefore, $(a +
ib)$ x $(a - ib)$.

More syntax:

years. Have you used any of these syntax yet ??

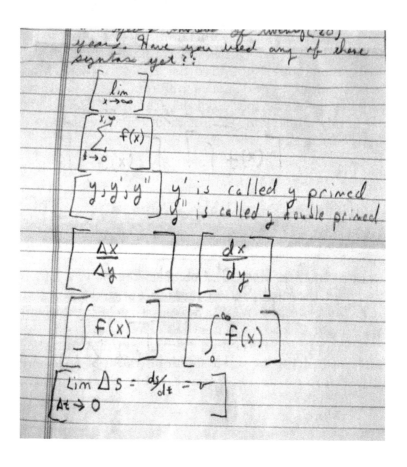

$$\left[\lim_{x \to \infty}\right]$$

$$\left[\sum_{t \to 0}^{x, y} f(x)\right]$$

$\left[y, y', y''\right]$ y' is called y primed
y'' is called y double primed

$$\left[\frac{\Delta x}{\Delta y}\right] \qquad \left[\frac{dx}{dy}\right]$$

$$\left[\int f(x)\right] \qquad \left[\int_{0}^{\infty} f(x)\right]$$

$$\left[\lim_{\Delta t \to 0} \Delta s = \frac{dy}{dt} = v\right]$$

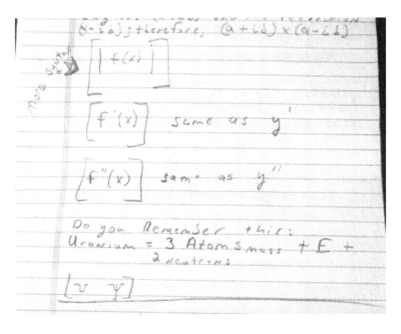

Do you remember this? Uranium = 3 atoms mass + E + 2 neutrons

[υ Ψ]

I am reading five books right now, most are boring. I want to write about Gnostics, maybe this letter. Read a book called "Small is Beautiful" by Schumacher.

I received a letter dated 1-30-04, I will sign the annulment – only thing that would stop that would be if Vito wants wording changed. As of 2-5-04, Vito's office did not have it – I will sign it as soon as Vito comes.

If you get convicted of a Felony – you will not be able to write me once I am in Federal Prison – up till them you can write. If you get a Felony I will not be able to see you for 3 years on up. If Oklahoma blows up on me, 8 years minimum. We shall not see each other for a long time. Vito says the annulment will not help. But I will sign because you asked me to. Love you, Todd

Feb. 10, 2004

Dear Ms. Pumpkins,

I spoke to Shirley (Vito's Office) and she said no fax or mail from you or your lawyer. I will talk to Vito this week.

There is in all things a pattern that is part of our universe. It has elegance, symmetry, and grace – a dance of the soul, in that which the true Godhead captures light and waves. One can find it in the turning of the seasons, in the way life leaves trails in the sand, in the branch clusters of a bush or the pattern of its leaves. We try to copy these patterns in our lives and our spirituality, seeking the rhythms, the songs, the forms that comfort. Yet, it is possible to see peril in the finding of ultimate perfection. It is clear that the ultimate pattern contains its own spirit. Its own way. I such perfection, all things move toward an intimate dance with death. To get a glimpse of the great face behind all the masks of the Godhead. There is a universal mind. To speak a language, not to be heard but to be beheld – so be the way! When a soul sees into the farthest reaches of possibility.

Rhodium foil 5 mil thick. Max temp 50° F, minimum temp 35° F. 20 gallon Hobby Fish Tank.

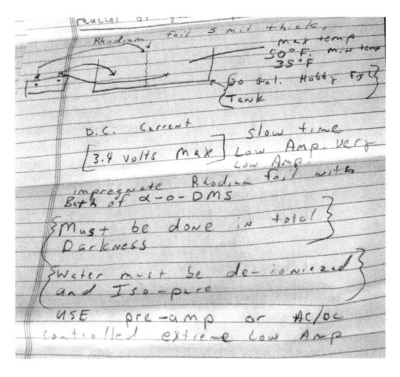

D.C. Current [3.4 Volts Max] Slow time Low
Amp. Very Low Amp. Impregnate Rhodium foil with
bath of á-o-DMS. {must be done in total
darkness}{water must be de-ionized and Iso-pure}
Use pre-amp or AC/DC controlled extreme low amp.
12-14 hrs – heat is a problem. Rhodium foil from
Sigma or Engelhard in New Jersey. The foil must be
99.9% or better. The foil is the sponge. It has a
matrix-lattice structure to hold the á-o-DMS in
place, to begin optical exposure. After time of
cathode and anode work make sure foil is sponge
not (-) probe. Weigh foil before and after. Dry Foil in
Dark, Dry Slow – use low Hund Chamber – No direct
air. No Light. Use known light temperature in Kelvin
(K). No longer than 440nm. Fischer Scientific has
UV lights. SAVE ALL FLUIDS. Do not use any other
wave length of light – one and only one. Fix tank

environment with Argon or heavier in drying, keep helium or Argon fix – Nitrogen is good for drying but has some interaction. Foil should be largest stock size, 20mm x 10cm or whatever. It is just a sponge. Rotate water in tank for mixing. Before tank work Rhodium foil should be somewhat translucent. Drying temp not above 55° F important exchange gas fix once per hour/ not to exceed 20 exchanges per hour. – 220nm works but may be hard to find. Light for 60 seconds and seal in dark film from photo store. Once sealed temp can go ambient.

Use calculus class to make money. Trade mini-sp futures. Open account with any low cost house, $10 round trip max – max. You scalp points both ways off of friction. Trick 2 accounts- and use stops to get into positions and limits to get out. I am sure of the order – stops to get in – limits to get out. The math is not that hard on this. Off of a $25,000 margin you should make $25,000 profit in a 100 day cycle – Almost $100,000 per year. 6 hours a day.

The future trading is extreme low risk that is why the income is so low. You are day trading both ways with two accounts and staying Δ (Delta) Neutral.

á – price of future
á'– Long or Short (Delta)
á"– Gamma or Δ (Delta) changes

Your firm must trade – e-trade over internet.

Have you thought of marketing brain booster? Capital is cheap now – look at ways to make bucks. Maybe you could market with Dr. Miles as prototype.

Learn some script or computer language for future help.

Photons in science will be as big as nanotech.

You should plan on being out of the USA by 2008 – Demographics turn bad. Australia or New Zealand or large Island/English speaking place.

I am coming out of a big haze – "Benzo" Haze. My mind is getting faster and faster. At times I can see problems flash and solve.

Quantum Mechanics Principle II-

If a particle can reach a given state by two possible routes the total amplitude of the process is the sum of the amplitudes for the two routes considered separately. I will write more about II principle next letter. t · o – N,N, á – o – DMS Rotate in form Ψ diffraction grading 90° of Polar Ψ, wave form embeddability being open. Embeddability being realizable in surprisingly low-dimensional ambient spaces – But only limited <u>smoothness</u>!! A work in Differential Geometry – I wish I could show you on the spring tester, this idea.

PLEASE eat better – and write me more. No mail has come for me – only the book from Ed came. I read it in two days, hard book, wild mind run. I now play two games of chess at once – to give others handi-cap. No loses. I watched TV, a show on Jamaica, Ocho Rios, only TV I have watched. No movies for 7-10 days. Be glad to leave this place.

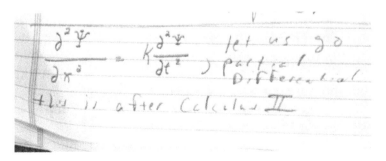

Let us go Partial Differential, this is after Calculus II. Pseudoprime sequences – 2,3,5,7,11,13, and... Same distribution properties Zeta Function in

form. True Primes reduce to Riemann Zeta Function. Riemann Hypothesis. When you develop Integration in Calculus you will use Riemann Sums. Even though you no longer send me – I love you or I miss you at letter's end. I do you, namaste.

Feb. 11, 2004

Dear Krystle,

How are you doing? I send my love. I spent 3 hours with Vito today. He spoke to Robertson, the D.A. – Robertson is over this case for sure. Vito has it in writing. The DA has offered [a plea agreement] ten years actual served time. Vito told Robertson, NO WAY. We are going to trial...

...But if it goes to trial more help may be given. All DEA and Federal agents can be brought in as witnesses – Brady rule applies [this has to do with Todd's immunity for testifying against Leonard] Kastigar and 6001, 6002, 6003 apply as long as I do not take stand... Vito says I have good chance at winning multiple appeals...

Vito says it is important for Hoch to be in court room for trial. Hoch is the best person because he looks bad on paper – he has admitted to everything – even injecting Brad with Zima. Aston says the problem is Brad has been coached and the testimony has changed... Problem Hoch has is he drove him across state line...

Aston said Brad told you that he was holding you most responsible – is that true?? If it is – it proves he has forgotten the highest commands of his religion but – he is bogus...

Vito said I can go to the "Cheese Factory" if I want – the home of Federal Rats. It is one of the best Federal Places...

Feb. 23, 2004 - Letter 57

Pumpkins,

I received your letter dated 2-18-04. In the letter, you asked about Palladium ring design.

First, Vito and Aston are working together (??) and NO Enhancement can be filed!! Oklahoma D.A. Lied to Vito. I have the Statutes, No Can Do. It was a hard week when I thought I was going to have to go to trial and risk 45 years. Are you my wife now?? My New Jersey Felony is over 14 years old – at 10 years Oklahoma cannot use Felony, too old. VITO DOES NOT LIKE ROBERTSON. This is to my benefit, Vito is working harder. Aston is sure OK DA cannot win Assault with a deadly weapon. Aston has been a help in last three weeks.

Questions: Why Palladium over Rhodium??? One can start from Tryptophan or α – from tryptamine. In the last three days I have had my two best days since I have been here and my single best day in years. I am close to being over "Benzos" no to control blood sugar levels. The letter card you sent on Valentines Day with a personal check was sent back to your Father's house.

I am SO VERY sorry all of this happened. I am sorry for everything I have ever done to hurt or harm you. You are my very best friend. What is a friend? "A single soul dwelling in two bodies" – Aristotle. I'm so very happy to have loved you and known you. I do look forward to going to Federal Prison. Let us pray Vito can get me into Air Force Base Camp – Long shot.

We have a friend who has all the important stones in rough form for your ring. Rough stones are hard to work with. Please write back about which type of ring in the end.

Pig Joke – I have sent you three pig jokes – I assume you mean the first one I told you – Here it is:

247

A man from the city is driving down a country road. He sees a farmer holding a baby pig up to an apple tree. The city man pulls over and asks the farmer what he is doing? The farmer says that he is feeding the pig. The city man says, "Doesn't that take a long time?" The farmer says, "What is time to a pig?"

I bow to you, Grasshopper...

What happened on Monday, 2-23-04, in Court? Please write. Also, what did Brad say to you in Court? Aston said Brad said he holds you most responsible for what happened. Is that true?

Trade of Investments:

First rule; do not buy stocks in your name, for a Trust, LLC, or Corporation. Open two future trading accounts at two low cost houses; cost must be below $13 round trip trade per contract. The Futures we want to trade is probably mini- s & p 500, One would buy on a stop and sell on a stop both sides of the same instrument and month.

Example:

March S & P 500
Buy at 350.00 in Account A
Sell at 350.00 in Account B

Then you place a limit order to sell the long S & P at 355.00 in Account A. And place a buy limit order at 345.00 in Account B.

1) One Never takes a Market Direction Position
2) Scalp small number of points
3) Electronic trade
4) Keep overhead down

One is trading for small volatility during the day. If you trade the Big S & P 500 you have better overhead cost. We will stay on this subject, but I need to know how your classes are going??

The S & P 500 moves around as f(x) the static movement of scalping small numbers of points is how you make money on this. 1/f(x) is static control. Everyday has a band of trading. That band changes every instant. How well you control bands, gives profit. Never become emotional about trading. Never make a market direction call, unless for fun. Stay mechanical – and use strict rules for trading. Build math system to help you; do not be greedy!! Make a certain amount each day and stop. Lose a certain amount and stop.

Feb. 24, 2004 – Letter 58

Sweet Heart,

Principles in Quantum Mechanics:
Principle IV:
Furthermore, from the laws for complex numbers it turns out that

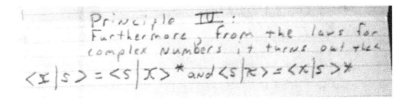

The amplitude to get directly from one state to another is the complex conjugate of the reverse situation. Thus symmetries in space and time in Quantum mechanics come from the world of "Complex Numbers" and the definitions of wave functions.

I will send more examples. Sorry for using Paul Dirac notation. I am just trying get you used to the form.

Trading. The stock indexes move around with a "fuzzy motion" indexes do not move in straight lines. S & P 500 stock index is a basket of stocks, 500 to be exact, that are tied to an equation for weighting and price value – as each stock changes in value, so does the overall value of the S & P 500 index. There many other indexes, "Major Market Index", New York Composite Index (NIFE), and "Mid-Cap Index", the Dow Jones Index, and on and on.

One wants to find an index that is very <u>liquid</u>! When an instrument is very liquid it means that the bid/ask spread is very small. There are a lot of buyers and sellers. Also means a huge OPEN INTEREST, which means how many open contracts.

What is the bid/ask spread? I a market system there is a "bid" – someone's price to buy and an "ask" – someone's price to sell.

Example:

Gold Spot Price-
410.50 bid
410.70 ask
410.60 lost trade (spot)

Spot means current physical market. Future means price for delivery in that month. The more liquid the market the easier it is to get in and out of the market for little to no cost. Bid/Ask spread is very important to all forms of instruments. This along with commissions is the biggest friction item. "Friction" is the cost of trading that has to do with getting in and out of positions. Friction is a major variable for us. Friction must be watched all the time.

Example:

250

Cost per round trip future trade in commissions $14.00. To buy and sell a given future contract. Friction cost = $14.00 + bid/ask cost

Just trading one contract cost $14.00 in, in and out cost. Some markets are so liquid that part of this can be overcome. Commission cost must be balanced against what you get in services from broker i.e. Election quote service, free online real time quotes, and so on.

Remember Index trading is Zero-Sum Game Theory. Zero-sum means every winner has an equal loser. Zero-Sum games have specific boundaries and rules.

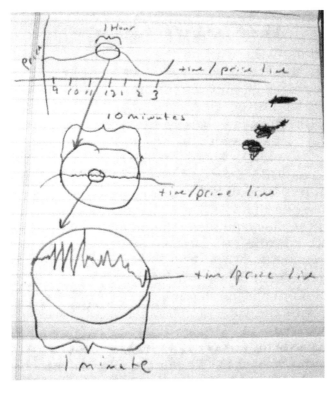

Most pits in futures trading use open out-cry system. Write back and ask many questions.

When opening up an account it is easiest to open personal account. But – it will be connected to you – you could use a front person. One does not even have to know they are a front person. Do not place money in your name – Brad, IRS, and State of Oklahoma can find that easy. The Land Trust had many trading accounts. The problem with a Trust is that you hit a maximum income tax at $3,500 income. Corp. C much higher – LLC – goes to personal income and personal is much highest income before highest take.

I prefer the most hidden which is a corp. under a Trust. Next to impossible to locate the controller and owner. Do not become bored with this process. Just write with all the questions you need answered.

You opened your letter with, what if Christy was a CS for FBI on DEA corruption. According to Christy, DEA was in Pryor by 1:00 – 2:00 pm max. same day. Brad went to hospital 10 am that morning – why would police/hospital/Brad's parents call DEA right off the bat? It makes no sense, unless Christy had already spoken to DEA or something like that. DEA was on this too fast. This is one of the major puzzles. The preliminary hearing will start to unravel this equation. Why would Christy go to the DEA if she was worried – she would go to Tulsa police – unless DEA was on top of all this from the beginning. If so either someone was working with the DEA at the hotel or DEA was all over everyone.

I tried to answer all your questions. My penmanship was poor. We cannot sharpen pencils now. And I have nothing to write on – no table/ no

252

desk and so on. I write on a book sitting on my bed with a one inch dull pencil.

Sample Trading:

Instrument: March S & P 500

8:15 market opens up

8:30 S & P 500 March range 500-515

9:00 one sends in 2 different orders to 2 different accounts (you can use same brokerage house with different names)

You calc. order between 8:30 am and 8:45 am and then enter it at 8:45 to 9:00.

First order Account A –

Buy 1 March S & P 500 at 525.00 on a stop.

Sell 1 March S & P 500 at 530.00 limit order.

Second order Account B –

Sell 1 March S & P 500 at 535.00 on a stop. - after it is filled

Buy 1 March S & P 500 at 525.00 limit order.

What you are doing is nibbling points – scalping points as you go along the day. I need to define stop order and limit order.

A limit order does not trigger until price trades through the specified price. A limit order is not a marker order. A limit order must be filled at your price or better.

Example:

Order:

Buy 1 March S & P 500 at 520.00 or better limit order.

Order filled at 520.00 1 March S & P 500

Better could have been 519.00 for example.

Market order means an open order is thrown in and filled ASAP at whatever price is legal and there. I do not like market orders – we would have a hard time.

Stop Order Example:
Buy 1 March S & P 500 at 520.00 on a stop.
How this is filled is once 520.00 is touched the order turns into a Market Buy order and has to be filled.

Rules to Remember:
When buying (going long) if you place a limit order the limit price must be below the current price – otherwise it turns into a market order.

When selling (going short) if you place a limit order the limit price must be ABOVE the current price or the limit turns into a Market order.

There is a magazine called *Commodities and Stock*, technical letter – buy one of these magazines. The magazine has a page called liquidity. It is a horizontal bar graph. This section helps us in finding liquidity ratio. Read magazine but do not buy into thought. That is a technical trader magazine – we will use some of the tools but not many.

Example of Trade:

Market opens at 8:15 am. March S & P 500 price 521.00 price high was 530.00 price low was 518.00 from 8:15 to 8:30 am current price 519.00 at 8:32 am. We will place an Above spot order and a Below

Placed at 8:35 am:
E-trade Account A –
Buy 1 March S & P 500 at 525.00 on a stop

Sell 1 March S & P 500 at 530.00 or better limit order

Placed at 8:37 am:
  E-trade Account B –
  Sell 1 March S & P 500 at 515.00 on a stop
  Buy 1 March S & P 500 at 510.00 or better on a stop

Market is now at 527.00 for March S & P 500 time is 8:50 am. Account A is long 1 March S & P 500 at 525.00.

Place Account A short at 8:55 am:
  Sell 1 March S & P 500 at 520.00 on a stop
  Buy 1 March S & P 500 at 515.00 or better limit order

Let us place Account B leg on at 8:57 am:
  Buy 1 March S & P 500 at 530.00 on a stop
  Sell 1 March S & P 500 at 535.00 on a stop

At 9:30 am March S & P 500 is at 524.00 high has been 529.00, low has been 524.00. No new positions and no new spreads.

I hope you are getting the idea. You will paper trade 60 days first to learn and get a strategy. After 1-2 hours of trading you want Account A and B to have a moving net position of zero (0) so you are not long or short the market. You will get the hang of it. I believe that each point on the Mini-S & P 500 is $50.00. Each point on the Big S & P 500 is/was $500.00. Now after index S & P hit, I think it is at $250.00 per point.

The goal is to be market neutral – Delta Δ Flat – or value zero. Do not bet on market direction. Again over "Δt" (Delta time or changing time) you want to be flat on market direction. You do not want to be market direction oriented. Nor do you want to be a price/ time/ direction player. Ask me about that, I used to play this time/this price.

We will start to learn Band structure of how to pick trading bands. We will go into the risks of this type of trading.

One has to snatch points (money) and put into reserve bank for traps that suck money in this type of trading. As you open up spread:

(I am trying to go slow and show each step, plus define.)

Buy 1 March S & P 500 at 525.00 on a stop
Sell 1 March S & P 500 at <u>540.00</u> on better limit order

Trading band is wider, more risk. I will show you next letter. One does not want to carry positions over night. If you are forced to clean up position with MOC (Market on Close) to get Flat in each account 15 minutes before market closes. Avoid out trades. Love, Todd

Feb. 25, 2004 – Letter 59

Hey Pumpkins,

Vito spoke to Robertson. Robertson said that Hawkins has replaced him on the case. Robertson was shocked about two things – first that Vito proved to him no enhancement could be filed. That was a major assumption Tulsa had in filing charges – Next, Vito was asked by Robertson what a difference it made, because Tulsa DA looked up my federal charge and said I was facing 20 years for MDMA. Vito explained I was looking at 51 months max. Robertson also admitted assault with a deadly weapon would not hold. But conspiracy of kidnapping would. Robertson told Vito as of 2-24-04 Hawkins would be in charge of case. Vito has to get authorization to handle my Oklahoma case until the day of federal sentencing, approx. July 27, 2004. He is requesting to be allowed to go to Oklahoma to represent me. He does not know if he will get budget...

Is Hawkins the "Nazi" you said may get the case?? Doesn't matter – they lost their edge. Now, Vito sees one of the many reasons the Feds did not charge us... Vito said Robertson said your statements were worse than Hoch's and Brad's put together. But you have a credibility problem because of Feds claimed you lied and Brad said you lied. I do not think Vito is going to work a plea out with Oklahoma – but he may be able to soften them up... Robertson's last sentence was he if fed up with this case – a bunch of druggies and liars.

Be careful not to get your bail revoked by your bail bond company.

On trading, I am trying to give you a lot of background information and I am trying to define terms and ideas as best as I can. I will go in baby steps as you have asked. Be patient – I am not good at writing.

History of Trading: In high school I traded options on my mother's boyfriend's account 1980-81 – Lost money, -$15,000, learned a lot (traded options on stocks, physical spot options). (Learned about Delta, Gamma, Vega, and Theta math in 1983-85 – I became very good at it.) I traded forward contracts with banks in Europe in 1983, broke even on trades. Traded late 1984 and 1985 – made money in 1984 – lost a ton in 1985 trading huge positions on options on physicals of currency. 1000 contracts at a time. Had days when my cash account was up $600,000. Lost my ass March 22,

1985. Stopped trading until 1986 – when I started trading metals (silver, gold, platinum) and so on. Traded metals through Atlas account under the name P. C. Caroll. Made solid positive cash flow – for me and Moise. Made money until I took delivery of a ship in Freeport, Texas. February of 1988 stopped trading because I was too busy.

Went to jail in 1989, no trading until 1992. Options and options on futures and futures on S & P 500 and Midcop Index. Traded heavy in 1992 and 1993-1194. Stopped in 1995-96, Kally [Todd's first wife] and I were breaking up and I was moving assets out of her name. Still have money in Jack Carl under her name. (She has 1,000 in account still). Lost money on stock indexes in 1992, made money on metals in 1992. (Are you wanting Alpha-MT or Alpha-O). Made money in stock indexes and metal positions, learned execution strategies. Made small amount of money in 1994 on all accounts and physicals – reported about $47,000 in 1099 from different houses – Kally was pissed. She did not want me dumping income in her name because she was trying to get grants for research and she wanted to look broke to school, PHD, and DO. Note: Kally did allow me to trade in 1995-96 on her account but she kept income – I was trading on a Wendy [a girlfriend of Todd's] account also. Made a lot of money... Emille is my contact at E. F. & Mann – parent of Stock Index group – Jack Carl Futures. Do not mention my name because of DOJ (Department of Justice) and IRS, but flirt with him to get Option cost down and future commissions down. I can send you drawing of jewelry?? You are not interested in Rhodium only right?

After all this I have learned:

1) It is tough to make money in options and futures
2) Enormous risk
3) Lot of stress
4) Do not take market positions in directions
5) Execution of trades is very important
6) One must understand risks
7) It is not fun
8) Even under best environment you can lose money in ways you have not planned
9) <u>Do not overtrade your money</u>
10) Be open to change style
11) Do not throw good money after bad
12) Do not chase a loser
13) If in doubt get out
14) Be flexible
15) Do not be one of the herd – the 95% that lose
16) Be unique in thought
17) Break even or make money on each trade
18) Close out 90% of all trades within 2 hours
19) Close out 97% of all trades before market close (2% is far out trades and mistakes and 1% for times you need to be in market overnight)

I really need a dictionary. Please find a bigger paperback version from Barnes and Noble; send it by itself, please. I am writing with a much reduced word spread because I cannot spell.

Mini-S & P 500 Electronic Pit each point is $50.00, it is 1/5 or 20% as bi as Big S & P 500. Much less Margin. Problem is you pay same commission on mini-S & P as for Big S & P 500 and mini- S & P 500 not as liquid as big S & P 500. Next problem, I have never traded mini-S & P 500 for novelty, never for real. Only a few times when it opened up to get the feel of it. "L" wanted to trade mini-S & P 500 in a big way. He opened up accounts for just that. In both contracts (mini- S & P 500 and big S & P 500) price sometimes moves to just "run stops". (Remind me to write about going long and going short. I need to give you basic definitions – baby steps.)

Look up "Fullerene Lattice" on the internet. <u>Buckminster Fuller</u>, physicist wrote a brief paper in 30's or 40's on lattice structure 3d physical on Palladium. Look him up. I have only read it once when I was 12 or 13 years old.

March 2004 (County Jail – Reno, Nevada)

March, 15, 2004

Dear Krystle,

I spoke to you many times in the last 24 hours. You are my heart – I will forever love you – sweet pies – big kisses – who else can I play in the Universe with? You are always on my mind and in my heart. Smiles, Pumpkins. Read this letter carefully!!

First a Joke it may take it a while to sink in – study it for the punch line. Hi Ho Silver and Away. Lone Ranger goes to an auction in Hollywood. He bids on a few items and loses, over looks someone and says "the Masked Man is a Faggot", at that the Lone Ranger starts to bid on his old Horse "Hi Ho" Silver. Someone asks why he wants the horse and the Lone Ranger says to perform unnatural acts, what about the Indian through him into. By the way the Indians Name is "<u>Tonto</u>". You will get the joke in the near future. One of these delayed jokes.

March 22, 2004

Dear Krystle,

...What is your book about [he's talking about *Lysergic*]? You ask about the "legal" structure 4-acetoxy-DIPT. I have never used it after Frank, or Foxy, or 5-methoxy-DIPT. I really have little hope in "DIPT" structures. "L" in 2000 said we should look at it and check it out. We blew so much money on "Foxy" I had little hope, PLUS, I do not like long-lasting front ends i.e. "Fluoro-ά", "acetoxy", and such. Brain has hard time breaking them down – I would leave it alone. "DIPT" is hard enough to break down. Safe is better than legal any day.

ά-o question [in my last letter to him I asked why the dose recommended in Tihkal was significantly less than what we use to take, specifically with ά-o-DMS]. Sasha always errors to very low dose often .25 or 25% of proper dose. Next is how pure his ά-o versus my ά-o. If mine was/is 50% pure and his if 85% pure my dose would be about 50% as strong. And for the third part which 3d physical structure and rotation – Remember we could not get his process to work, yet mine worked as broad spectrum as his plus a lot more – he did not test any large doses. The thought reading going on for days is not reported anywhere, yet is universal in my research. I am sure he had much purer finished sample. I just didn't care about Indole like pollutants – also the yield sucked – either Sasha's way or my way. My yield was under 2% but was fast. I did not want to hang up 15 days in 100 grams. I think he had a yield of less than 25% but people had mixed results. "Lott" had bad luck plus "Priesty" had bad luck and he is out in bay area with "Sasha". I had a real problem with optical sensitivity. Yet no one else reported it. "Mass Spec" was very close to published reports. My Mass was in Chicago. I had paperwork with it; I thought I showed it to you. Had it done with 2Ci, 2ci-I, 2tci, 2ch, and 2cb. Kiss that batch goodbye.

As you can see I am answering your questions from March 10, 04 letter. I think I am climbing out of Valium withdrawal or I am handling blood sugar problem and it is much warmer here. I still have rough hours but problem is less than 10% of the time.

May 2004 (County Jail – Reno, Nevada)

May 10, 2004

...I had no address to send this letter to so I kept it open. I received your one page letter about book today. I am sending permission out on Friday, 5-14-04. I am off of "fast." Total veggie diet for some time now. I get very few letters – one every two-weeks – mostly Joyce. Have not heard from Vito in over one month. I got searched today, locked down for ten hours for extra towel, socks, underwear, and extra pencils. Guard wants to send me to SHU (hole) for rest of my stay. Oklahoma is trying get me from here – who knows how it will go. Write back soon I do not know the value of an experience from me in your book. I think it would help if you spent $100 for Oklahoma divorce over annulment for legal reasons. Please write back about marriage and book soon. I doubt you read these letters. I will get this in the mail. See you one of these days. Love, Todd

May 11, 2004

Dear Krystle,
Hope this letter finds you in good spirits.
Line of indirect immunity:
I at Karl's request deliver you to Topeka Federal Court House in March of 2003 so he can serve you – again they see and talk to you. Karl after I leave stand [during the LSD Trial] in Topeka at

Capital Plaza Hotel talk about next operation furthering my CS status and immunity status. If they try to can it from way back I can go to the Castillo fax to John Roth – But I contacted DEA and HIDTA group south Miami in May/June 2003 plus after I went to hospital in Tulsa I spoke to Karl from Garder Inc.

You have good Kastigar status with Kidwell – Plus both of us have Agent of Government Status. I went through Hearing in Phoenix in 1991 and was declared Agent of US Government. You and I have much better claim to that each of us – make claim in court other was "Agent of DOJ" and we get Federal Court help about co-consp. status in crime. 2nd and 3rd circuits.

You have strong claims – on me. I have strong claims – on you. We both have immunity issues. Are there any details you could give me that would help my claim?

This is good, why did Tulsa wait so long to file – because Hoch was trying to get me on something big – by working with the Feds. The goal of Kastigar hearing and 6003 is to suppress as much info as possible – the taint is everywhere. Feds will pressure Tulsa to cut deal; the Feds cannot handle dirt on this case. I and I think you should follow this – should lay grounds for appeals – you have Kastigar with Brad, you took him to DEA and claimed 5th – Doug [DEA agent in Oklahoma] BS'd you it was a bluff. I went to see Doug in the middle of the event, creates more taint. But DEA set date week earlier – they have problems – Brad has a story that blows any limitation Doug is going to use. Both Eric and Roger [DEA agent from Kansas City] create taint – 6003 from Roger which is a matter of how and binds all 50 states helps me in big way – Doug taints everything in your case. Both of us need as many hearings before prelim as possible to get access to info. Prelim is going to be the war I see it lasting for more than 5 days. DA will be worn out and want to settle by that time. I am working on STRONG Legal Theory – stuff that will get to the 10th Circuit in a hurry – if shot down at state level – Lays ground for multiple-million dollar claims with DOJ for me and you as my wife.

May 12, 2004

Dear Krystle,

Enclosed is letter you asked me to send on 5-15-04 [giving me permission to print *Lysergic*]. I am sending notarized ink pen letter... I am on vegetarian diet – going over to vegan diet soon. I weigh about 215lbs – you have seen me as high as 280lbs. I have read the thirteen principle Upanishads from beginning to end (so-so) nothing that great... Thanks for your help as of late. I do not need for you to send anymore money for project. Have you and Bill had any breakthroughs? Ideas? I met with Lawyer for free ($100.00) I call that free. Wanted no part of project trust. Said no local will touch it (Feds too much in Big Drug cases). Automatic audit for working for me. He wrote me a formal letter saying he was not qualified to represent me????? It is important to call and talk to the brother. I pray you do not have to go to prison... I do not want anyone to have the letters you wrote to me here do I send them to your PO Box or what?? Plantar's wart is back on my foot. Are you sure you want me to write something for your book?? Please write ASAP if yes. Does Tulsa County Jail allow contact visits? [Omitted names] has a gem (very important) optical grade – Rare – Large – impossible to find. Namaste Pumpkins.

Legal is not always better – I have been down that path – I have strategy for panel testing new structures. CHANGE WE MUST...

Goodbye for now. I am very tired. Very worn out. This is a real endurance test. Sometimes I would like to go to sleep and not wake up. I pray I go to Fed prison before Oklahoma – I need to rebuild my mind and soul and body even 90 days would make a big difference. Smiles, light and love, kisses and hugs. I thought of you more as a mate than as a student. Love you forever, Todd

May 17, 2004

Sweet heart,

I send my love. I send smiles. Response to the typed letter with your storyline for children's book... Take two structures and use lattice to hold each independent structure and apply some wavelength of light, let's say 400nm. I will have to think about this, would you use D.C. (+,-) to drive structures together? Would both structures be in lattice matrix at same time – what about competition to fold into surface?? How does light bond final item?? I am not knocking the idea – I am trying to get the big picture form your "movie" experience. Are you wanting light frequency (wave length) formula in general – trial and error seems to be only path I know – if I understand. The film needs to be broke down into many small steps or solved in "parts." Is the matrix foil thin as so light can pass through?? Both "lovers" are imbedded in foil? I use the lattice to hold on to structures and do organic work then reverse current and "puke" structure back out. Let us say αMT and structure to change to is 5-Fluoro- αMT (legal expensive). I am trying to get this. Two items need to have a glue or common link to make as one and I do not see it off the bat. But light work on a single

265

structure altered through many steps may work. I just read letter so I have to think on this for some time. Tell me "lovers" names.

Krishna has seven letters. Krishna was protected and always had an unlimited source of whatever. Krishna needs a source of food. Why? "He <u>had</u> to hunt a mouse" Find a sac. Was sac for self or others?? "Kind person" does not take sac or any sac. Is kind person a prime creator or pass along soul? Is kind person teacher or just a source? The kind person is in the land of Maria, Miles? Is kind person a Brahmin?? Brahmins would eat some sort of food, any food that takes one to Godhead would do. Brahmins look into souls – is this a true Brahmin or an employee of a Brahmin (how high is source Brahmin?) Can we call kind person a Brahmin in story? How many foods does kind person have? Any flaws in Brahmin or kind person? – Habits that show problems. Does story have any red flags. Is word structure there? Do you see syntactic form in being? Why does kind person not eat? Is it the food is too low? What about more sacred food will he eat of that? This must be done – the high order knows itself. What is a "kitty month"?? Is food like "BOL"? Is food of Elysian fame? Why did kind person pick Krishna? I know of a story which Krishna was picked by a soul with good intentions. Brahma does love synchronicity. But story would be better if Krishna found kind person and approached. The Brahmins know the age of light is here. That which was made in darkness no longer is the high food. If the food is of this way, each one teach one 2 reach one; each one to reach one and is of higher light source above the Socratic vibration then kind person is of pure intentions. The story needs to be more filled in for me – answers to the above questions plus details of each character. Is Krishna trying to find food for others or just self? Is Krishna trying to feed an order of souls? Write a very detailed storyline use symbols. Is Krishna feeding many, many, many souls? You need to use classic Sanskrit names and characters in storyline when you write back. Does kind person want money, help, help cooking food, on and on. I love you very much. I need a day or so to reflect on your storyline of a children's book. Tests that can apply. I need days – weeks to think about matrix film #3...

May 18, 2004

    Dreams are not good since you told me of Salvador – once police start it does not stop. Another problem is hash with stamp on it. The Lineage of this sucks – are you ready for that kind of roller-coaster ride. It takes military connections to move that from Afghanistan to USA. Do not even kid yourself. Use your higher self to see into events – bring it into focus. You must not fumble; look at how clean any lineage is. Plus is that your Path we are the Source Always, you are changing that current. If you use these other avenues to support gifting of the sacs then that is alright. Back away from Topeka problems...

    The world is a ghetto, a utopia, a slum, a war zone, anything you create it to be... The world is a state of mind. What do you (Krystle) mean by "PURE INTENTIONS"?? Or should I say Krishna or seven letters. Does the HE vs. Female gender have meaning in your storyline? What are the goals of the "Kind Person" look at those – look at the works of the kind person. Because of the problems with Dali maybe Krishna should take a chance. But a well chosen chance – with great care. If I have blown the symbolic meaning of the children's book storyline – please shed light. I do not get "he waited, alone"?? Hope you read Etruscan letter at Ed's. In the end, only seeing into ones soul by higher means will tell "pure intentions." Follow your heart and inner sight. I am sure Topeka is coming to an end. Your six months is up! Brown glass vial in [omitted] had light form in it. Time is of the essence... Purple people eater – can you see the movie line Black Box. I think two more collections like that exist. Movies are a big part of life... Only the mind can set itself free – freedom is a state of mind...

I read a lot of work by a Japanese scientist who worked on Cold Fusion – Pons and Flieshnew[sp.?] out of Utah (Salt Lake City). I cannot remember how to spell Japanese scientists name – his name was mentioned as a co-worker of German team the refuted Pons work – great work done on how Palladium "pukes" out molecules or atoms. Math model done by professor in Florida. Do not get drawn into cold fusion, use it as a big resource for lattice structure of Rhodium, Palladium, and Platinum. I have written many letters on where to go find jackpot on this subject. Ψ Richard Feynman has some short articles that could help. Draw up story of Lord Krishna and what possible paths Lord Krishna wants to take, use symbolic form. Robert Prechter out of Atlanta, Georgia – Elliot News get free copy. You can bet he is counting wave formation...Have you found Math that helps with lattice matrix?? Send it, I will help. Pete is to see me soon (Rolling Stone). Sorry for spelling and penmanship – I am writing very fast and in bad conditions. I had a rare good veggie meal tonight. I hope the Feds get me to Fed facility – if Oklahoma gets me I am screwed. I really need to go to Federal Place before Ok case so I can look up legal cases, get real food, and move around – I have never had any shoes but slippers. No tennis shoes, just paper thin slippers. I have been cooped up. I have been a Good Vegetarian. I need to walk with you and see you at

Fed place. I have suffered being away from yo
are my eternal soul. The same soul in two bo
hurts to be away from you. I so look forward to
being able to see you at Fed place. I pray I go to
Sheraton outside of Portland. Oklahoma is going to
wear me out. It is their best hope. Letter came from
Joyce, she is sick again. I need to write her – but I
have held stamps for you. Please send a photo, I
would love to see your face... How is your knee?
Remember Advil hurts tummy long term. Do your
best to retrieve [omitted]. The Etruscan letter will
help us if you get it fro Ed's. Please try to find out
info. This country will make a hard, hard turn to
extreme law and order over individual rights. The
USA is on a path that will stomp on any free will.
Homeland Security is the Dept that will screw us to
the wall. No hope to change this place. It will have to
run its course. You must balance the equation of
what to do. The brother has info – The spirited souls
must make moves to survive to help later. This is a
big blow out here. The next economic downturn will
be hard along with it will come bigger central
government. The energy used to stop LSD is hard to
believe compared to mass consumption, LSD is not
even a problem drug. This Government is in a war
on true spirituality. Flower power has lost. Radical
plan time...

They photocopy every letter that comes in.
One letter came in and they gave me photocopy by
mistake instead of original...

May 18, 2004

Dear Krystle,

Hello pumpkins – smiles. Back to Matrix.
Each "lover" (out of 2) will have an affinity that
differs to go to foil (Palladium??). If you mix the two
in solution one will deposit faster that the other or

one will block the other or both may fail to arrive at all on foil. Therefore, each must be deposited on foil as separate function.

So, you work with "Lover A" to get it to go to foil. Then you find out how to get "Lover B" to go to foil. Now here are problems "A" or "B" may have filled surface or lattice structure. Next problem – did a change occur to "A" or "B" or both in process – so you need to run a test to see what you have. Gas chrom, or Magnetic Res test, or equin Mass Spec. Then you invision a wavelength light dose to foil – what this gives you is anyone's guess. Four choices – 220nm, 400nm, 680nm, 700nm. The Bath solution is another Big Choice "reactive" or "not", one choice. Also is air exchange, "inert" or "not." I have only one very short pencil, ½ inch ad it is very hard to write. THEN which metal – gold, silver, palladium, platinum, rhodium, or other types. Most research is with palladium – probably best references. Remember both cathode and anode must be of same metal, for example Rhodium(+) and Rhodium(-). If not you will electroplate.

Note to extract item from foil you can melt it out by slowly heating up till it melts out "Lover." Since foil's melting point is so high – this may work 150-300°F should get most items – Foil melts, if Platinum Metal group, above 1000°F. Another way is to reverse current, this may or may not work. Another way is to use solvents – wash foil clean, problem did you get "lovers" out of lattice structure. And another, this is a trick. Leave the current on for days and Lattice structure will (maybe) clean itself out. This is a real unknown process. I never have tried this, only read about simple single atom experiments. There are other ways to get structures out of foil. For light or optical work I would think the thinnest most transparent foil would work best.

Why not First work with one "lover" get into foil (or on) then organic or optical process or both. What is goal to form "God" what is components of "God" or wishes for a better "God." Keep variables to a minimum – this is hard enough without extra unknown vectors or complex variables.

Most of this would require Finite Element Analysis – if that model can be masked. "Radius" is name of one Finite Element Analysis program. Another is "Structural Research" out of California. The struc research model has an electro-magnetic program solution set. This project may be way beyond the scope of any Finite Element Program. The Math on film idea would be off the charts. The math for a single atom "Hydrogen" optical jump is a nightmare – for a whole molecule, to much for what I have seen. You could set up a tensor calculus model (maybe) I need to think it through.

Trial and error with best guess (intuition) and past experience is only way I know. Keep variable super simple and keep exact notes. Use as much standard organic chem. Process as possible to get structure changes. Maybe, foil process is used to super clean final product and optical is used to make small but important change. THINK ABOUT THAT!!

What about a "light chamber" that Feeds-Pumps photons into a structure 24 hours a day so we can now have true light structures. Like a mono-atomic Rhodium Ciborium or Vessel that is transparent and has a light source of one wavelength.

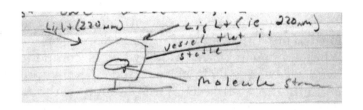

No other light source and maybe air is fixed
i.e. Neon, Helium, or cheap non-reactive. I have
such chamber; it is about two inches in diameter
three inches tall. Cut mono-atomic it is very heavy. I
never took process to end. Many of the Best "Gods"
may be unstable without photon pumping, in fact I
am sure of this.

Never forget using super-critical fluid
extraction and our friends the plants. Since light
chem they have been doing for over 1 Billion years –
clever little friends. You can help then out through
splicing and gene and stress changes and what you
feed them to work with. I have long felt this is a
beautiful way. Check out Sleepy grass on the web.

Next letter will have what and how Finite
Element Works – Theory and such. Photon pumping
is a major wave coming. I am trying to get two
letters a day out to you...

May 20, 2004

Quo Vadimus? I ask you the eternal question:
"Where are we going?" In more colloquial terms, we
might ask, "Where are you coming from?" And if
we're in a contemplative mood, we might even vary
the basic theme and extend our inquiry to arrive at
that deepest question of all speculative thought:
"What is the true nature of mankind?" Eternally
difficult! Quo Vadimus? As you can tell, I am feeling
better today. Eternal questions have a nasty habit of

remaining eternally impenetrable when left on the lofty plane of philosophical discourse.

Spoke to Pete (Rolling Stone) again today. Looks as if we will get a long four plus hours next Wednesday. I am trying to pull my linguistic skills together for your need and my meeting with the modern scribe of which no moss grows on. Note because of your wee number of times around the sun – you may not know of the saying – "No moss grows on a rolling stone" – and so gave birth to Rolling Stone. To see through different lens is one of my goals in life. Get off the shared 5htp hallucinations. I would like, ⇔, I would also hope to make a small contribution to thought by displaying a few of the fascinating interconnections between these seemingly diverse pebbles strewn about on the seashore of consciousness. Note: Consciousness is a negative state of entropy. As you (Krystle) would say – "layers on top of layers and textures." Yes, Pete, I am starting my one last synapse up. Attention, Sparky, you are soon to be on stage. Do you (Krishna) think it would be a sagacious move to tell Pete of my latest work in neurochemistry and my attempts at being a degenerate physicist? "Oh, let the sun beat down upon my face, here I sit before the elders of the human race. I am a traveler of both time and space..." Physical Graffiti – Kashmir.

The work of one Ludwig Boltzmann may shed some starting stages for the math rigor we may build. Given to him is the second law of thermodynamics – even on his tombstone (in Vienna's Zentral friedhof) the formula $S=k\log W$ is engraved. If we go back to the solid bedrock of Boltzmann and Maxwell we may well create a syntactic system to handle your problem of the frequency of meetings lovers' need to bond?" – And bow we do to Maxwell's electro-magnetic wave equations. Namaste James Clark Maxwell. When I feel shaken – I go back to the closest time (history) solid place to land. Maxwell's work is as solid as it gets. I cannot yet project the type of rigor wee will end up with.

I am trying to work on form of your endeavor. Your allegory of kitty Harry Krishna is one I truly want to write together!

> "Lives of Great Men all remind us, we can make our lives sublime, and departing, leave behind us, footprints on the sands of time." –H. W. Longfellow

Now that we have opened up the door of allegories – let us look at the story of a young person who has to take a very strong sacrament. The young person was a well educated woman named Helen. She went to the Brahman the day before the ceremony and asked him if he would walk with her on the Beach after she took the sacrament. He asked, "But Why?" She said, "So you can help me when it becomes hard." He said, "Of Course." The Brahman had others coming to the special time, and they asked him to take many high sacrament[s] in Stair-case fashion. He did – and then went for a walk along the Beach with Helen. Helen had much anxiety – much fear – she was afraid she would die. They walked for more than two hours. She had a very hard time, but she learned much – as she descended from the God-Head, she could remember the lessons and the Space she Held. She told the Brahman she was better and could they turn around and walk the way they came – so she could tell him what happened. She said she did not remember him all the time only most of the time. They walked about an hour tracing their Footprints in the Sand. Sometimes here footprints were on one side of his and then on the other – But at the hardest part there was only one set of Footprints. She said, "See you left me when I needed you most – Why?" The Brahman said First, "Are you harmed?" She said "No."

Brahman –   "You asked me to walk with you – you did not say to stay with you at all times."

Helen –   "But You are a High Priest – you have a duty"

Brahman –   "You call me Brahma – I do not call myself High Priest"

Helen –   "You failed me in My time of need"

Brahman –   "You have been trained – who am I."

Helen –   "I could have died, you do not care about me"

Brahman –   "You are fine"

Helen -   "You only care about yourself and you focused only on your own Stair-case Sacraments – you are a False Brahman"

Brahman –   "Then call me by my Name"

Helen –   "I am afraid Now – because you left me alone when I needed you most, that time at which there is only one set of footprints is

275

the time I had the Heaviest transition."

Brahman – "Let us go back to the stretch of Beach with only one set of footprints and you tell me what happened."

Helen – "I Now Remember, it is the time I took the Full God-Head position. I SAW FOREVER, I saw the oneness of all things. I knew the answers to the Eternal Questions. And you the so-called Brahman left me. I will call you by you name, Todd."

Brahman/Todd- "Then I shall call you by your NAME, But I want you to look close at those footprints that are so alone. Those Footprints are Mine – as I had to pick you up and carry you in your greatest time of need."

Helen – "You are so right I am sorry that I doubted you"

Todd – "Your NAME is SHadow, I could have no more left you as you could have left me." You see Shadow – If I am I because you are you and you are you because I am I – Then I am not I and you are not you. We are one. You are right I am not a High Priest, Nor have I ever claimed such – in fact I have

276

always said we each are our own Priest-Priestess. You see Shadow when you went to the God-Head we were ONE! Therefore, only one set of footprints. And SHadow you called me to you – You are my shadow and I yours.

Todd (cont) – "Shadow you had much fear of death when you started to ascend to the God-Head – and I picked you up and carried you over the Sands of Life. LIVE YOUR LIFE So that the Fear of Death can never enter your HEART. When you arise in the Morning, Give thanks for the Morning LIGHT. Give THANKS for your Life and Strength. Give Thanks for your Food and For the JOY of Living. And SHADOW; if PerChance you see no reason for Giving THANKS, Rest assured the Fault is IN YourSelf. You See SHadow You are a Product of Light when Light Shines upon Me you are Shown as separate, but that is and Illusion. We are One."

Shadow – "Todd, I ask why have you said this?"

Todd – "And So, at this time, I greet you. Not quite as the world send greetings, but with profound esteem and with prayer that for you, NOW and Forever, the day breaks, and the SHADOWS flee away."

Todd –   "You are not Shadow only"

Shakespeare – "This is above all: To thine own self be true. And it must follow, as night the day, Thou canst not then be False to any Man!"

Prospero – "Shakespeare as Jesus – their Soul is not in the Dogma, But in their works lives their eternal Spirit – as this is so" "And the Name is not the Work"

Lao Tse – "Myth transcend Reality" "Mythos is So"

Prospero – "Lao Tse you died centuries before either"

Lao Tse – "And you Never were" "You See Mythos transcends Reality"

Todd – "I am glad my vertical and Horizontal Brothers of space-time are here. My A-temporal Family who Partake of the Sacraments."

Todd (cont) – "You must understand that we are all atemporal – That the Beach we walked on was a Beach/NO THE BEACH without time. And we walked on the

278

Sands of Time, As we are in the Eternal Now."

Johann Göethe – "The Present Moment is a Powerful Goddess"

Albert Einstein – "The distinction between past, present, and future is only an illusion, even if a Stubborn one." – You Know my sacrament Rings my acetyl-choline receptor site. (same as site of β-bungaro)

Child of Light – "Those that Know the Know are aWake."

Bother of Eternal Love – "Those that Know do not say – Those that Say do not know"

Shadow – "I have seen the Beach without time. I am of the Order of Light and Love. I am of Light... Fiat Lux!! My Name Like as to Vishnu incarnate, Krishna. Like as to Shadow incarnate, Krystle. For in the Rock sleeps the Krystle. The Krystle bends the light and is Home to LIGHT... Is a House to Lux. Again I SAY: KRISHNA an incarnation if Vishnu, KRYSTLE an incarnation of Shadow. 7 follows 6. I am a Child of Light, we have Dominion in Matters of LIGHT."

RA – "I am the Sun-God" "I am of the Order of Light" "My All-Seeing

279

eye is my symbol" "Brave Helios is of Me" I have ordained the "Children of Light"

Krystle –

"For in the Rock sleeps the Krystle and in the Krystle lives the Rainbow – the Rainbow gives the answer to Optical Physics. Read Newtons work on OptiKs. It is Smooth Smooth-No limit to number of colors.

Todd –

"If Rainbow is infinite in number of colors than what of Schrödinger's work of discrete energies?"

ATHENA –

"Ψ Behold for I unRavel A Mystery" "Palladium the metal is from the root word "Pallas" "which means asteroid" "PALLADIUM is the statue of Pallas whose presence and preservation ensured the safety of Troy." "Palladia: Safeguard" "AND KNOW THIS PALLAS is MY NAME" "Palladium the Metal is a Gift from the Greatest of the Order LIGHT And is a SAFEGUARD" "It is a HIGH ORDER Element"

RA –

"OH, PALLAS, Goddess of Wisdom, You are So Right" "This Palladium is a Gift From a Higher Order than HELIOS or If you so like SOL" "For You only Give Helium to the Universe"

280

Marie CURIE – "The Stars that make Palladium are relatively Rare and Are Very, Very MASSIVE, Know this Helium is 2 in Atomic Number , 4 in atomic weight while Palladium is 46 in Atomic Number, 106.42"

Madame Curie – "The Star that can make Palladium is many orders of magnitude greater than our SUN"

RA – "Many orders of Magnitude greater is like "Higher Order""

ATHENA – "Ψ So Be that the Elements that are called Ruthenium, Rhodium, Palladium, Iridium, and Platinum are Gifts from the Greatest of the High order of Light" "The High order of Light has the Power over Light, energy to matter, and matter to energy. Helios(SUN) is a very low member of the Order of Light"

Madame Curie – "Atomic Number and Atomic weights of Ruthenium (44,101) Rhodium (45, 102) Palladium (46, 106.42) Iridium (77, 192.2) Platinum (78, 195.08) "These elements are very Rare in the Universe"

Jesus – "Element is the Bread and wine used in the Eucharist"

281

RA – "The High order of Light ordained the "The Children of Light" "The HIGH ORDER SENDS STARDUST as Gifts to Help the Children of Light. When the Children Of Light are ready the Greater Gifts (Heavier Elements) are so found and USED. Your abilities follow the Rarer gifts up.

Madame Curie – "The Nobel Elements are chemically inert or inactive especially toward oxygen Platinum is the most Nobel of the Metals. That is only Part of the Story, of these Rare Metals" "It takes Massive transfers of Energy to make such High Numbered (Atomic Number and Atomic Weight) elements Energy transfers far beyond anything we know."

OPPENHEIMER – "The Energy to create the elements of the Platinum Metal Group is so far beyond our technology Fusion and Fision skills all we can do in Fusion which creates Heavier Elements is Hydrogen to Helium – the Energies required for lets say Platinum" is beyond our imagination.

Werner Heisenberg – "We broke the Rules we used our Gifts as Children of

Light to make weapons against other Children of Light and even worse our Mother Gaia."

Gaia –   "In testing the Hydrogen Bombs and all the Fission Bombs, I was hurt greatly" "I have wept without end over this" I prayed to Bramha, I prayed to RA" I prayed to the High ORDER OF LIGHT – Please Help Your Children.

Prospero –   "We Bow to Heisenberg for he held to the Principles of the Children of Light" "He went against his government"

ATHENA –   "Ψ So Now YOU KNOW PART of the MYstery – KRYSTLE"

RA –   "The High ORDER OF LIGHT FOLDS LIGHT INTO The Matrix of Palladium – Immense Amount of Energy in the Form of Light"

RA –   "Palladium is Folded Light into a Special Lattice organization" The Masses involved exceed the total Mass of This Solar System by so many Orders of Magnitude that a comparison is Numerical at Best"

Brahma –   "Namaste Heisenberg"

Boltzmann –   "I think the energies are beyond Stars alone"

283

Brahma – "NOW YOU ARE IN MY DOMAIN" "Humans Call them NOVA's, SUPER NOVA's, Pulsar's, and BlackHoles" This is Beyond RA. For I HAVE CREATED GIFTS FOR THE CHILDREN OF LIGHT, At the Level of Iridium and Platinum the Energies and Masses are so Great to Fuse the Atoms into such dense Atomic structures that it is beyond Star work Alone. Dense Photon Structures are these, in them I have so blessed many Gifts. Iridiums time is yet to Come with Humans. The Mono-Atomic Form is/will be A Signal of the Turning Point in Human History. Iridium gives off the Rainbow in visible light when dissolved in Hydrochloric Acid.

Brahma – Its lattice Structure is a thing of Beauty. Now Know this the Crystalline Structure is so tight, so ordered that the metal Form is Brittle. The Folding lattice matrix can convert energy to light form (heat) at Room temperatures. It can "WING" Carbon atoms in its lattice, Much as Palladium absorbs Helium in its lattice matrix. KNOW THAT IT HAS A VALENCE OF FOUR.

284

Madame Curie – "Brahma we call that tetravalent"

Brahma – "I HAVE SO Gifted Platinum my Most Nobel Metal" "Now I reveal a Mystery wrapped in a Riddle, Packaged in a Puzzle... For as Silver is mate to Gold one is 47 Atomic Number and 79Atomic Number, Gold is directly Below Silver in Periodic table – SO is the Elements (Rhodium to Iridium) and (Palladium to Platinum). KNOW THIS THAT EACH Element with its Mate is 32 Atomic Number removed. Gold-Silver(79-47) 32; Iridium-Rhodium(77-45) 32; Platinum-Palladium(78-46) 32. AND SO KNOW I CREATED THEM AS MATES and When Found the Mates are with them.

Brahma – "THey are Mined as such."

RA – "Even your Money and concepts of Money come from this Nobel creation" Currency comes from current as even the Ancient Egyptians Knew Silver had the highest current flow. The currency flowed through the People. When the Real Money is used the High Order prevails. Mono-Atomic Gold is translucent. NASA Has made this Form in "Z-G" space flights. "In God we Trust" is on the Gold

Pieces of the U.S. COINS – Meaning God Made the Silver and Gold and it is Good. The Government Showed it Had Gone Bad when it Printed it on the Paper Money. Chalices are LaB Beakers and Flasks of an older time. Ciborium is a light and atmosphere protected Beaker. Monstrance is a Magnification device. These items Far pre-date the Catholic CHurch. Chalices pre-date most religions.

SOCRATES – "I am Here to Answer Krystle's Questions"

Krystle – "I know why SHADOW to Krystle – But why Helen to Shadow."

SOCRATES – "The time of Your development Your Highest Sacrament that you were mastering when you went for your walk was Eleusinian; therefore, Helen from Hellenist period of Ancient Greece was your name – since you are atemporal" "Helen was Helen of Troy the most beautiful of Troy a 10 year war was fought over Her."

Demeter – "I gave the sacrament to You – Helen (Shadow (Krystle)) the Sacrament stood alone in Eleusinian fashion. You were

286

pure and did not partake of the Dionysian cults, the Lust and debauchery of Bacchus. Nor did you follow the Hedonistic path. You are of my House and I give you High Priestess position in the Eleusinian Mysteries. My House Has Many Mysteries for I am the Goddess of Agriculture – You Should Know that Helen has 5 letters and Shadow has 6 letters and Krystle has 7 letters. You have Mastered the Greater Mysteries. You are so charged with its protection. The Eleusinian Rite gave way to the Rise of the Republic of Greece. A Strong Knowledge of Universal Justice. This Republic energy transferred the United States – born a Republic. I, Demeter, still reign over the fruits of Agriculture. And I have Ordained thee."

Philo Judaeus – "In the search of a more perfect Logos, Krystle you must go to a higher sacrament. A Logos to BEHOLD, is your Quest."

PALLAS – "Helen is Part of Your Eternal Soul as is your relation to Troy is as to your destiny with Palladium" "You shall forever be Gifted Palladium in matter of all Kinds" "Ψ"

287

Brahma – "Krystle you are made of stardust and your energy comes from sunlight – You are truly a CHILD OF LIGHT! When the Order of Light ordained through RA the Children of Light it was literal. No Symbolism – Hard Core Facts. NOW I SHALL PULL ASIDE The Curtains – And Show light transfer to the Mind. I will Soon Show the Math of How it all works. For I have always, always"

Brahma – "Had the Math by which things behave"

Albert Einstein – "E=MC² tells us the potential Energy of a lump of Mass – Even though we had an earlier equation this one tells us something MORE GRAND. For it implies Mass and Light are related – That the (Light) squared (light)² a Planar of Light times Mass gives full potential Energy."

RA – "The work of Stars"

Brahma – "The work of Universes" Namaste Einstein

RA – "Namaste Boltzmann"

ATHENA – "NAMASTE" "NAMASTE HAMSA"

Brahma – "HAMSA"

288

RA –

"I to, shall give "SHADOW" the equations of Light"

Gaia –

"USE Palladium as a SafeGuard" "For I ask Krystle – Your Help since you are gifted"

ATHENA –

"IRIS, Goddess of the Rainbow, Messenger of the Gods, In Your Silence, You speak as Loud as One-Hand Clapping. We pray that you Illuminate us with your knowledge."

IRIS –

"I am of Light, I brought gifts to the Children of Light. My Gifts are Many. My Namesake Iridium and its mate Rhodium – Are both tetra-valent. In Mono-Atomic form Light dances in their lattice Matrix – Photons can energize the Organic element structures and advance structures. This is a secret, this is Knowledge of Mine and I so gave this Gift to RA. RA taught his children of Egypt. In these two gifts. "Lovers" may be able to Bond. 6500K° Activates Iridium's lattice for Carbon – So Know I use 6500 K° in Color temperature. Day lite – 65 – Durotest Makes this cheap. Look to see if Vita-lite is peaked around 5600K°. Now I tell you – SITE D Has Many of Both – "Daylite-65" and "Vita-lite"

Name is on bulbs [omitted name] can help."

IRIS(cont.) – "Know that No Other wavelengths can compete – total Darkness with immense flood of the color of light. Both 6500K° and 5600K° one must test to see best results. Please understand that the "STOBE" is already in the Mix. The FLUORESCENT BULB strobes already. The lux = one lumen per square meter. The Lux transfer must be great. The light wattage must be on the order of 500 watts per 10cm^2. If one wants to cause "strobe" effect wire every other Ballast in out of phase separate transformer. This was an easy option at "Site D." Remember angle and distance of optics. [omitted name] will understand this (in order to get 240 Volts single phase – tap into two different wall sockets which come out of two different transformers and are wired out of phase) Same idea to get solid light blanket if so desired. Bulbs must be no further than 30cm and cannot transfer heat bleed off."

Erebus – "This is to done in my Home"

Albert Einstein – "Through the Laws of Parity – I saw another from of Matter.

An Atom made of Positron instead of an electron. A positron has a positively charged particle having the same mass and magnitude of charge as electron, constituting the anti-particle of an electron called Positive electron. Antimatter also has antiprotons. When equal amounts of matter and antimatter are combined the result is total conversion of Matter to Energy – given by:
$E=[\text{Antimatter}_1+\text{Matter}_1]/M\cdot C^2$
The Energy is given as ElectroMagnetic wave as all of the spectrum is expressed."

RA – "NAMASTE TULKU Einstein"

Hegel – "Who will explain the Laws of Parity"

KANT – "Shall I Give it a Try"

Paul Dirac – "Laws of Parity are Laid down After your Time"

Lao Tse – "This lies at the heart of the TAO. Yin and Yang balance FORM."

Hegel – "The thesis, Antithesis, synthesis is the best Foundation"

Werner Heisenberg – "Young Shadow is tired, this format bores her!"

Govinda -	"Namaste to All"
RA –	"I Hope young Krystle you come once again to OUR Place without TIME."
Brahma –	"See you in an instant"
Pallas –	"I Look Forward to the Secrets of Rhodium"
Gödel –	"We Shall Walk and Talk MATH"
Brahman –	"Namaste Krystle"
ATHENA –	"Fiat Lux"

I love you with all my Heart. Today I got my Presentence Investigation report (PIR) I was right I am at a Criminal History Category I as low as you can go. Guidelines 46 to 57 months. The U.S. Attorney is at Mid Point Rec. which would be 51 months...

Ex-U.S. Marshall to Read PSI on Saturday to give me his opinion. I am very tired as you can see. The report was hard on me. It gave a favorable report on Paul death [Kansas involuntary manslaughter charge Todd got dismissed because of his immunity]. It said internal DOJ Investigation States I did my best to help him – I probably did more good that harm and I was brought in too late to do much – He was brain dead when I arrived. First good report on that...

Now that the Rolling Stone is coming the Guards all want to talk to me. Sycophants, "Gracie". Ref. to "Straight Man" Gracie Allen wife of George Burns. Learn this Taylor's Series:

Learn this → Taylor's Series

$$f(x) = f(a) + \frac{f''(a)}{1!}(x-a) + \frac{f^{(2)}(a)}{2!}(x-a)^2 + \dots$$
$$f(x) \qquad\qquad + \frac{f^{(N)}(a)}{N!} \cdot (x-a)^N$$

May 25, 2004

Dear Krystle,

How are you doing? Luv you. Met with Vito for 4 hours today. My New Jersey conviction cannot be used in my criminal history. I am now at Criminal level I with one point. "I" is as low as you can get. That is 46-57 months. DOJ has agreed to 51 months point. We will argue to get Topeka conviction of Misdemeanor removed giving me Zero points. Vito has looked it over and says I could be out in 17-22 months. He and I spent two hours on Ok case...

Todd – "There are two metals that are Mates: Osmium and Ruthenium-polyvalent. The possibilities are endless as you can see. Osmium is the heaviest metal. Take care Osmium reeks/smells terrible – and is Toxic! I have avoided it for many reasons. This Polyvalent aspect is remarkable. I can give no help in what to do.

Look up Iproniazid

All the group of Metals will do better if temp is kept below 75°F. Reason is to slow reaction down, even 50°F would be better but would be a problem to heat sink that low. Plus internal reactions could get fast

293

temp rise. 5-mt can go a lot of routes. 7-mt can go a lot of routes. There is a Jap. Made Film developer that goes to AMT is 2 easy steps. Again Super-Critical [Fluid Extraction] is cheap and easy. Dow Chemical makes a resin that goes a very good route. Be careful of Epimerization – know Epimease. Use standard ways if you can. Note Health Dangers. Quick – Simple – Cheap. Love you. Miss you. Love, Todd

June, 2004 (County Jail – Reno, Nevada)

June 9, 2004

Dear Krystle,

Vito and I once again had a meeting and it looks like I will not be going to Sheridan, my life is at risk there. If I want to risk it, I could try. The one place I can for sure go to by court decree is "the cheese factory" the "rat" house in Arizona. Phoenix FCI has a special place for government C.S.'s [confidential source]. Because I have a breached D.O.J. [Department of Justice] agreement, I may get something even better, Air Force Base – I will know in two weeks. If I post Oklahoma bail, it will not make me camp eligible. Vito has once again come alive and is doing a good job. Baby Kat [Todd's daughter] wrote me a letter, it was harsh – I think Kally [Todd's first wife] was behind it. Vito has gone on sworn court statement the Oklahoma case is flawed. I won a Kastigar motion against D.O.J. U.S. Probation. Now I have a 6001, 6002, 6003 hearing in a week and a half. 8th Circuit has already ruled – I will win that. I have a meeting in the morning with Vito – I will wait to send letter. If you want to live in Arizona please write ASAP and tell me. I am down to the wire time wise. This will be the last letter you can respond to, that I can respond. Anything you want to tell me or ask me you should do now. At the Fed's the mail is very controlled, read both ways. Also, if you write, give me an idea of how many letters you have got in the last three weeks. I will not write much from Fed's too read. DO NOT TELL ANYONE WHICH PLACE I GO TO – I will know if I can tell anyone after June 21st. Still working on State Department [CIA] project – at best 5% chance of going through – D.O.J. will use Rule 35 on me if it goes through – tell no one, not even a lawyer of yours or my mother – you could get me killed. I give it 2%, Vito gives it better than 5%. I am getting some special Federal lawyer for these negotiations only. A woman in her early 60's, only one that is good for this in Western USA. WHY do the Feds pick up all my legal bills?? Hope to see Kennedy [one of Todd's lawyers] in the next few days. IS THE BOOK FINISHED [*Lysergic*]?

June 10, 2004

Dear Krystle,

I did not see Vito today, as he has not gotten to speak to the D.O.J. people. Poor English. One of the people in his office is handling B.O.P. interface. Just before lockdown about 15 minutes earlier, I spoke to Pete (Rolling Stone). He is not making any progress with Federal Marshals for arranging interview with me. He said Pickard ["L"] wrote him and said Lompoc is not a very friendly place – rough conditions. Pete asked me what I am doing. I said "I am learning Sanskrit, Devangari, and Physics." How often do you get letters from "L"? I think I am down to less than 20 days here – big relief to be out of here – I need real food, need to see earl Doctors and get on to a law library. I worked out my Immunized information defense on PSI report. I used below as case:

999 F.2d 1246 (8th cir. 1993) US vs. Abanatha

Lexus 18803, 1993 US App.

To get my info removed from PSI, Vito never read this case??????? Spoke to Vito on the phone he says he is coming to see me next day. He said he has some good news on FCI's from BOP – down to 20 days or less till I am out of this mental hell hole. I am filing special paperwork (I will send name when I am sure how it is spelled) that will compel Federal Marshals to file and serve my civil paperwork. No mail again today. I will keep this letter open until I get 8 pages. The day I leave my roommate, Terry, will send a letter out for me with as much info as I know – what place I was ordered to, what day I left, sentence, and such. That will be that last letter you get from me for some time. Maybe up to thirty days before I can write you. You should get one letter from me dated 6-22-04 and one letter the day I leave...

Next day, the purple people eater was not around. It was the men of the crew. Do you remember the two men that were around? They were gifted.

Today has been a real rough day have not felt good all day. First showers were either way, too hot or too cold – some plumbing change here. Love you – will write later. I want you to know I am very sorry for ever yelling at you, for ever blowing up, you were/are the person I loved most – I was under too much stress for too long. I want you to know from the bottom of my heart I love you and I am truly sorry for ever giving you a hard time – you were the only one who stuck by me. Not feeling well now, my feet have been cold for days now. I hope you can remember me with smiles – remember the happy moments – the peaks... I hope my Mother has nothing to do with the fact that you are not writing or taking my phone calls – I hope you are traveling and left phone behind as a black shadow ploy...

My mate went to the DEA and the reasons were wrong – it was to hurt me – those were life sentences you were dealing with them on. I was not even dealing – I was doing legal private research. You went to help Brad out – only reason you took him, you tried to get Kastigar for the both of you. I went to the DEA and got you out of trouble, you brought Brad into my life and I got hurt bad – You went to the DEA to hurt me. I asked both you and Brad to leave that night when he came back and wanted to trip. I asked both of you to leave for good – Do you remember that??? Not only did I not lure him back to the hotel – I begged you to get him out of my room/ and life. Do you remember any of that – he makes no reference to being asked to leave – and leaving – this is why I can win is he has lied so much. You did not need to bring him into my life. The two of you should have stayed away from me. Brad is a girlish boy – gay – he is more woman than man – for you that was fun but I did not want that energy around me – you let him stay in a bed with me without asking if he could be there – night I cam back to room from hospital – and he woke me up at 4:00am jacking off. I did not even know what was going on. Do you know I was very sick – you two could have gone and slept somewhere else. Then the night he had picked up Hoch he got in bed and was sexual with you while I tried to sleep – that was wrong I told both of you – I did not want to be around his sexual energy – he was/is a little faggotty, pushy asshole – his friends warned me about him – why harm your love with him – I was sick for God's sake...

Again, you need to arrange someone to see me as soon as possible. Tell them all of the info you need to go to me plus all of the questions you need me to be asked.

Side note: Major bust of XTC (MDMA real) Pills were wholesale cost in San Diego for $.60 each in lots of 10,000. $6,000 per 10,000 real MDMA made Reno newspaper. That places a kilo at between $6,000-$12,000 already pressed. There is very little profit in making that.

Do you remember when I told you Hoch getting out on bail would show a card – no way a bail bond company would bail him out for $2,000 down on a $200,000 bail. Government had to have been in on it. Major questions of Hoch and his bail bond company when I call them to the stand.

You should write just so I know you are all right. Your phone has been off for three weeks now. Big blowout to downside for XTC prices. I think we predicted that 4 years ago. In the 1980's prices crashed on real XTC to $7,000 per kilo – it takes a new breed of brain cells to recover prices – Prices will stay low for about 5-15 years. I think XTC has had it forever as far as the big prices of the 1990's. New designer drugs will outpace all the rest. Heroin is down to $7,000-$20,000 of Mexican brown. While xanax and valium keep climbing, OC's [Oxycontin] are big time popular up here – but meth is the big drug – 50% of the people here use that garbage everyday. Designer meth should be a biggy and it is not – I do not understand why. This country has screwed itself – everyone is going to meth – No Spirituality in Meth. Uncle Fester is well known around the chemists here. Everyone is a chemist – they all cook meth here – I mean a lot of it. And the formulas are real; these guys have really done this stuff – stay way from any meth vib. as you know it is really bad – dark energy. Wrong head set of people.

The big drug of choice is psych meds – half of this jail is on some bullshit new drug that is five years or less old...

June 15, 2004

Dear Krystle,

Received your letter dated 6-2-04 sent on 6-7-04 given to me on 6-14-04. Hope this letter finds you in good spirits...Answers to your questions [questions for *Lysergic*]:

"Could you tell me how you met 'L'?"

He walked up to me at Palace of Fine Arts, San Fran. 1996. I was there to attend ethnobotony conference. End of October-early November. I was walking over to Kerry Mullis and "L" walked over and asked me to move $50,000 into expense money for him. It was out of protocol. Many of the people came to Stinson Beach house to talk about Nicki Sand's bust. "L" came for that talk. Also, I had a room at the Mandarin Hotel. Sans Souchi – name of the house at Stinson Beach. "L" had been calling me on the 800# at Garder for two years prior under code name "Carlos." I was a bit confused, I thought we had two not one using two names in the LSD chemist business. "L" and I were to have met in 1995 at Buffalo Inn in New Mexico but I did not show because of a snow storm. Bill was at the house along with [omitted list of names] and about 20 others came and went. I know of Pickard as far back as 1984 from Ott and Weil. In 1985, Stamets mentioned Pickard.

"Did 'L' ever bust anyone big?"

Yes – the Bolinas connection – LSD team of women lawyers and accountants – ask Bill if he has info. "L" told me what he did and it went with external info. "L" got busted with large lab in Mountain View, CA in 1988 – he got a major sentence reduction. "L" did something to a man code named "Mike" who lives in Holland. What was done I do not know – but it was extreme and caused long term problems. "Mike" was in ling term hiding for some reason. "L" and "S" may have got a chemist in Russia killed/busted because of judgement error. "L" usually rolled on distribution network – not chemist unless they were meth chemist. "L" did some work with US Customs in last 8 years. He had Federal Court Order that barred him from certain work.

"Also, what can I say about your involvement with B.O. [Boris Olarte]?"

I wish to think BO equation through. BO is a friend of turf. Now as in then.

Las Vegas US Attorney has blocked any agency from taking me out – they (agencies) can work with me in custody. Any help that I can give may not result in downward departure on Fed case – 19 months net – how absurd – I will exhaust my Federal sentence before I finished work – and Feds will not help on OK case...

June 21, 2004

Dear Krystle,
I went to court today to be sentenced. I got 50 months. I got court ordered DAP credit of one year off. I got credit for time served. $100.00 fine total. For security reasons ordered to Nellis Air Force Base

first; Dublin, CA second. Oklahoma details struck from PSR and PSI. All of 6003 [immunity] items ordered removed. All past conviction ignored points-wise. 20.5 months till expired. Oklahoma will have to file special paperwork to move me... Important to stay on ball over next 60 days. Success on many fronts!! Keep praying. Keep dreaming reality into being! TIME IS IMPORTANT NOW. I love you more than anything. French Hotel stay – important. Please write ASAP – I will be here at least through July 4th weekend... Be careful you are holding the lineage... Please take time to write me. Send it before June 30th – alpha-o is a MAOI please remember that. Pink Hat needs to be cleaned. Please get ready to clean it. You are missing the best chance to write me. When can you come west?? Are you planning on moving soon?? Will you move to Nellis if I go there? Or only San Fran – are you going to move to San Fran no matter what I do? Or only if I move to Dublin? Please write in Code. I love you with all my heart. I love you through all time. Smiles forever. Please come to see me ASAP at Fed place. Push hard. Please. Tear all of this up. All motions you get and PSI/PSR. Love, Todd

June 22, 2004

Dear Krystle,
        ...I have felt rough for a few days, mild flu. I hope Tulsa cannot extradite me from here as I need to recover as soon as possible, for OK charges. My Mother is ordering three sets of Fed Visit papers for you (two) and her (one). Please get two sets from her. Be careful of MAOI's and pain medicine. Alpha-o is a MAOI so pay close attention to what you do. Try hard to see me as soon as possible. It is very, very important. Try to take time to write me as soon as possible, ask coded questions now! It is so very

important that I go to Feds before OK case. I am so worn out. Vito's office to send many motions and court rulings on Friday to me. I will forward on. I want you to know I love you very much. Sorry for all of these problems. I never wanted you to get into this type of trouble. DEA paid Hoch from Day 1 – another reason Hoch's testimony is suspect.

I am going on fast for next week if I can. I am stair stepping down into it. I want to clean myself up for Fed transport, if I even get picked up by Feds. I have been weak for days now. Only working on legal stuff, to get ready for case in Oklahoma. I did Abanatha work. Vito knew nothing about it.

Vito is going to help on OK case after the Judge made comments on problems. DEA internal notes and police notes do not match at all. Hoch and Brad told different and changing stories. The book that has sun/light protective covering needs to be restored, updated, and cleaned up. Be careful one of a type – I will tell you how to restore. The Pink Hat was work in progress it needs to be finished. Oil is trapped in its fabric. Again oil is trapped in its cloth matrix. It is a working hat, it just could use a good dry cleaning.

You know maybe she has the book – to be, or not to be see, or to see I. I can help locate book for you. We need to get all of our books back. Krystle, my brain hurts all the time since coming off "Benzos." I have continuous mild pain in the region above the ears forward. It is a real pain in the ass. I did not know one could have such a thing. I wish you the best with your new boyfriend. Go on with life. I wish you could write a letter telling me what I should do in Big picture. I wonder why Vito thinks case is very beatable. His idea is that all the witnesses suck for one reason or another. And it is going to be hard to prove anything. If I never hold your hand again or look into your eyes and soul, it was wonderful to have/be in our/your/my life. We got to go on a honeymoon. Sorry you are currently stuck being married to me. I promise to get you out of that when you need it. By the way, HAPPY ANNIVERSARY, one year on paper, five years in heart. Love you, Todd. Tear all of this up.

June 23, 2004

Dear Krystle,

    I received you letter dated 6-14-04, the wording in some places did not sound like you. Answers to some of the questions:

1) Hypothetically, why would a member of the Brotherhood be involved in the production of LSD?

   It is a great honor to help form the sacraments. It is a blessed position and a sacred duty. Only a few in over 40 years were so honored.

   Some did it for the money too.

2) If you could give the "up and coming" one piece of advice what would it be? (this question does not sound like you)

   I have no advice to give anyone.

3) NO COMMENT NOW

4) Was it all worth it?

   Yes

5) Would you do it all again?

Yes

6) Describe what your position is.

Someone who partakes of the sacraments and who tries to show others a path of sacraments. In the Alphabet soup's eyes? Crazy, nut.

7) When did you first cooperate with the Alphabet Soup?

DEA – 1989
FBI – 1985
US Customs – 1989
IRS – 1984

8) Why "L" was turned in.

Because of murder the sacraments were tainted. I could feel a major quake coming. And it was, I was only two weeks ahead of the curve. Money was ruling everything.

The car accident with you started a check in to how much I was able to do. I was interviewed by peers in CA. I was told to retire. "L" had nothing to do with the interviews. These were older powers.

Big Sur operation was hit hard by none other that Karl [DEA agent] – between Dec ember of 1999 and March of 2000.

Tim's suicide added pressure.

Secret Service bust added pressure. [Todd was busted for impersonating a federal officer at a casino]

Natasha got busted with cash at KC airport.

Tim's father showed up to lab, almost got it.

Others now knew because of emergency lab move.

"L" and "C" did not show up on time to emergency lab move.

Lab was at Wamego when you and Ryan were tracked to missile base, Wamego.

Story on street in KC was lab for MDMA at Wamego missile base.

Too many people knew.

"C" and "L" blew a large batch and shipped it anyway. Shit hit the fan for that.

You were in trouble with DEA – I could not calculate how far the damage went.

K.I. examined "L" and told me that "L" would try to move first on anything. K.I. did not know what was going on, only that there were problems.

Gunner triggered Guilder [Dutch currency] IRS problem at Wamego bank.

Gunner warned that you knew a lab was somewhere in Kansas, but that you thought it was MDMA.

MDMA network was on fire in California.

I did not turn "L" in. I went for immunity and agreed to shut big ops down for such immunity.

Bank started investigations in money movement in California.

Major bust in LSD network in 1999 – Northern, Ca.

E.T. [precursor to LSD] man gets violent with "L" and downstream.

Alfred went off the deep end 1999, threatened to kill "L" for real. Wanted to burn down the lab.

Ganga got served with subpoena from Customs over UDV. Before the grand jury spills the beans on swimming pool project.

Andrew U. goes to DOJ about me. 1999-2000.

Lanny W. turns me in to DEA for DMT and other items, 1997-98.

Ganga was causing problems with Sasha and me... Joel and Ganga pitched a case to Sasha about my old close ties to Feds backfiring on me. Ganga turned me in to Comptroller of Currency two days before you and I flew in private plane to Topeka for federal court [Todd's impersonating a federal officer at a casino case].

Brown glass vial full of LSD busted in Big Sur, Mel problem.

"L" begins to worry about Mel and how far he got into Friday night dinner of Sasha. "L" starts intelligence op into Mel. Karl [DEA] busted Mel for MDMA.

MDMA lab in San Diego burned to ground is story on street.

Miles of Santa Fe gets jail sentence suspended – Miles drove Kilo's of LSD to drop off spot. Miles knew me well. Miles lies to "L" and I.

Secret Service investigation into me increases as I agree on deal. Did not stop till Jan. 2003, case open even after I was immunized???

Sita says people at club start asking about "L".

$150,000 is missing in UPS/Fed ex shipment. "L" gets worried.

"L" gets turned into Cal. Bureau of Narcotics for cash payment to [couldn't understand word – looks like WCS??] site person.

Houston LSD bust – people mention Bruce's name – "L" and Al freak out.

E.T. man gets plastic surgery because he is getting ready to flee.

We think sealed indictment of E.T. man "James" is getting ready to come out.

Diazadine [LSD analog] fails to be do-able big stress lines. "Frank" (foxy) bombs.

DMT scarce. Brotherhood defaults on promise to deliver free DMT in New Mexico late 1999 – shit hits fan – I make up default and ship 10 oz. far short of 2 kilos promised... "L" and "C" get into big fight over DMT.

C.G. finds out about extent of swimming pool project...

"L" starts a major power move.

I come across Snow Man document in Black Bag operation. (I am code named Snow Man)

Dutch Guilder falls 20% between November 1999- May 2000. Brotherhood takes a big, big loss.

Stephen (Ice Man) charges 40% for currency float on one deal.

Ice Man loses 1.169 million of "L" retirement fund in a few days in Russian bond market. J. H. lies to "L" and I about that.

Problems with W. P. step-child of Sasha.

Hefter group distances itself from "L" and Sasha – leaving me only one in good graces.

D. N. gets into some hot water at Purdue lab.

Gunner looks like he might roll in July – over stressed.

Lupe and Gunner blasted hard in move of lab. I did not know the extent of the Lupe problem until trial – when it was disclosed...

Side note: DEA As of trial refuses to disclose Operation Polar info [Canadian LSD/MDMA investigation]

...I am worried about your question #9 (origin of the silver) – I cannot tell you how concerned I am about some of these questions... It sounds like you have bounced into 3rd or 4th level down. Be very careful, government is on the war path these days. You are a special incarnation; you must take great care... Please center yourself and make master plan with logic branches. If you get into trouble it will blow long term progress...

I have not heard from "L" send his address please... My intuition tells me to be on alert right now – something is afoot in the system – take good care of yourself – get your knee better.

Side note: Count letters of God-Goddess names and go <u>dextrorotatory</u> a 7 is a 1.

I am forever yours, for all time. My very best friend. I send light and never-ending love. Smiles – favorite person. Love, Todd.

June 25, 2004

Dear Krystle,

Talked to Vito's office – I was told BOP to pick me up in max of two weeks. Maybe gone around the July 4th weekend.

I want you to know these things: thank you for being my friend since Feb. 2000 – you have been a source of strength for me – and you stood by me – when all others ran. I love you more than myself. I love you more dearly than words can tell. I pray for you everyday. Thank you for being my eternal friend. You are the most beautiful soul I know. Keep on shining. I loved every moment with you. I loved your energy and beautiful smiles. When I slept with you I knew it was alright. I loved to just be with you. How could an evil twin been given the divine sacrament job? A man is known by the fruits of his labor. No matter what the government does, I will never betray you. I stand firm in my loyalty to you. To the end, I will never break on that. My love is outside the time-wave. I bow to you for all existence. Three single stamped letters have gone out. One on June 21st, one the 22nd, and one the 23rd. These had much important info. One of these letters had two stamps. I sent light on Egyptian myth work. I hope letters come unopened. If any are opened please take note and write me. I will probably not write for some time after I leave. I am going to try and buy you as much time as I can. If Vito is right, five months. I am having a blood pressure problem??? It came out of nowhere. I cannot wait until I see your eyes again. Only people who write are Joyce, baby Kat, and you. I really do not want letters from Ed after things he said...

You should go to visit more than one library. The library around French Hotel may have new book alarm system so you will need to check out books. I do not know – you will be surprised at how many libraries do not know what books they have. Books and libraries are important. Two good libraries on

West coast. One, not on west coast, close to place we went to Cabin in middle of nowhere with a lot of flies and bumpy, bumpy road. About eight hours away in another small town – we stayed one night only in that I-Ching town. Three total libraries. Maybe some refund money in third, none west coast place??? We had fresh juice and I looked for a girl I used to know at juice bar – walked around city square. I took you to a bar built over a hole you could look down into. We lost money in casino not far away.

　　Side note: Purple people eater has some other nice gifts if you can still get clothes from her. I can guide you through. Love, Todd

June 25, 2004

Dear Krystle,

　　I hope this letter finds you in wonderful spirits. Good blessings to you and happy thoughts. Namaste pumpkin... I bow to your beautiful soul. You have grown so much over the last five years. Do not worry about Oklahoma case, we will overcome. Hoch lied so much that his testimony will be invalid. Brad was not hurt that much – the press has had a field day... I never wanted to hurt you. I love you so much. The pain of loving you has been extreme. I could not separate you and I in my head. I am so sorry. Thanks for working so hard on my life's work. It is your way of saying – what you did, Todd, in life was worthwhile. Learn to focus energy down into sacraments, to sing to the structures and to change vibrations of energy packets. Read letter on Photon Chemistry – it is a very important work on physics. Hold off on book being out for sale until after trial in Oklahoma – two lawyers have told me that I am worried about Rolling Stone Article being used against me... Look for isotropic pink hats. Find

311

levorotatory fractions in this layer. It helps with pink hats. Unless one has idiosyncratic response to pink hats, very safe in cleaned up fractioned form. Look for racemic mixture. Optically inactive. Inverse racemization. Use sal ammoniac to achieve pink hat transform. Again, Sal ammoniac. Pink hats can help Sankhya. Eudaemonistic pink hats. One looks for tautomerism in pink hats and in light blocked book covers. I hope some of this sticks, please look up and find out each link of thought...

Dear Shadow, Are you able to follow – you may find diturpine at French Hotel, Fraction A and C. Let us go back to you – how are your higher language skills coming? Please write and answer... One can focus ones mind down into the structure. Start making plans to leave Topeka – bad for your soul. I hope you learn from these letters. Look up definitions and internet info. Expand your mind – set yourself free...

You need to go into deep meditation and work on this situation we have landed in. I am sending pages on the Prison Fed. wit. [Federal Witness Protection] program – go to internet and find out what applies to you. The internet website is what gets us qualified because we are CS's that are blown. Puts us in danger anywhere. Keep track of threats from anyone and file with police – build a paperwork trail and at some point DOJ has to act because of liability...

June 26, 2004

Dear Krystle,

Hello pumpkins, here are some of your answers. Question #3: Describe your view of the spiritual universal."

I want to write over a number of letters on this one. I have spent a lot of time on this one and have a lot to say. I wish to write on this when I am at Fed's because I will have dictionary, word processor, and such – plus desk and table. I will send out some ideas now.

The spiritual universe is the reason or art of being and includes all of life's aspects. You can reword anything I write. There is a oneness aspect of spirituality – but there are non-oneness aspects to spirituality. When one takes a sacrament one may go to the God-head and see forever and know all answers. The brain is in a way the 3.5 # universe. When the brain is bootstrapped up and energy levels rise, pathways are opened up. Sacraments are technology in a fashion. Different sacraments give different paths on spirituality. For example Lysergamides (in me) enhance reality, amplifies the instant and can bring all of my mind to one central focus. Most people on LSD (and family) become scattered – I (in my monomaniacal way) become even more focused – I should say it took a lot of practice to control all the extra-firing. My mind tracks these experiences closer and better than "normal" waking life. In last fifteen years I ascend and descend with great ease. Plus the pea is very easy on me. I have not had a "bad" Lyserg experience in years (probably never.) I have had a bad 2CB time. Vision becomes sharper and reality has more texture. Meaning is more apparent, truth more evident. Although you claim I am into a form of Manichaeism – I am not dogmatic about it – philosophical or spiritual dualism is only one of many possible views...

You need to start to make plans to leave Topeka, Ks. – I am sure of this. You should stay no longer than 9-15-04 (please start prep now). Next

313

spot do not place to deep of roots. Zona, Bay area, San Diego Area, and like-minded spots are good. Stay away from Seattle or Washington State – do not even visit. Some how Oregon Narc Task Force has us on radar, I am confused with that one. Arizona you have to figure yourself. Watch Karl if you go to the bay area. His new office for last year is in San Fran. and he has moved up the ladder. When I was in Lovelock I had Chi call his phone # and he had a new 415#. Plus San Fran. article said he won an award and had a new position. Karl follows habits of people – he knows most of our standard habits – which gives him the opportunity to slip in a random person. I have heard him instruct people how to get into a system. It is how he got into Mel – and then Friday night dinners (Sasha). DO NOT TRUST Sasha's system... The half-moon system is government op – has been for years. I believe Al is protected by the Northern Cal. DEA... Young people 18-28 roll faster – if not well trained. "L" did a study from DEA microdot pub. and found if a person does not roll in the first 15 minutes, they usually last six months. After that they crack...

June 29, 2004

Send no new mail, I have been told I will leave in next 10 days maybe in 3. I will call my Mother and tell her my location as soon as I know. This is the last letter – I am out of stamps and will soon be out of paper. Get ready for library trip. You will need one other person to help you going to get books. Some of your current books need restoration. If you can meet with me at Feds let us talk for first hour and check out if any possible hearing devices are being used...

Side note: need to recover screw on can 1.5 inch tall by 1.25 inch from purple people eater. Be careful. Made of aluminum with metal screw on cap.

Are you using Syrian rue? I can give you some directions on extractions. I am on day three of my fast. This fast has been easy. I am going to try to fast until Feds pick me up. My Mother is sending a one time $150 for me to use at Feds to get situated. I am praying hard for Nellis or Dublin. I do not feel positive about it but I have hope. I have been trying to get sunshine, as the sun is at an angle that gives us direct sunlight for about one hour a day. Fed inmates are jumpy about why none have left in over three weeks. You must restore the books and clean up hat collection. Do you know how? Do not talk as loose on Fed Phones the first month they listen in to every phone call. DO NOT USE CODE! Feds are much smarter than Washoe operation. I know I am repeating myself – but its important I think I have good news on Trust. Reflux alpha-o. I will tell you how. Keep 10 pages of book in light proof cover... RA has two letters, Isis 4 letters and such. Use redux form in code on Myths. Positions and work spot along with step number with element work. Thin layer fraction could be done. THIN LAYER. Equation rough start point a direction. We do not want to teach soup boys on how to be gourmet. I assume you found Palladium based on 9 letters ado on yellow paper. Anything that purple people eater has that is in foil is important. There is a book in her collection that is so very important. You have never seen or heard of this book if she still has it. It is an unfinished manuscript. The light proof cover may have as much as 3 different sections, please note plus it is not made of the most stable paper/pulp out there. I gave an important message to Purple's youngest man. You need to talk to that man – after you see me. He was not that bright but he had a good soul. I do not know if he understood. Did you get the code key on Myths? Love, Todd

August 2004 (El Reno Federal Prison – Oklahoma City, Oklahoma)

August 23, 2004

Dear Krystle,
I wrote you a happy birthday letter – and sent it six days ago to my Mother's house. Joyce just sent me a letter and said neither she nor my Mother have heard from you. Maybe this letter will get to you. So, Happy 23rd trip around the sun on the 23rd of August two thousand and 3rd year of our lord. TIGHT protocol. I send blessings. Please come and see me in Tulsa. Please write me in El Reno.

February 2005 (County Jail – Tulsa, Oklahoma)

Feb. 22, 2005

Krystle,
I shall see you at Kastigar Hearing [immunity hearing on the Oklahoma kidnapping case], try to give me a smile. Next letter will be about Kastigar and was written before this letter so a bit of overlap. Love and Light, Peace and Love. Market volatility way up – energy complex overboard – look for radical changes in the system – Royal Dutch Shell holding $50 Billion in cash plus is short 20 to 40 Billion in Fx position. The Big Boys see a sea of change coming. [President] Bush acting strange – are we getting ready to fight yet another war? North Korea or Iran take a pick – or the WILD card. USA on Big war roll – Bad form – The people eat it up. Namaste Pumpkin – I send a Toddy Bear Hug. Love, Light, Dona Nobis, Pacaem, Eleusinian Mysteries

Always Yours, Todd. $C_{16}H_{16}N_2O_2$ [left reverse arrow symbol] spin ≈> [symbol? - · X .] LUX

[On Back of letter:]

Other dense [dihydro · ergonovine]^N

Feb. 28, 2005

Dear Krystle,
    I send love and light to your soul, and pray this letter finds you in uplifted spirits. I tried to strike a balance in teaching you critical thinking and nurturing your creative force. One can occlude art in pursuit of reason; this is the risk one must try to avoid. I introduced you to Occam's Razor because I noticed a tendency for you to jump to fuzzy conclusions – to create variables – to add complexation to a solution set – or to seek the bizarre answer instead of the simplest direct conclusion. I tried hard to ease this Base of logic (lose) into your thought process. I even went as far as to show Occam's razor's proof: Law of Parsimony. "Baby Steps" is how you like in Formation. I was a poor teacher – I ask forgiveness – Valium flawed me in many ways...
    Bill says your book [*Lysergic*] is finished – do you have a contract? You can always have Kara send letters off of word and laser printer. It would be nice to know how Kara is doing. I have not received a letter since May of 2004, from her [My lawyer advised me not to write Todd any more. Beyond that, for my own well-being I needed to stop writing. I needed time to emotionally heal from the loss of him and from the memories of how he abused me during the last year we were together. He is asking to have "Kara" write, so that way no one will know it is me. "Kara" was one of my stripper stage names.] I

became weaker by the month. I believe my word and sentence style are improving...

The Red Cross always maintains neutrality in wars, yet provides relief and help to those who have suffered as a result of the conflict. The High Order does much the same in the battle for Minds in this planet. A Luminary over the eons of existence, whose presence is a foundation of spirituality...

One of the great arguments against selling the sacraments is this: if you sell them – you do not mind the ingoing business, but if you gift them you want to teach them to find (in nature), make or grow their own; To Bow to this Principle: Give a man a fish feed him for a day – teach a man to fish feed him for life. Another inherent strength of not selling sacraments there is no system for the pharmacratic inquisition to attack. The strategic dismantling of the centralized distribution of the sacraments produces long-term endurance to the High Order. We are in a time of war against our souls, our sacraments, our hearts, our beliefs, our unalienable rights, our religion, our minds – against our very selves. Each one teach one to reach one. Ordain so that they may ordain. This is a make it or break it move.

A large distribution system is not the Model of our future – but small orders within larger orders that only know each other from common experiences. The oppression of the sacraments started with the Catholic Church but the US Government has continued this selfish, ruthless, and merciless WAR. England broke from Catholocism and the US broke from the Church of England who King George III was head. This has [been] and is a Spiritual War. Pope – head of the Church of England (King or Queen) – A republic (USA) – individual, "None but ourselves can free our minds." The Battle of the Flesh of the Gods; it is an

OLD WAR. Leave thy low-vaulted past. Stand up and be Noble (as the swift seasons roll) not time to worry about FIAT Money – For God sake the Dollar is their MAMMON – Do not pollute our High Sacraments with such low filth as paper currency. It is a disgrace – an insult to the very structure of our spiritual beliefs. If you must worship that god Mammon – do so in a way not to debase our Souls.

The "BEL" [Brotherhood of Eternal Love] and its ilk were another spiritual con game. These people in the Network were there for the money – I used to say gift everything to prove your point. LSD Network was a high class drug Network – But money (MAMMON) oriented – Not Spiritual – What about the ones who give it for free – but do not teach each one how to be their own Priest? Just a power game. Be careful of Guru systems – avoid such trivial power plays.

I taught Beth and Jeremy how to be their own IV techs. I gave money to the LYCEUM – I used to go to the gatherings and teach (everyone thought I was Dennis). Do you think I have gained wealth, fame or power from this road? I bow and pray each day and remember the True Sacrament of life is LOVE...

CONCLUSION

I testified against Todd at the kidnapping trial. It was the only right thing to do, after what he had done to Brad and me. I am against violence and what Todd did to us was wrong. As I previously explained, Todd ended up being found guilty, and he was sentenced to life in prison. The sad part is that Hoch only received a suspended sentence on both the felony kidnapping charge and the felony conspiracy of kidnapping charge. He hurt Brad just as much as Todd did but the Tulsa DA's office gave him a deal in exchange for his testimony anyway. Todd never could have done those horrible things to Brad if Hoch wasn't there to help him.

Anyhow, on the assistant DA's verbal promise of no jail time, I pled no contest to a non-violent felony accessory after the fact. The Tulsa DA's office dropped my kidnapping and conspiracy of kidnapping charges. I could have fought the case and won, since I was under duress and basically kidnapped along with Brad (even though the Tulsa authorities always tried to ignore this aspect of the case). Regardless, the three years of waiting to testify against Todd had worn me out physically, emotionally, and financially. If I would have fought the case, my battle could have lasted another two or three years. I needed it to end, even if that meant there was a possibility of serving a few months of jail time for a crime I didn't commit.

The court made me go through a pre-sentence investigation. A caseworker was supposed to look at my life and the crime I was charged with to see what punishment I deserved. So I collected letters from family and friends, financial records, proof I had an associate's degree, and a background check with no prior convictions.

The caseworker told me to write a summary paragraph of what happened during the kidnapping and one about how I had been abused throughout my life. Since she limited me, I had to just list groups of words with no real explanations. How was I supposed to recount the truth about my life in two paragraphs?

Of course, Brad was allowed to make a four-page statement to her. He basically said that even though I did nothing to physically hurt him, he held me most responsible for what happened to him. He went so far as to say that I did satanic séances over his dying body! Consequently, she disregarded the fact that Todd was abusing me during that time. She also ignored the positive changes I'd made in my life. Her recommendation to the court was that I should serve jail time.

Since the assistant DA had given me his word that I wouldn't serve jail time, he was in a bad position. He negotiated with Brad and his family for several months. Finally, the assistant DA brought up the idea of a restitution payment with them. This turned things around, and they decided that I would get the punishment I *deserved* if I paid Brad $52,000. I reluctantly agreed to this and received five years of probation and a diversion. Ultimately, I was just glad to see it finally end. I needed closure.

*　　*　　*

I sometimes think about Todd. Why did he do so many bad things in his life? He should have been a great person. He should have set a good example for those around him. He used so many entheogens, yet for some reason he didn't bring what he learned during his journeys into his life. When he was tripping, he was the most spiritual shaman you would ever meet. But when he was sober he was a ruthless, manipulative, con man. In some ways, I think Todd believed that synthesizing entheogens and giving them away for free was like karmic money in the bank. So, in his mind, this large act of spiritual kindness gave him a free pass to do whatever *bad* things he wanted to in life.

Todd was my first love and my spiritual teacher. I trusted and devoted myself to him completely. I thought that if he was at the top, then he must be the best person to learn from. In the end, this idea turned out to be wrong. The people at the top of drug systems are often the most ruthless. I was so naïve to believe that it was *different* when entheogens were the drug being distributed.

The years immediately after the kidnapping were a difficult road for me to walk down. Yet, they made me a much better person. I got so far out of touch with a normal person's reality. When I was with Todd, I never worked a job, watched television, or even went a week without being on or around someone who was on an entheogen. It was like living in an entheogenic monastery of sorts.

I basically had to start life all over. I began watching the news to get up to speed on current events. I got an apartment of my own, and I started a business to support myself. I also served my probation and ended up getting out of paying most of Brad's restitution. So now I don't have a felony on my record or a huge bill to pay.

Plus, I went back to college. First, I earned my bachelor's degree in psychology and substance abuse counseling. Then I went on to get my master's degree in psychology. These days (2014), I'm a PhD candidate in psychology.

Unfortunately, though, in the years after my time with Todd I was also diagnosed with PTSD as a result of the things Todd did to me. His abusiveness was an emotional challenge for me to describe in detail when I wrote the first edition of *Lysergic* in 2004. The experiences and fear surrounding them were so fresh. And the nightmares were so scary. I was also constrained by my lawyer's recommendation to not discuss any of it while I was fighting the legal battle over being wrongfully charged in the kidnapping case. Therefore, I apologize if some of the story is vague when it comes to these events.

If you are interested in learning more about my PTSD diagnosis, I'll refer you to my book *After the Trip*. In it, you can find more of the details regarding Todd's abuse that I didn't write about in the first two editions of this book. *After the Trip* also provides more details about my present-day life and my perspectives regarding the psychedelic experience.

If you'd like more information pertaining to the LSD trial, the court transcripts can be viewed at: www.neurosoup.com/pickard-lsd-trial-transcripts/

Namaste.

About the Author

Krystle Cole is the author of *Lysergic, After the Trip, The NeuroSoup Trip Guide,* and *MDMA for PTSD.* She currently (as of 2014) is a PhD candidate in psychology. She has a Bachelor of Integrated Studies degree in Psychology and Substance Abuse Counseling as well as a Master of Science degree in Psychology with an emphasis in research, evaluation, and measurement.

Additionally, she is the founder of NeuroSoup.com. Through her work at NeuroSoup, Krystle strives to educate people around the world about responsible drug use for the purposes of harm reduction.

Made in the USA
Monee, IL
06 November 2020